The Civilization of the American Indian Series

Indians and Intruders
in Central California, 1769–1849

Indians and Intruders
in Central California, 1769–1849

BY GEORGE HARWOOD PHILLIPS

University of Oklahoma Press : Norman and London

By George Harwood Phillips

Chiefs and Challengers: Indian Resistance and Cooperation in Southern California
  (Berkeley, 1975)
The Enduring Struggle: Indians in California History (San Francisco, 1981)
Indians and Intruders in Central California, 1769–1849

Library of Congress Cataloging-in-Publication Data

Phillips, George Harwood.
  Indians and intruders in central California, 1769–1849 / by George
Harwood Phillips.
    p.   cm.—(The Civilization of the American Indian series ;
  v. 207)
  Includes bibliographical references and index.
  ISBN 0–8061–2446–6 (alk. paper)
    1. Indians of North America—California—History.   2. Indians of
  North America—California—Government relations.   3. Spain—
  Colonies—America—Administration.   4. California—History—To
  1846.   5. California—History—1846–1850.   I. Title.   II. Series.
  E78.C15P47   1993
  979.4′00497—dc20   92–54134
                                                                    CIP

Indians and Intruders in Central California, 1769–1849 is Volume 207 in The
Civilization of the American Indian Series.

The paper in this book meets the guidelines for permanence and durability of
the Committee on Production Guidelines for Book Longevity of the Council on
Library Resources, Inc. ∞

1 2 3 4 5 6 7 8 9 10

Contents

Illustrations

Maps

Preface

ONE cannot write a book about Indian-white interaction in the interior of central California without acknowledging the enormous debt owed to Sherburne Cook. A man of unlimited curiosity and master of several disciplines, Cook set high standards for those who followed. The three monographs he published in 1943 form the basis upon which all subsequent studies of Indian-white contact in central California must be measured. Entitled "The Indian versus the Spanish Mission," "The Physical and Demographic Reaction of the Nonmission Indians in Colonial and Provincial California," and "The American Invasion," they and three other essays were posthumously republished in 1976 as *The Conflict between the California Indian and White Civilization*.

Although written many years ago, the monographs hold up well because the research is sound and the insights profound. Cook, however, could not fully develop all the themes he identified, nor could he always support the generalizations he formulated. And he lacked access to important documents that have since been collected and made available. I am sure Cook would admit that he had the first but not the last say on the history of Indian-white relations in California.

Perhaps believing he had preempted the field, few scholars immediately followed his lead and example. But in recent years anthropologists such as James Bennyhoff and historians such as Albert Hurtado have published important works on interior Indians. Cook, who died in 1974, would be proud to know that the field of investigation he initiated in the 1940s is, after a long slumber, showing remarkable signs of vitality.

In a crucial way, Cook influenced my decision to write this

book. In 1960 and 1962, he published in *Anthropological Records* many of the diaries, letters, and reports written by Spanish and Mexican governmental officials, religious authorities, and common citizens who penetrated the San Joaquin Valley. Before their publication, some of these documents had been used by historians but mainly to trace the routes taken by those probing the interior. Information regarding Indian culture and activity was largely overlooked. Since their publication, the documents have been selectively used by anthropologists and historians but not in any systematic way. They were, in effect, waiting to be culled.

Extracting data about Indians from documents written by non-Indians takes time, and, as they say, time is money. Fortunately, several institutions and organizations provided me with much-appreciated financial support: the Graduate School of the University of Colorado, the Douglas A. Bean Memorial Fund (administered by the Department of History at Colorado), the American Philosophical Society, and the Sourisseau Academy of the Department of History, San Jose State University.

Because the assistance given me by several individuals took time, energy and probably years off their lives, special recognition is warranted. Pat Murphy typed the first draft, Donn Headley the second, Clara Dean the third, and, coming full circle, Pat Murphy the fourth. Their efforts are greatly appreciated. Thanks also to Bob Ferry, Melvid Hernández, and Rubén Pelayo for translating Spanish documents, to Linda Jankov for drawing and Diane Lorenz for modifying the fine maps, and to Randy Millikan for reviewing the maps and suggesting changes in the location of Indian political units. Historians James Rawls, David Weber, and Donald Cutter shared documents and ideas. Anthropologists Randy Millikan and John Johnson carefully examined the manuscript, pointing out where I had erred and pointing to data I had overlooked. Someday, perhaps I can return the favor. Others reading part or all of the manuscript and offering suggestions for its improvement include Lowell Bean, Randall Dean, Norris Hundley, and Harry Lawton. Thanks one and all. I also would like to express my gratitude to Fr. Francis Guest, who was most generous in providing me with accommodations at Mission Santa Barbara while I conducted research in the mission's archives. Individuals not mentioned here will be acknowledged in the future when, barring senility, sudden wealth, academic fatigue, or marriage, two follow-up volumes appear.

I am especially grateful to Jeannette Henry Costo and the late Rupert Costo. Not only did they endow a chair in American Indian History at the University of California, Riverside, but they also supported my candidacy to be its second holder. Provided with a generous salary, travel funds, a research assistant (Donn Headley), and free time, I was able to advance the publication date and enhance the quality of this book.

Alfreda Mitre, then director of the Native American Students' Association, and the faculty and staffs of the departments of history and anthropology at Riverside made my stay intellectually stimulating and socially enjoyable. The students who took the two courses I taught on American Indian history also deserve mention. They demonstrated a keen interest in the subject and even found humor in my jokes.

A short time after I left Riverside, Rupert Costo died. In his memory I dedicate this book.

GEORGE HARWOOD PHILLIPS

Boulder, Colorado

Indians and Intruders
in Central California, 1769–1849

CHAPTER 1

Ethnohistorical Considerations

IN 1962 the British social anthropologist E. E. Evans-Pritchard encouraged his colleagues to consider the historical dimensions of the peoples they study. Concerned with the structures and functions of tribal societies, most social anthropologists then paid only cursory attention to the change these societies underwent after contact with whites. This neglect could be corrected, Evans-Pritchard argued, only if documentary sources and oral traditions were used.[1]

Evans-Pritchard also had some advice for historians: "It is understandable that in the past they should have restricted their activities to European history, but it is no longer so in the world in which we live today. When, instead of adding to our knowledge of Charles the Bold and the Conciliar movement, they show more initiative and write histories of non-European peoples and cultures they will better appreciate how relevant to their studies is our own research." Rhetorically, he asked how many scholars then in England could write the histories of India, China, and Africa that dealt with the indigenous peoples of those regions.[2]

At the time he wrote, however, several British historians were investigating the histories of non-European peoples, especially African peoples, and when their research appeared in print a short time later, the changes he called for were well underway.[3] And not all British anthropologists agreed they were ahistorical and unaware of the effect European colonialism had on tribal peoples.[4] According to I. M. Lewis, "the majority of monographs based on field research in the structual-functional tradition have included some excursions into history, however unsophisticated or unsystematic these may seem to the orthodox historian."[5]

Whereas anthropologists have expressed some interest in history and historical methodologies, until recently few historians have acknowledged that anthropology has much to offer them. An exception is Keith Thomas, who some years ago claimed that those studying Great Britain could gain much from an examination of the anthropological literature:

Where can one find a better explanation of the Divine Rights of Kings than in Evans-Pritchard's analysis of the kingship of the Shilluk of Sudan? Where is there a closer analogy with the medieval and Elizabethan world-picture than in the Tikopia conception of the future life . . . ? The emphasis upon the binding force of oaths among the Kikuyu is reminiscent of seventeenth-century England, where the oath provided the sanction for almost every form of legal, official or ecclesiastical arrangement. The Cargo cults of Melanesia are obviously analagous with such millenarian movements as that of the Fifth Monarchy Men in England.[6]

Thomas reasoned that the historian "familiar with the findings of the anthropologists is in a better position to ask intelligent questions of his material."[7]

More so than historians, anthropologists have identified the common ground shared by the two disciplines. William Fenton noted that "it is the ethnologist's business to delineate patterns, forms, and processes of culture history. But such attempts at descriptive integration . . . are also characteristic of the work of the historian."[8] Alfred Kroeber understood that historians, like anthropologists, employ synchronic analyses. Occasionally they halt the "narrative flow in order to hold a . . . period steady while they review the state of institutions, arts, manners, attitudes, and values . . . in the country or area they are dealing with." Temporarily, "the pervasive regularities of human behavior" take precedent over diachronic developments.[9]

According to Robert Anderson,

historians are remarkably like anthropologists in their concern with culture studied holistically and comparatively. They typically study societies as integrated wholes even though they rarely use an explicit model of functional integration. They typically make comparative assessments, even though they rarely use any systematic technique for comparison. One finds, as a result, much implicit theory in their work, and it merits looking into.[10]

It would be inaccurate, in the words of Claude Lévi-Strauss, to claim that "the historian and the anthropologist travel in opposite directions. On the contrary, they both go the same way. The fact that their journey together appears to each of them in a different light—to the historian, transition from the explicit to the implicit; to the anthropologist, transition from the particular to the universal—does not in the least alter the identical character of their fundamental approach."[11] Marshall Sahlins wrote that "practice clearly has gone beyond the theoretical differences that are supposed to divide anthropology and history. Anthropologists rise from the abstract structure to the explication of the concrete event. Historians devalue the unique event in favor of underlying recurrent structures."[12]

Even the sources used by anthropologists and historians are not as distinct as they may appear. Kroeber pointed out that "ethnographic accounts are usually based not on search and exploitation of already extant documents, but on newly made documents resulting from face-to-face interviews and observations."[13] What does the historian do, Lévi-Strauss queried, "when he studies documents if not to surround himself with the testimony of amateur ethnographers, who were often as far removed from the culture they described as is the modern investigator from Polynesians or Pygmies?"[14]

Although the basic kinds of sources used by anthropologists and historians have not drastically changed over time, the theories they employ and themes they develop often derive from the intellectual climate current at a particular time. Historians long have acknowledged that their views of the past are influenced by their perceptions of the present, most professing that each generation should rewrite its history. But neither are anthropologists immune from the influences of contemporary life. As Evans-Pritchard explained: "What anthropologists inquire into, observe, and record, and the inferences they draw from their observations, also change from generation to generation."[15]

That many anthropologists and historians have been greatly influenced by the recent activities of non-Europeans is to state the obvious. As African, Asian, and Pacific peoples have achieved independence from their European colonizers, and as American Indians, Australian Aborigines, and other minority groups have sought more recognition and rights within their respective countries, interest has been generated regarding the historical interaction of intruding and indigenous peoples. In their investigations of interethnic relations, anthropologists and historians increasingly have employed the term "ethnohistory."[16]

Gregory Dening has suggested that the term also implies a reaction to, even a rejection of, the old ways of doing things: "Ethnohistory is the bastard child of history and anthropology, born out of the snobbish reluctance of historians to be interested in anyone who was not white and did not wear a crown and born too out of the intransigent belief of anthropologists that to understand anyone they must be alive, in remote places and in dire danger of disappearing."[17]

That a true hybrid discipline will emerge is unlikely because most scholars calling themselves ethnohistorians were trained either as anthropologists or as historians. Their research usually is designed to fulfill the goals dictated by their respective disciplines. Anthropologists use written documents to corroborate the data gained from field work. Historians draw upon the cultural information produced by anthropologists to support the data derived from the written sources. As noted by William Sturtevant, "when historians and anthropologists read each others' writings it is usually in search of specific data on a culture of mutual concern rather than through interest in the theory and method of the other field."[18]

Ethnohistorians from each discipline bring to the study of American Indians strengths and weaknesses. On the one hand, historians have been trained to investigate intersocietal activity within large regions and thus conceptually are well prepared to examine Indian-white and inter-Indian relations over time.[19] But many are methodologically ill prepared to understand the activities and behavior of nonliterate peoples. On the other hand, anthropologists are well prepared to investigate distinct, usually small-scale groups, but many lack the training necessary to fully appreciate the dynamics of multisocietal interaction, especially when Euroamerican societies are involved. Bruce Trigger admitted that "the anthropologist usually knows little about the complex economic and political relationships among the European powers who were in contact with the Indians."[20]

The two disciplines are restrictive in other ways as well. Because anthropologists of the American Indian tend to place the people they study in culture or linguistic areas, they often overlook processes of interaction. The Huron, for example, have been placed in the Northeast Culture Area, but they traded with the Cree, who have been classified as a subarctic people. Because historians of the Indian often present their data within time frames exclusively created to trace and analyze Euroamerican activity, they often fail to understand that the historical watersheds occurring in Indian and Euroamerican societies seldom intersected. The American revolution may have ended British rule, but it did not end Cherokee independence.

Particularly detrimental in appreciating the importance of the Indian in shaping postcontact North American history has been the widespread application of the frontier thesis. Formulated by Frederick Jackson Turner in 1893 and perpetuated by his many followers, the thesis relegates Indians to "the frontier," a vaguely defined area repeatedly penetrated by westward-moving whites.[21] As pointed out by Francis Jennings, this kind of history presents "only one side of the frontier. . . . The Indians who appear in it are cardboard figures set up to be knocked down. It cannot be anything else so long as the frontier is conceived as a line of separation constantly being pushed 'back.' "[22]

Modifying the concept of the frontier to encompass distinct cultures had been undertaken with some vigor. To Robin Wells, an anthropologist, the frontier is "a dynamic social network of a particular kind which covers an extensive geographical area and which links a number of culturally diverse societies."[23] To Jack Forbes, a historian, the frontier is a situation that involves "more than momentary contact between two ethnic, cultural or national groups."[24]

More specifically, historians Leonard Thompson and Howard Lamar have conceptualized the frontier "not as a boundary or line, but as a territory or zone of interpenetration between two previously distinct societies. Usually, one of the societies is indigenous to the region, or at least has occupied it for many generations; the other is intrusive. The frontier 'opens' in a given zone when the first representatives of the intrusive society arrive; it 'closes' when a single political authority has established hegemony over the zone."[25]

By identifying the frontier first *as* a zone and then by claiming the frontier opens and closes *in* a zone under certain conditions, these historians regard the frontier as both a region and a process. In this regard, Thompson and Lamar have failed to overcome some of the concerns issued by Walker Wyman and Clifton Kroeber in an earlier publication. "Considering the great variety of frontiers," they wrote, "it is small wonder that historians have no fixed meaning of the term. They have considered it a place, or a process, or a situation."[26]

Because the frontier of one people is the homeland of another, the addition of this elusive term to the study of interethnic relations clouds rather than clarifies the issues under discussion. Alfonso Ortiz, an anthropologist, proposed that "we dispense with the notion of the frontier altogether when talking about historical encounters between peoples . . . because it is possible to make so much mischief with this notion."[27] By abandoning the term, we also dispense with the difficult task of attempting to identify when the "frontier" opened and closed in a particular zone. Instead, we can discuss a zone's different phases. The history of one zone might comprise several phases, that of another only two or three; some phases lasted decades, others only a few years. But whatever the time frame applied to a particular zone, it would be determined not by a conventional period in North American history (although coincidence should not be ruled out) but rather by the processes of interaction established between intruding and indigenous peoples.

Ideally, a zone of interaction would be defined by its geographical unity, cultural uniformity, and historical continuity. A river system, coastal strip, or interior valley, of course, are never perfect geographical entities, but they can provide spatial frameworks in which to investigate Indian-white interaction. Because most zones comprised more than one indigenous society, political unity may be lacking, but cultural similarities, such as common subsistence patterns, might be present. Whether different Indian societies located in a particular zone shared a common culture and a territory with well-defined features, however, is not as important as their sharing a common past with one another and with the Euroamericans with whom they interacted.

The extent and availability of the cultural and historical evidence will determine to a large degree whether the processes of interaction in a particular zone can be truly comprehended. Because some Indian peoples have been extensively studied by anthropologists, ethnohistorians have access to an abundance of data regarding material culture, spiritual beliefs, social organization, and economic systems. Other peoples dispersed or disappeared before much information was recorded. In some cases, the oral traditions Indians have transmitted over time provide ethnohistorians with the values and viewpoints of the people being investigated. In other cases, so devastating was the Euroamerican impact that Indians remember little of their distant past.

Ethnohistorians concerned with Indian-white interaction must rely heavily upon documentary evidence. Contrary to established opinion, those who left accounts of Indians did not always portray them in negative and stereotypical ways. Few appreciated or understood Indian culture to any significant degree, and many expressed their ignorance and bigotry in no uncertain terms. But others demonstrated concern and occasionally respect for the peoples they encountered. True, their descriptions often were determined by the relationship then existing between Indians and whites. Conflict is not conducive to objectivity. But even those repeatedly suffering from Indian attacks usually left behind more information than opinion. Over the course of some five hundred years of Indian-white contact, a vast body of data has accumulated. Much of this evidence has been either ignored or employed to rationalize Euroamerican expansion and conquest, but it exists nevertheless. The problem is not the amount of historical evidence; the problem is that much of it lies buried in bits and pieces in the diaries, journals, and reports that deal mainly with other matters. As any ethnohistorian will attest, it is much easier to write about those who produced the documents than about those intermittently mentioned in them.

Furthermore, writing the history of any culture relying mainly on documents produced by another is, in the words of Trigger,

different from writing the history of a literate people who have abundantly documented their own activities. Admittedly, it may not be so different from trying to understand the history of illiterate peasantries or working classes in Europe using documentation produced almost exclusively by the state, the clergy, and the upper classes. Yet, in dealing with native people, there is the additional challenge of studying wholly alien cultures. Ethnohistorians require not only all the skills of a good conventional historian but also a sound knowledge of ethnology, if they are to be able to evaluate sources and interpret them with reasonable understanding of the perceptions and motivations of the native people involved.[28]

The vast majority of North American historians, of course, are concerned with issues having nothing to do with Indians. But those studying the colonial period, western expansion, and particular regions who overlook Indian activity may be doing themselves a disservice. According to Trigger, "the price of ignoring native history has been not simply a one-sided understanding of relations between native peoples and Europeans. In some cases it has resulted in serious misunderstanding of the internal dynamics of European colonialism."[29]

The price of downplaying or overlooking Euroamerican activity, advocated by some, is equally costly to our understanding of interethnic relations.[30] At different times and places, Indians and whites interacted with such intensity that to ignore the latter is to trivialize the activities and influences of the former. As explained by Trigger, "if we are to understand the total situation, we must attempt to achieve a . . . dispassionate understanding of the motives of European groups . . . who interacted with the Indians."[31] Dening put it this way: "To know the native one must know the intruder. . . . In the ethnohistory of culture contact . . . we are concerned to write the anthropology and the history of those moments when native and intruding cultures are conjoined. Neither can be known independently of that moment. They are both changed by it and change all the subsequent moments."[32]

Maintaining a perfect balance between the activities of Indians and Euroamericans, it should be admitted, is difficult if not impossible to achieve, although the imbalance is partially corrected when the processes of interaction are investigated within a zone of interaction. When a region occupied by Indian peoples is selected as the spatial framework for the investigation, the ethnohistorian acknowledges the historical importance of the "original" inhabitants. But only against a backdrop of conventional chronology can Indian activity be followed. Comprehending the strategies implemented by the Indians is impossible without tracing the activities undertaken by the intruders.

Because those penetrating a zone usually were bent upon domination and exploitation, prominent figures in North American history—the explorer, missionary, trapper, and pioneer—are cast in a different light. The task of the ethnohistorian, however, is not to replace one set of "heroes" with another. It is, rather, to present an accurate description of the process of interaction and a careful analysis of the ramifications it produced in the different societies under investigation.

Most of the activity examined in this study transpired in the vast region the Spanish called the Tulares but now known as the

San Joaquin Valley. Although comprising only half of the great Central Valley, it contains ample geographical unity to fulfill the territorial requirement for a zone of interaction. Because most of the Indian peoples residing in the zone spoke Penutian languages, because all subsisted upon the abundant wild plant and animal life, and because all were organized in relatively sedentary village communities, cultural uniformity was extensive. Most importantly, the valley represents a zone of interaction because, much

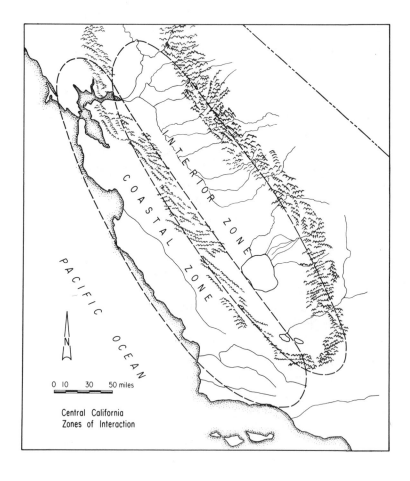

Central California
Zones of Interaction

more than other interior regions, it was repeatedly penetrated by intruders beginning in the last third of the eighteenth century. The coastal region from where most of the intruders came also constitutes a zone of interaction. Because Indians in this zone were first to experience the consequences of colonization, understanding its history is crucial to comprehending the nature of Indian-white interaction in the interior. The historical processes unfolding in the two zones further intersected when Indians from the coast fled to the interior to reorder their lives and later when Indians from the interior intruded upon the lands occupied by the Euroamericans.

Just as geographical features rather than the concept of the culture area determined the spatial framework of this study, the dynamics of Indian-white contact rather than traditional periods in California history determined its temporal framework. Unlike many ethnohistorical studies, it ends not with the defeat, dispersal, or destruction of Indian peoples but with the conclusion of a particular phase in the history of a zone of interaction.

CHAPTER 2

Indian Occupation

In old times water covered all this earth. . . . Chicken Hawk . . . was God's son. Every morning he would go around looking for the earth. First God made four ducks, two large and two somewhat smaller. He didn't like these as they were quite useless, just floating around on the water all the time. The ducks, however, kept diving down under the water to try to find the bottom. God thought it was time they all had some earth to live on; he asked Chicken Hawk to take care of the matter.

Chicken Hawk asked the ducks what they were doing. They told him they were trying to touch bottom. Hawk told them to continue trying, for if they could get some earth they could make the world. The two larger ducks tried again and came up exhausted. Then the larger of the smallest pair went down; he failed though he was nearly unconscious when he returned. Finally the very smallest black one went down. He went down, down, down; he thought he'd drown. He reached the bottom and seized the earth with both his hands. As he came up the rush of passing water washed all the sand out of his fists. When he reached the surface he was almost dead. Hawk picked him up, scraped the sand from under his fingernails. This he took to his father.

God told his son to take the sand and go far back toward the east, and as he traveled westward again to drop one grain of sand at a time. Chicken Hawk did this. As the grains were dropped they grew up into mountains which pushed the water westward to the place it now occupies. The ocean's home used to be where the Sierra Nevada Mountains are standing.[1]

This Yokuts creation myth shares much with the geologic record regarding the formation of the Central Valley. Some 140 million years ago the interior of California formed part of a vast shallow sea floor. Eventually, a batholith of crystalline rock emerged in the eastern portion of the sea, forming a mountain range. During the following ninety million years, residue from these mountains was transported westward down ancient streams to the sea, where it formed a sedimentary pavement on the floor. About fifty million years ago, the western edge of the sea floor warped into the geographical predecessor of the Coast Range. The peaks of this range remained above sea level for only a short period before again becoming part of the sea floor.[2]

During the ensuing thirty-seven million years, the batholith evolved into a low plain that sloped to the west. Uplifting of sev-

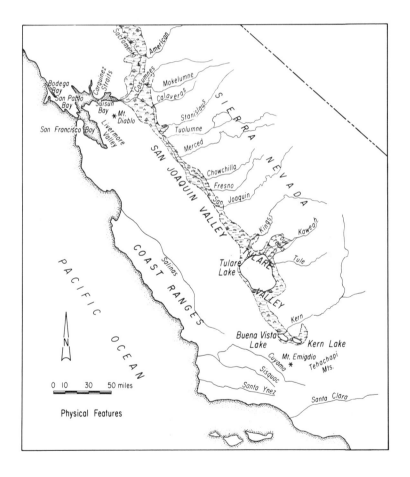

Physical Features

eral thousand feet on the eastern side of the batholith caused a steepening of the western plain, creating the Sierra Nevada. Between the mountains and the sea lay the Central Valley. The western edge of the valley was later formed when the Coast Range reemerged.[3]

Then God made one man and one woman for each tribe and put them where their home is now. At this time brothers and sisters married each other. God did not like this so he made a road so that the tribes could travel about and marry among each other. Men began to walk on this road. . . . When they first met each other they'd ask each other who they were and where they were going. They were all friendly, asked one another to visit, and intertribal marriage resulted.[4]

The movement and interaction of peoples mentioned in the legend corresponds with the archeological record which postulates that Indians arrived in California in waves. The first wave probably occurred between 10,000 and 9,000 B.C., resulting in the occupation of parts of the coast and the interior of southern California.[5] As members of the Paleo-Indian culture, the first occupants relied heavily upon big game for subsistence, in particular bison, mammoth, antelope, camelids, deer, sloth, and an early species of the horse. They hunted and trapped smaller game such as rabbits, lizards, and tortoises and probably collected some of the plant life as well. But as big game hunters, the Paleo-Indians are best known.[6]

Paleo-Indians arrived in California when North America was experiencing the last glaciation of the Pleistocene. As the earth began to warm, rainfall decreased and ground water evaporated. The grazing areas available to the large herds shrank dramatically. By the end of the Pleistocene (9,000 B.C.), the large animals had disappeared and with them the Paleo-Indian culture.[7]

Then God dropped acorns, manzanita, and all seeds that were needed. In the spring the salmon came; they were dried and taken home. . . . The Indians moved about to gather acorns. Everything was free.[8]

The use of acorns, seeds, and fish referred to in the legend was the salient feature of the Archaic Culture which followed the Paleo-Indian. The disappearance of the big game forced Indians to experiment with the environment, to develop a more diffuse

Gathering seeds in the San Joaquin Valley, by S. Eastman from a sketch by E. M. Kern, 1865. Courtesy of The Bancroft Library, University of California, Berkeley.

economy. By about 3000 B.C., they had become dependent upon a variety of plant species.[9] It was during the Archaic, moreover, that Indians established permanent settlement in the northern reaches of the San Joaquin Valley. This occurred between 3500 and 2500 B.C.[10]

Those occupying the delta area, where the San Joaquin and Sacramento rivers converge, hunted deer and other small mammals for meat and hides and fished for salmon.[11] They gathered hard seeds from the grasslands and chaparral, grinding them on milling slabs. The mortars and pestles found at their sites suggest they also consumed acorns. The olivella and abalone shell ornaments located in graves indicate trade connections with coastal groups. Charmstones carved from steatite and other materials identify the delta people as the originators of spiritual beliefs that eventually spread throughout the Central Valley.[12]

By about 1700 B.C., settlements in the delta had increased in size and numbers, and Indians increasingly relied upon salmon and acorns for subsistence. They manufactured more milling tools than before and depended more heavily upon trade than had their predecessors. Instead of burying their dead in a horizontal position, as was the former tradition, they interred them with knees lifted toward the chest.[13]

Settlements continued to grow in the delta. By A.D. 500, the acorn and salmon had become the most important food staples. Villages located along the San Joaquin and Sacramento rivers and in the delta contained large pit-houses and storage facilities. Indians manufactured from bones a variety of practical artifacts, such as awls, needles, and barbed harpoon heads.[14]

Linguistic evidence indicates that these Indians were the ancestors of the Miwok. They spoke Penutian, a language stock that appeared in California about the time the delta first was settled.[15] The Penutian speakers who later spread southwards became known as Yokuts. Upon arriving at the southern end of the valley, they met Chumash Indians, who spoke a Hokan language.[16] Sometime after A.D. 1000, speakers of an Uto-Aztecan language crossed the Sierra Nevada from the east and settled in the western foothills, eventually becoming known as the Monache (or West-ern Mono).[17] Other Uto-Aztecan speakers, the Kitanemuk, occu-pied Antelope Valley and later, about A.D. 1700, spread into the Tehachapi Mountains.[18]

The occupation of most of the San Joaquin Valley and adjacent foothills indicates that the region contained an abundance of nat-ural food resources. The animal life of the area probably had changed little when first observed by literate visitors. To be found in the interior, James Carson noted in 1852, were

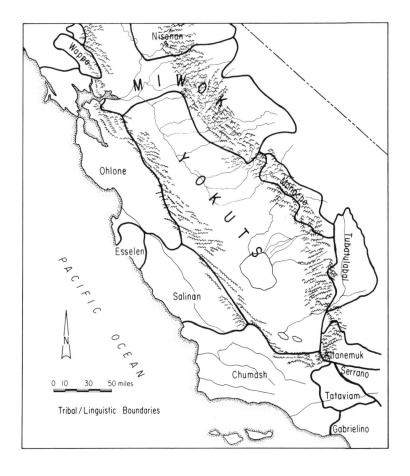

elk, antelope, black tail and red deer, grizzly and brown bear, black and gray wolves, coyotes, ocelots, California lions, wildcats, beaver, otter, mink, weasels, ferrets, hare, rabbits, grey & red foxes, grey & ground squirrels, kangaroo rats, badgers, skunks, muskrats, hedgehogs, and many species of small animals not here mentioned; swan, geese, brant and over twenty different description of ducks also cover the plains and waters in countless myriads from the first of October until the first of April, besides millions of grocus (sand hill crane), plover, snipe and quail.[19]

As reported in 1851 by an anonymous traveler to the Tulare Lake region,

The abundance of fish of all kinds in these waters is absolutely astonishing. The waters seem alive with them, and the variety is as great as the quality of most of them is good. Pike, perch, bass, salmon, grout, eels, suckers, and many other kinds . . . are caught with the greatest ease. . . .

The quality of game which frequent these magnificent sheets of water, and build their nests and hatch their young among the tules, is immense. Large flocks of geese, swans, pelicans, cranes, ducks, teal and curlews, can be seen at every point.[20]

The kinds of food resources consumed by the Indians were determined by the ecological zones in which they lived. The lake peoples (Yokuts) relied heavily upon the fish and waterfowl found exclusively in this particular environment. The foothill peoples of the lower levels of the Sierra Nevada (Yokuts, Miwok, Monache) occupied an area containing a great variety of wild foods. Because they lived along streams or on ridges between streams, they had easy access to fish, but they also harvested the wild plants that grew in the woodland, grassland, and chaparral vegetation zones. The valley peoples (Yokuts and Miwok) tended to cluster along the San Joaquin River and its tributaries, fish being their most important staple. The delta peoples (Miwok) also relied heavily upon fish.[21]

Indians also hunted and trapped a variety of large and small game. In the foothills they stalked the Columbian black-tailed and California mule deer, and in the valley the tule elk and the pronghorn antelope.[22] Indians shot them from blinds at lakes and waterholes and snared them in nooses placed along trails. They also flushed rodents and ground squirrels from their holes by smoke and water and drove rabbits into nets stretched over a wide area.[23]

Fishing for salmon in the southern Sacramento Valley, by J. R. Bartlett, 1854. Courtesy of The Bancroft Library, University of California, Berkeley.

Regarding all the plant life available to interior Indians, the acorn was perhaps the most important. Of the nearly twenty species of oak, Indians used nine as food, although some of these were of marginal value. Especially important were the valley oak, blue oak, maul oak, and black oak. Indians preferred some species to others, but availability and abundance, not preference, often dictated which oaks were harvested.[24]

The valley oak was found not only throughout the valley floor but also in the foothills of the Sierra Nevada to elevations of about fifteen hundred feet. It failed to grow in dense stands and thus was not as numerous as some of the other species, but it produced a large crop. Every third year Indians could expect an abundant harvest from this species. In a good year, one tree might produce five hundred pounds of acorns.[25]

On the dry, rocky hillsides in the Sierra Nevada foothills, between five hundred and two thousand feet, grew the blue oak. Smaller than the valley oak, the average blue oak produced only about 160 pounds of acorns per season. The maul oak was found in the Sierra Nevada between fifteen hundred and five thousand feet, its crop size averaging between 150 and 200 pounds per tree. Sharing the same habitat was the black oak, which produced between 200 and 300 pounds per tree in a good year. It was, moreover, a reliable tree, producing at least one good crop in every two years.[26]

Harvesting, transporting, and storing the acorns were relatively easy tasks. Indians knocked the acorns from the trees with long poles and stored them in large baskets inside dwellings or in large wattle granaries on platforms built a few feet above the ground.[27]

Before the acorns could be eaten, the tannic acid had to be removed. One method, probably the first devised, was to bury the unshelled acorns in mud for several months, thereby neutralizing the acid. Only when the technique of leaching was invented, however, did the acorn become a truly important staple. The nuts were shelled and then pounded into a meal. The meal was placed either in a basket or in a sand-lined hole in the ground. Hot water poured over the meal leached the tannic acid.[28]

Sometimes the meal was baked into a cake on a flat stone in a fire. More commonly, it was mixed with water in a watertight basket. Hot stones, continually added, kept the water boiling. The meal was either drunk or eaten with a spoon.[29] Spanish clover, pond lily roots, mushrooms, tree fungi, and small seeds often were mixed with the meal to enhance its flavor.[30]

As recalled by an American settler, George Stewart, Indians made use of many plant species:

Several plants, such as burr-clover, sorrel, and Indian lettuce, and edible roots, were consumed in quantities without cooking. Leaves of a number of plants were boiled and eaten as greens. A kind of soup was made of the seeds of the peppergrass. Berries of various kinds were eaten fresh or dried. Some varieties known to be poisonous when first picked were cooked in a manner to render them harmless. The bulbs of many plants were eaten raw, but other kinds were cooked before eating. Fungi growing on oak, cottonwood, and willow trees were eaten fresh or roasted, and were considered delicacies.[31]

The anonymous visitor to Tulare Lake observed Indians putting the tules, or bulrushes, to good use, noting that "the green roots are used for food, and when ground into pulp and baked into cakes, are very palatable, and seem to be nutritious." Tules were useful in other ways as well: "the dry roots serve for fuel; from the stalks baskets are made; while more than one Indian conceals his nakedness under a mat of them." No one could ask for "a better bed than a mass of fresh-pulled tules."[32]

As a source of medicine, some plants were indispensable. "The Indians, and particularly the women, had a remarkable knowledge of the medicinal properties of plants," Stewart recalled. "They prepared purgatives, emetics, poultices, decoctions of various kinds, and ate roots of some plants and leaves and stems of others for the beneficial effects of their juices."[33] The Chumash used a root, *Lomatium californicum,* that grew in the mountains. Called *chuchupate* or "plant of great virtue," the Indians, according to the Spanish explorer José Longinos Martínez, ascribed to it "a cure for all kinds of headaches by merely smelling it, and for pains in the stomach by chewing a little of it and swallowing the saliva."[34] The Chumash also believed that when worn or carried, the root would protect the individual from rattlesnakes.[35]

Of great spiritual importance to the Chumash and to the peoples residing in the southern San Joaquin Valley was a species of the hallucinogenic plant *Datura,* commonly called jimsonweed. Preparing the concoction took special skill, because the root was poisonous. The dose swallowed to induce a vision was only slightly less than the lethal amount. The age of the plant, the kind of soil in which it had grown, the size of the root, and the season in which it was harvested were factors the preparer took into consideration. Too strong to ingest late in the year, it was consumed by the Yokuts and Kitanemuk only during the winter and early spring. Those who took Datura attempted to make contact with a supernatural guardian, the dream helper, who would assist them in becoming more proficient at a particular task, communicating with the dead, viewing the future, overcoming unhappiness, or curing illness.[36]

Indians not only devised a variety of ways to procure and use the natural food and medicinal resources of California, but also consciously manipulated the environment to ensure that nature's supply would be available and accessible. Indians regularly burned brush, thus producing parkland environments which lessened the likelihood of wildfires, increased animal and plant productivity, and improved the flow of springs.[37] Martínez noted that the Indians "have the custom of burning the brush, for two purposes: one for hunting rabbits and hares . . . ; second, so that with the first light rain or dew the shoots will come up."[38] "At times," Stewart recalled, "when there was no danger of a prairie-fire large clumps of tall bushy weed were set on fire at the windward side, and hares, rabbits, coyotes, skunks, and other animals, as they ran out, were shot by hunters who had previously surrounded the place."[39]

Because of the abundance of wild plant and animal foods, Indians of the valley, although hunter-gatherers, lived a remarkably sedentary existence. Hamlets and villages were designed to be permanent. An American traveler, Stephen Powers, noted that the Yokuts resided in houses, "conical or wedge-shaped, generally made of tule, and just enough hollowed out within so that the inmates may sleep with the head higher than the feet, all in perfect alignment, and with a continuous awning of brushwood stretching along in front."[40]

The residents of every village constructed at least one *temescal,* or sweathouse. The Spanish explorer Francisco Garcés described the temescal as

an underground room covered with sticks and grass after the manner of an oven; it has no more than one opening, which in some (cases) is in the roof and in others at the side. The hour of entering therein is either during the morning, or during the evening. When once the persons are inside, they kindle a fire; and . . . they . . . sweat until the earth grows wet; when indeed they can endure no more they climb out by means of their ladder of sticks and throw themselves into the river.[41]

Bathing cleansed the body, but it also guaranteed good health and a long life.[42]

Living a healthy existence in a bountiful land, the Indians of California increased to over three hundred thousand by the time of European contact.[43] How a people relying exclusively on nature for subsistence could have grown so large confused some of the early visitors. Late in his life, J. J. Warner recalled a journey through the San Joaquin Valley during the winter of 1832–33:

Yokuts lodges, by Stephen Powers, 1877. Courtesy of The Bancroft Library, University of California, Berkeley.

The banks of the Sacramento and San Joaquin, and the numerous tributaries of these rivers, and the Tule Lake, were at this time studded with Indians villages of from one to twelve hundred inhabitants each. The population of this extensive valley was so great that it caused surprise, and required a close investigation into the nature of a country that without cultivation, could afford the means of subsistence to so great a community.

His "close investigation" revealed a correlation between food resources and population density. Warner acknowledged the importance of fish, fowl, and game to the Indians but also realized that "the demand for food would have been but partially satisfied had they not brought the vegetable kingdom under contribution. . . . So great was the number of inhabitants, that no source from which subsistence could be derived in this most abundant and productive valley, was neglected."[44]

The densest populations were located near rivers and lakes. The Kings and Kaweah rivers and the Tulare Lake basin carried a population of over twenty thousand. Another seven thousand persons resided in the less-watered areas of the southern San Joaquin Valley. Some forty thousand individuals settled along the San Joaquin River and its tributaries—the Fresno, Chowchilla, Merced, Tuolumne, Stanislaus, Calaveras, Mokelumne, and Cosumnes. Nine thousand persons occupied the delta area; another four thousand resided in the foothills of the Sierra Nevada. Thus, the population of the San Joaquin Valley and adjacent foothills grew to approximately eighty thousand.[45]

In important ways, population density was linked to the types of social organization Indians developed in California. Those who first arrived in the region were organized into bands. Most bands comprised fewer than one hundred persons, thus allowing all members to know one another intimately. As Indians improved their knowledge of procuring and processing wild foods, societies grew in size and density. The intimacy characteristic of band organization gave way to impersonal relationships, which forced Indians to erect a system that furnished a set of symbols which allowed the individual to act in prescribed ways to other mem-

bers of the society. Kinship principles, in particular the lineage/
clan system, provided this set of symbols.[46]

The areas most heavily settled contained Indians with the
strongest kinship systems.[47] For example, the Miwok who resided along the rivers and in the delta possessed well-developed
lineages. Comprised of males and their offspring, and called *nena*,
each lineage was associated with either the land or the water moiety. An Indian belonging to a nena in the land moiety had to
marry someone from a nena in the water moiety. Residence was
patrilocal; wives left their natal settlements to live with their
husbands.[48]

Apparently, the male members of each nena, along with their
wives, resided in a single hamlet. Land immediately adjacent to
the hamlet, usually containing a stream or spring, belonged to the
nena and was used in common. The convergence of kinship organization and territory meant that the nena formed the basic political unit among the Miwok.[49] A headman governed the nena but
acted only with the consensus of all adult male members, especially the elders. Regulating trade, directing relations with other
groups, settling disputes, and teaching morality were some of his
duties.[50]

Yokuts residing immediately to the south of the Miwok, especially those settled along the major rivers, probably employed the
lineage as their basic political unit and thus differed little in this
regard from their neighbors to the north. But those residing south
of the San Joaquin River possessed lineages that lacked distinct
territories and exclusive political functions. Many, if not most, of
the southern Yokuts were organized into territorial units, each
comprising several lineages. Furthermore, unlike the Miwok lineage in which all members resided in a single hamlet, members of
several lineages often resided in a single village. Kin, therefore,
were diffused throughout the political unit.[51]

A chief governed each unit, and his duties were manifold. He
authorized trading and food-gathering expeditions, directed the
intertribal mourning ceremony, sanctioned punishment, provided assistance to those in need, and advised individuals with

personal problems. Assisting the chief were members of his lineage and those who formed a staff called the *wina'tum*. The staff served as an ad hoc police force during large gatherings, managed the distribution of food, and regulated ceremonies.[52]

A shaman also assisted in the regulation of the social order. Usually a friend and associate of the chief, he occupied an important position in Yokuts society. As both doctor and priest, the shaman administered to the sick by prescribing medicines for common ailments and by employing the supernatural powers he

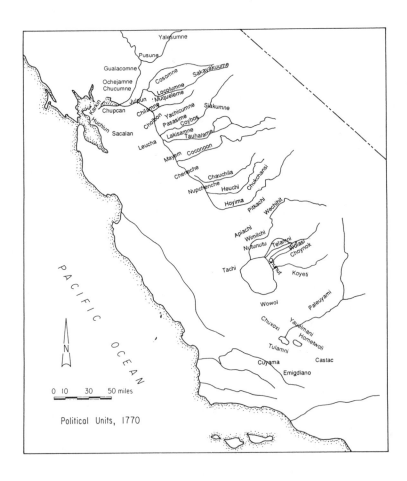

claimed to possess.[53] If the shaman lost three patients, however, he could be put to death by relatives of the deceased. Some shamans became famous beyond their own communities and traveled widely to serve the needy.[54] Yokuts also traveled long distances to trade. A Spanish priest, Antonio Ripoll, remembered parties of twenty or thirty men and women arriving once a year along the coast with a thick sugar called *panocha*. Made from honey-dew and sweet carisa cane and wild tobacco mixed with lime, it was chewed.[55] The Yokuts also provided the Chumash with herbs, seeds, salt from salt grass, and obsidian.[56] The Yokuts brought back to their villages a variety of products. While in the Tulare Valley, Garcés spotted small baskets, knives of flint, and vessels with inlays of mother-of-pearl obtained from coastal peoples with whom "they carried on much commerce."[57] The Chumash also supplied the southern Yokuts with beads and ornaments made from a variety of shells.[58]

Yokuts seldom crossed the Sierra Nevada to the lands occupied by Paiutes.[59] But Owens Valley Paiutes sent trading expeditions east across the mountains. For salt, pine nuts, obsidian, rabbit-skin blankets, balls of tobacco, and buckskins, they acquired manzanita berries, baskets, and strings of shells. Paiutes who resided at Mono Lake also ventured eastwards, exchanging baskets, pine nuts, and salt for acorns, manzanita berries, and elderberries. The Paiute traders often wintered in the Yosemite Valley, where they married Miwok women.[60]

The permanent establishment of Paiutes (the Monache) on the western side of the Sierra Nevada may have resulted from a trading expedition stranded because of early snow storms.[61] The northern Yokuts living in the foothills of the Sierra Nevada supplied the Monache with acorns, willow-bark baskets, and shell beads. They received, in turn, rabbit-skin blankets, moccasins, rock salt, and piñon seeds.[62] The Monache rarely traveled across the mountains to trade but exchanged with neighboring Yokuts the products Paiutes brought to them.[63] They became, in effect, middlemen in a trans-Sierra economic system.

Perhaps the single most prevalent cause of intersocietal conflict resulted from economic competition. The intrusion by members of one group into another's territory to hunt, fish, or harvest was grounds for retaliation. Martínez noted that wars "always originate over the rights of boundaries or places where they gather seeds."[64] Along the eastern side of the San Joaquin Valley, where Uto-Aztecan speakers (Monache) and Penutian speakers (Yokuts and Miwok) shared common borders and the same food resources, battles often took place.[65]

Conflicts also erupted between coastal and interior peoples. In 1879 an Indian, Juan Estevan Pico, told Stephen Bowers about an ancient fight between Yokuts from the southern San Joaquin Valley and the Chumash from the Point Mugu area. A woman belonging to a Yokuts group had been unfaithful to her Chumash husband and was, along with her lover, condemned to death. Three times the Yokuts warned the Chumash that the execution would lead to war. As recorded by Bowers, "the man and woman were killed and their bodies burned according to the laws and customs of the Santa Barbara Indians. Four hundred Tejon [Yokuts] Indians at once set out to avenge the death of the woman by punishing the Magu [sic] people; but in the encounter they were badly defeated and left some seventy of their dead on the field."[66]

The Indians first venturing into the San Joaquin Valley acquired through trial and error the knowledge necessary to use much of the plant and animal resources the region produced in abundance and variety. This expertise allowed them to spread throughout the valley, to settle in permanent villages, and to establish social systems based on kinship principles and territorial identity. Warfare flared periodically, political boundaries expanded and contracted, but apparently the social landscape remained stable over extended periods.

Unlike the Indians residing in the coastal zone who experienced occasional contact with European seamen during the sixteenth and seventeenth centuries, those in the San Joaquin Valley remained isolated from the beginning of European interest in the region. But they were soon to realize that geography could offer them only partial protection. Three years after the Spaniards planted their first settlement, they penetrated the interior. Initially, they came to explore rather than to exploit, but a precedent was established that became the basis for increasingly intensive interaction.

CHAPTER 3

Spanish Penetration

SPANISH colonization of Alta California began in 1769 with the founding of a mission and presidio in the San Diego area. Although initiating a process that ultimately resulted in the establishment of twenty-one missions, four presidios, three pueblos, and a few privately owned ranchos, the Spanish military and religious personnel occupying San Diego represented an empire in steep decline. Because the monarchy lacked the men, money, and motivation to militarily conquer and effectively populate California, the task of bringing the region under the flag of Spain fell largely to Franciscan missionaries.[1]

The Franciscans arrived in the region with a well-developed colonizing ideology which had taken shape over several centuries. Precedent, experience, and law dictated, at least in theory, how the Indians were to be treated. By persuasion and example, the missionaries would convince the Indians, whom they labeled gentiles, to abandon their traditional culture for a life that embraced Catholicism, agriculture, the Spanish language, and Iberian political institutions.[2] After a period of tutelage and baptism, the gentiles would become neophytes and would be transformed into loyal subjects of the king and dedicated believers in Christ. Ultimately, they would govern themselves in villages created from the missions. The Franciscans would then move on to other regions to begin the process anew.[3]

During the 1770s several Spanish settlements took hold along the central California coastline. In 1770 a presidio and Mission San Carlos Borromeo were established at Monterey among the Ohlone. In 1771 and 1772 Mission San Antonio de Padua opened in Salinan territory and San Luís Obispo de Tolosa in that of the

Chumash. At the tip of the San Francisco peninsula, Mission San Francisco de Asís and a presidio were planted among the Ohlone in 1776.[4] From these and subsequent settlements, the Spanish ventured into the San Joaquin Valley.

Two army deserters were the first Spaniards to enter the interior.[5] Ordered to bring them in, Captain Pedro Fages passed through the Cañada de las Uvas to Buena Vista Lake in early 1772. From the village of Tulamniu of the Tulamni (Yokuts), he explored the surrounding country. Unsuccessful in apprehending the deserters, Fages nevertheless gained important geographical and ethnographical knowledge. He noted, for example, that "in their villages the natives live in the winter in very large squares, the families divided from each other, and outside they have very large houses in the form of hemispheres, where they keep their seeds and utensils. They are people of very good features and of a superior height, and are very frank and liberal." He remained only a short time in the Tulare Valley before departing for the coast.[6]

Fages returned to the interior in March. Accompanied by Father Juan Crespí and twelve soldiers, he left the presidio at Monterey on the twentieth. As the party moved northwards along the east side of San Francisco Bay, it passed through the territories of several Ohlone groups, such as the Huchiun. At the Carquinez Strait, the Spaniards entered land controlled by the Karkin, from whom the name of the strait was taken. Crespí reported that "on the banks on the other side we made out many villages, whose Indians called to us and invited us to go to their country, but we were prevented by a stretch of water about a quarter of a league wide; and many of them seeing that we were going away, came to this side, crossing over on rafts, and gave us some of their wild food."[7]

Continuing along the southern shore of the strait, they "came to five large villages of very mild heathen, with pleasant faces, . . . all with long hair which they tied with twine. We were well received by them all and presented with some of their wild food." Once past the strait to Suisun Bay, the Spaniards turned to the southeast, entering Miwok territory, where they encountered four Indians, who "shouted at us, making signs that we should go and receive a bow trimmed with feathers, the pelt of an animal, and arrows which they had thrust into the ground. The captain went forward with a soldier and received their presents." Fages reciprocated with beads, which pleased the Indians.[8]

While crossing a spur of Mount Diablo, they sighted the juncture of the San Joaquin and Sacramento rivers and proceeded there at once to take note of the land and waterways. On their way back to Monterey, the Spaniards passed through the Livermore Valley and came upon three small villages. "As soon as the heathen caught sight of us," recalled Crespí, "they ran away, shouting and panic-stricken without knowing what had happened."[9]

Early in 1776, Captain Juan Bautista de Anza, Father Pedro Font, and twelve soldiers traversed the same area Fages and Crespí had explored in 1772. As recounted by Font, a short distance from the entrance to the Carquinez Strait

thirty-eight Indians came to us unarmed, peaceful, and very happy to see us. At first they stopped and sat down on a small hill near the camp. Then one came, and behind him another, and so they came in single file. . . . They were very obliging, bringing us firewood, and very talkative. . . . After they had been a while with us they bade us goodbye and we made signs to them that they should go and get us some fish with two hooks which I gave them. They apparently understood us clearly, but they brought us nothing and showed very little appreciation for the hooks, because their method of fishing is with nets.[10]

The next day a delegation of Indians arrived at the Spaniards' camp. Font described the ceremonial nature of the meeting:

At sunrise the ten Indians came, one behind another, singing and dancing. One carried the air, making music with a little stick, rather long and split in the middle, which he struck against his hand and which sounded something like a castanet. They reached the camp and continued their singing and dancing for a little while. Then they stopped dancing, all making a step in unison, shaking the body and saying dryly and

in one voice, "Ha, ha, ha!" Next they sat down on the ground and sig-
nalled to us that we must sit down also. So we sat down in front of them,
the commander, I, and the commissary. Now an Indian arose and presented the commander with a string of cacomites [bulbs], and again sat
down. Shortly afterward he rose again and made me a present of another
string of cacomites and again sat down. In this way they went making us
their little presents, another Indian giving me a very large root of chuchupate, which he began to eat, telling me by signs that it was good.[11]

The ceremony concluded, Spaniards and Indians set out for a
nearby village. The Indians began to sing but were interrupted by
Father Font chanting the *Alabado,* which he did every morning of
the journey. Once he had finished, the Indians commenced singing again but this time "in a higher key, as if they wished to
respond to our chant." Near the village, the Spaniards were
greeted by three Indians carrying "long poles with feathers on the
end, and some long and narrow strips of skin with hair on, which
looked to me like rabbit skin, hanging like a pennant, this being
their sign of peace." Once in the village, the Spaniards presented
the residents with glass beads and received cacomites in return.
Font wrote in his journal that the Indians "were apparently sad
because we were leaving, and I was moved to tenderness at seeing
the joy with which we were welcomed by those poor Indians."[12]
Passing beyond the Carquinez Strait, they spotted Indians in
tule boats. Anza offered to trade beads for fish. The Indians
ignored the offer until shown a colored handkerchief. Font
recounted that he had not seen "in any other place Indians like
these, so desirous of clothing . . . , for they preferred any old rag
to all the glass beads, which others are so fond of."[13]
Turning southeastwards, the Spaniards encountered other
Indians who sought their possessions:

They showed themselves to be somewhat crafty and thievish, for as soon
as one stolen thing was taken from their hands they stole another, and
we did not have eyes enough to watch and care for everything. So we
resorted to the expedient of putting them out of the camp and telling
them goodbye in a good-natured way, but this did not succeed, and one
of them even became impudent with the commander, who thus far had

shown great patience with them. So, half angry, he took from the Indian a stick which he had in his hands, gave him a light blow with it and then threw the stick far away. Thereupon all departed, talking rapidly and shouting loudly, which I suspected was a matter of threatening.[14]

Close to the mouth of the San Joaquin River, the Spaniards entered a village of the Julpun (Miwok). Its houses "were not of grass and dilapidated like those we had seen during this journey, but rather large, round, and well made, like those of the Channel, and made of tule mats with a framework of slender poles inside, and with doors." Communication proved to be difficult, and initially the women feared to leave their houses. Finally, an Indian climbed to the top of the temescal and erected a long pole with feathers and a strip of rabbit skin. Font interpreted this to be a sign of peace. Spaniards and Indians exchanged glass beads for "feathers, little sticks, and other gewgaws esteemed by them."[15] From this village the Spaniards followed a branch of the San Joaquin River upstream, passing an abandoned settlement, to a tule swamp. Unable to cross the river to reach the Sierra Nevada, they returned to Monterey.[16]

Later in 1776, three expeditions explored the same area. The first two, organized at the presidio of San Francisco, were to meet at Carquinez Strait on September 26. When the overland party failed to arrive at the designated time, the other sailed through the strait, stopping at villages of the Chupcan (Miwok) to trade tobacco for fish. The Spaniards explored the lower San Joaquin and Sacramento rivers before returning to San Francisco. The overland party, meanwhile, marched directly to the San Joaquin, following it upstream for several days. Indians the Spaniards met on the journey offered seeds and fish and were given beads in return. The third expedition explored the same general area in early December. It crossed the west and middle branches of the San Joaquin, land controlled by the Julpun, to the junction of the Mokelumne and Cosumnes rivers, where the Indians were described as brave and robust.[17]

Another Spaniard entered the San Joaquin Valley in 1776. In

March, Father Francisco Garcés had arrived at Mission San Gabriel from the Colorado River. With three Indian guides, he journeyed to a village in the Tehachapi Mountains. Named San Pasqual by Garcés, it was probably a Kitanemuk settlement. Most of the residents fled when the party approached, but returned when they realized that only one of the visitors was a Spaniard.[18] A previous encounter with Spaniards had not gone well. In February the Anza-Font expedition had passed along the coast on its way to Monterey. A total of 240 persons, including twenty-nine wives of the soldiers, comprised the expedition. All were mounted, and they herded some three hundred head of cattle.[19] In April, Anza and twenty-one men returned by the same route.[20] They robbed the Kitanemuk of baskets of seeds and other valuables.[21] The Indians may have been on a food-collecting expedition when contact was made.

Once he convinced the villagers he was a Spaniard who came from the east and thus "did harm to no one," Garcés was warmly received. Invited to the lodge of the village elite, Garcés

recited the rosary . . . of Maria Santisima, singing the hymn . . . with the Indian Sevastian and the two Jamajabs [Mohave] who accompanied me from the beginning, and who already knew the Ave Maria. . . . A little while after the service began the wife of the chief arose, took a basket . . . of seed . . . and scattered it over the Santo Cristo I wore on my breast; the same did other women, and they even threw some of this seed . . . on the fire, in order that there should be a bright light. Having finished the praying and singing I seated myself by the captain and the rest of the elders of the rancheria, who had assembled as soon as I began the services. They smoked the tobacco that I gave them, and begged me to exhibit again . . . the breviary, compass-needle, and other little things, manifesting great delight throughout.[22]

Apparently, Garcés and his companions tasted the Datura plant, being given an extremely bitter paste to eat which caused two of the Indians to vomit violently. The villagers found this very amusing. Garcés noted in his journal that they drank this gruel "to cure fatigue, and consequently it is customary to offer it to all their guests."[23]

Accompanied by several Indians, including the leader of the village, Garcés passed into the San Joaquin Valley. At a village east of Kern and Buena Vista lakes, his guides and companions refused to go farther because they were near Indians who "were very bad, and no relations of theirs." But Garcés persuaded an old man to escort him to the Kern River where it exits the mountains. The current being too strong to cross, they followed the river downstream to a village where the inhabitants "were obsequious to us." Three guides from this village escorted Garcés to a crossing. The villagers held "a great feast over my arrival, and having regaled me well I reciprocated to them all with tobacco and glass beads, congratulating myself on seeing the people so affable and affectionate. The young men are fine fellows, and the women comely and clean, bathing themselves every little while."[24]

Continuing northwards, Garcés camped with Indians who "showed me every attention." On May 2, he and another guide reached a village where an old man persuaded the Spaniard to give him his crucifix. The following day, Garcés visited a village of 150 souls, many of whom sought to kiss his Saint Christopher medal. The Spaniard was surprised when an Indian begged him in Spanish for paper to make cigars with: "I wondered much, and on questioning him he told me that he was from the sea where there were padres like myself. . . . When he took to kiss the Santo Cristo, he did so with great veneration, and set himself to preach to the rest. I had a suspicion that he might be some Christian who had just fled from the missions of Monte-Rey, since he made signs of shooting and of flogging."[25]

If correct in his assessment, Garcés spoke with one of the first mission neophytes to take up residence in the interior. He also spoke with Indians from a village to the north who admitted killing two Spaniards who had mistreated their women. As recounted by Garcés, the Indians "had cut off the hands, had laid open the breast and all the body . . . and scattered the remains."[26] Presumably, those executed were the deserters Fages had sought a few years before.

After baptizing a young boy who was near death and visiting a nearby village, Garcés, against the wishes of his hosts, decided to turn back. At a village where the residents also pleaded with him to stay, Garcés heard about a Spaniard married to an Indian woman who lived somewhere to the east. An Indian told the priest that the Spaniard "wore on the breast a certain round thing that I conceived should be some medal or reliquary, . . . that he . . . already had a little son; that he was of a good heart, and was much in request of all, living . . . like the rest of the Indians."[27]

On May 7, Garcés was back on the Kern. A village downstream

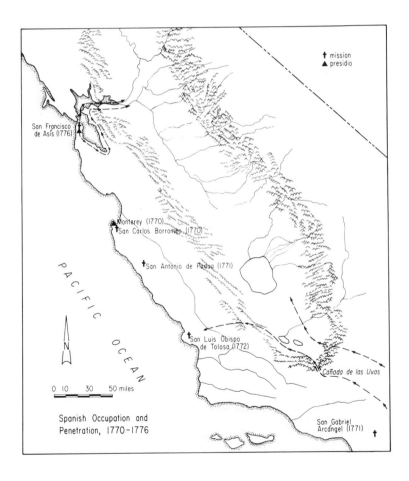

† mission
▲ presidio

San Francisco de Asís (1776)

▲Monterey (1770)
†San Carlos Borromeo (1770)

†San Antonio de Padua (1771)

PACIFIC OCEAN

N

0 10   30   50 miles

†San Luis Obispo de Tolosa (1772)

Cañada de las Uvas

Spanish Occupation and Penetration, 1770–1776

San Gabriel Arcángel (1771) †

from the one previously visited caught his attention as an ideal site for a future mission. Although the Indians expressed friendship and provided him with game and fish, an old man refused to kiss his crucifix, asserting the "shells and tobacco were good, but that el Cristo was not, and that he held it in great dread." This rejection caused Garcés to question the feasibility of establishing missions in the interior. He envisioned "a scene of the highest felicity and docility shifting in an instant to one of mishaps and fatalities."[28]

Back in the village he called San Pasqual, Garcés again spoke with its leader, "intent upon persuading him that the Españoles were a good people; to which he would by no means assent." The Indian reminded Garcés that Spaniards had stolen valuables from his people. The following day Garcés departed for the Mohave Desert, having traveled in the Tulare Valley for over three weeks.[29]

Seeking geographical information rather than political domination, the Spaniards who initially penetrated the San Joaquin Valley made, on the whole, a favorable impression on the people they encountered. They exhibited remarkable restraint in dealing with individuals whose behavior they found peculiar, and they deferred to Indian customs and ceremonies, especially when the meetings first occurred. Although some Indians found the Spaniards terrifying, most expressed not awe but curiosity. Keenly interested in the material items the Spanish possessed, the Indians demonstrated an eagerness to trade that surprised and even unsettled the explorers.

To the Spanish, the San Joaquin Valley was a region they would occupy sooner or later, but changes affecting the coastal Indian populations prompted them to modify their policies and accelerate their timetable. They entered the valley in search of mission recruits long before they were prepared to establish permanent settlement there. Only a small percentage of the Indian population of the San Joaquin Valley experienced incorporation and conversion, but all interior peoples were profoundly affected by developments evolving in the coastal zone.

CHAPTER 4

Hostile Interaction

FROM the late 1770s to the late 1780s, Spanish occupation of the coastal zone increased dramatically. The pueblo of San José de Guadalupe and nearby Mission Santa Clara de Asís were founded among the Ohlone in 1777. A presidio at Santa Bárbara and Mission San Buenaventura were established among the Chumash in 1782. Missions Santa Bárbara and La Purísima Concepción were opened in 1786 and 1787 respectively, also among the Chumash. From these and the earlier settlements, the Spanish continued to penetrate the interior.[1]

As they explored the San Joaquin Valley, Spaniards sometimes intruded into inter-Indian affairs. In August 1790, for example, Indians from the Chumash village of Najayalewa, located northeast of Mission Santa Bárbara on the Santa Ynéz River, killed three men and a woman who resided in or near the southern end of Tulare Valley. A large revenge party quickly formed, including eight Yauelmani (Yokuts) from the village of Loasu and thirty-nine Castec (Chumash). Evidently, the Indians formulated their plans at the Chumash village of Matapuan, whose leader, Tucha-chana, commanded the party.[2]

At the same time the revenge party was forming, a Spanish military contingent was heading towards the Tulare Valley. On August 24, the commandant of the presidio at Santa Bárbara had dispatched nine soldiers and an Indian interpreter to apprehend a neophyte, Domingo, who recently had fled from Mission San Buenaventura. Domingo's destination was a village in the San Emigdio area. The commandant feared Domingo would incite the villagers to attack Indians friendly to the Spanish.[3]

Five days later, the Spanish, supported by fifteen Indians from

Najahalewa and a few others, made camp in San Emigdio. They explored the immediate area for precious stones. Two soldiers investigated a nearby gully, while nine Spaniards and three Indians searched for a vein near the trail they had followed. Two other soldiers remained in camp.[4]

Neophytes from San Buenaventura, in the meantime, had warned the Indians comprising the revenge party that Spanish soldiers were moving inland.[5] Some of the Indians wanted to avoid the Spaniards, but the leader of the village of Loasu sought revenge for the crimes committed many years ago by the two army deserters.[6] The Indians attacked the Spaniards in the gully but were driven off. They killed the two guarding the camp and appropriated cloaks, ponchos, five shotguns, riding gear, and a horse.[7]

The Spaniards who had gone to search for the vein returned to camp, buried the dead, and retreated to an area near Mission San Buenaventura, where, shortly, they were joined by the two sol-

Ohlone Indians fighting a Spaniard, by Tomás de Suria, 1791. Courtesy of The Bancroft Library, University of California, Berkeley.

diers who had survived the attack in the gully. On September 1, the party returned to Santa Bárbara. The commandant wrote to the governor, claiming that Domingo, the runaway neophyte, must have participated in the attack because only someone familiar with stock could have caught and saddled the horse the Spaniards lost.[8] Whoever was responsible may have introduced the first horse to the Tulare Valley.

The fight also represents the first significant violent encounter between coastal Spaniards and interior Indians, a point not lost on the commandant, who requested from the governor soldiers to punish the Indians. It would not be just, he reasoned, if "they get away without a lesson."[9] But the party entrusted to teach the lesson returned with only two prisoners, Soxollue and Samallá.[10] In mid-September, another Spanish contingent penetrated the interior, apparently to the village where the Indians had launched their revenge party. The Spaniards returned to the presidio at Santa Bárbara with three prisoners who subsequently were released. Domingo turned himself in at Mission San Buenaventura and promptly was imprisoned at the presidio at Santa Bárbara.[11] Interrogated by the commandant, Domingo claimed he had received permission to leave the mission to visit his mother and had not participated in the attack on the soldiers.[12] Domingo, Soxollue, and Samallá were absolved of all crimes and released.[13]

Because the Spanish increasingly relied on neophytes to assist in the apprehension of fugitives, disputes erupted between mission Indians and the so-called gentiles. In early January 1797, the priest at San Luís Obispo sent a party of neophytes into the interior to locate the wife of an Indian who had converted and resided at the mission. The Spanish suspected she had poisoned her baptized daughter who had died at the mission. Somewhere near the edge of the Tulare Valley, the neophytes captured the woman.[14]

On its way back to the mission, the party paused at a village, where two neophytes insulted an old man and his two sons. The three villagers killed one of the neophytes, Toribio, and burned his body.[15] On January 8, a military contingent was dispatched to apprehend the three, but it failed in its mission.[16] Later in the month, another party brought the old man and his sons to the mission, where they confessed to the murder.[17]

More troubling to the Spanish than gentiles murdering neophytes was gentiles protecting them. Thus, in July 1797, when it was reported that gentiles at a village north of San José were harboring runaways and encouraging neophytes to rebel, the Spanish responded immediately. On the fifteenth, three soldiers and twenty-five civilians contacted the Sacalan (Miwok). Sergeant Pedro Amador recorded what transpired:

Although we repeatedly told them that we did not wish to fight but only to take away the Christians, they admitted to no persuasion but began to shoot so as to kill one of our horses and wound two others. Seeing this opposition, we used our weapons in order to subdue them so that they would surrender. Some were killed, for they refused for two hours to give up. Finally, it was necessary to dismount and throw them back with swords and lances.[18]

The Spaniards captured thirty-two gentiles and neophytes. After explaining the purpose of his mission, Amador released the gentiles but kept the neophytes under guard. The following day the Spaniards surprised three Huchiun (Ohlone) villages, rounding up more fugitives. They returned to Mission San José with eighty-three neophytes and nine gentiles.[19]

At the same time the Spanish were sending expeditions into the interior, they also were expanding their coastal settlements. In 1791, Mission Santa Cruz was founded among the Ohlone and Nuestra Señora de la Soledad along the Esselen-Salinan border. Four more missions were established in 1797: San José and San Juan Bautista among the Ohlone, San Miguel Arcángel among the Salinan, and south of the San Joaquin Valley, San Fernando Rey de España.[20]

Early in the nineteenth century several of the older missions ceased to grow. Mission Santa Bárbara achieved its maximum number of neophytes (1792) in 1803; La Purísima (1520) in 1804; San Antonio (1296), San Luís Obispo (961), and Soledad

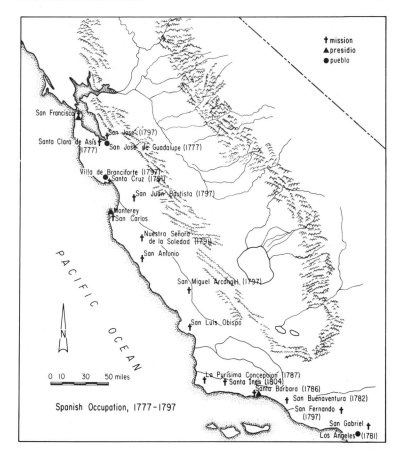

Spanish Occupation, 1777–1797

(688) in 1805.[21] Those missions soon experienced rapid population decline. The introduction of European diseases from which the Indians initially had no immunity accounts in large measure for this development.[22]

The decline of the coastal population forced the Franciscans to increasingly probe the interior for mission recruits. In late 1803, for example, Father Juan Martín of Mission San Miguel, accompanied by a soldier, journeyed to the village of Cholam of the Tachi (Yokuts), seeking from the local leader, Guchapa, children to take back to the mission. Guchapa refused, ordered the Spaniards out of his village, and told the padre that he was not afraid of soldiers. The following month, the commandant of the presidio at Monterey sent fifteen soldiers to the village. They returned in early January with Guchapa, his son, two other Indian leaders, and two neophytes. Guchapa negotiated his own release by promising to bring to the presidio all fugitive neophytes then in his village. He left his son as hostage.[23]

The following year, Father Martín again sought children for his mission. Informed by neophytes returning from Tulare Lake that gentiles in the area were willing to have their children baptized, the missionary, in the company of two soldiers, proceeded to the territory of the Wowol (Yokuts). At the village of Bubal, Martín was offered some two hundred children to take to the mission. Unsure whether all Indians approved of this, he sent for the headman, Chape, who was absent at the time. Chape returned at once and prohibited the release of the children; Father Martín retreated to his mission empty-handed.[24]

Even when successful in recruiting Indians from the interior, the padres found it extremely difficult to keep them in the missions. In their biennial report issued December 31, 1804, the Franciscans at San Miguel admitted that "it is the painful experience of the missionaries that such Christians, very much attached to their Tulare homes, leave the Mission, and in consequence lose the holy Mass and offend God, and hide in the Tulares region where they cannot be taken out without peril and without troops."[25]

The padres did not exaggerate the dangers. In January 1805, Father Pedro de la Cueva of Mission San José, accompanied by two soldiers and a few neophytes, journeyed into the hills south of Livermore Valley. At the village of Asiremes, where two dying neophytes supposedly sought last rites, he found no Indians. Continuing eastwards, the party experienced determined resistance from the Leucha (Yokuts), who killed three neophytes and wounded the padre and a soldier.[26]

Later in the month a military force consisting of eighteen soldiers and fifteen civilians located Indians responsible for the attack. In the ensuing fight, they killed five and captured thirty-nine. Apparently, the success of this encounter affected neighboring Indian groups. A leader from a village on the San Joaquin River visited the Spanish encampment to proclaim his innocence regarding the attack on Father Cueva. Fugitives residing at several villages returned to their missions.[27]

In July 1806, Father José María de Zalvidea and Lieutenant Francisco María Ruiz, supported by a few soldiers, departed from Santa Bárbara for the Tulare Lake region. The padre sought to promote friendship with the local Indians and to search for mission sites. The expedition stopped at several Chumash villages, where Zalvidea offered baptismal rites to a group of predominantly old women. Near the Cuyama River the Spaniards spotted a wild horse.[28] If yet to penetrate the San Joaquin Valley, wild horses soon would diffuse over much of the interior.[29]

A few days later, the Spaniards arrived at the Chumash village of Malapoa, where Zalvidea baptized an eighty-year-old woman, christening her María Rufina. At a nearby settlement he baptized five old women and an old man. At the village of Tulamniu, in the territory of the Tulamni (Yokuts), the missionary baptized another old woman.[30]

With several Indians, including the headman of Tulamniu village, to guide them, the Spaniards departed on the twenty-sixth for the village of Pohalin Tinliu at the southern end of Kern Lake and in the territory of the Hometwoli (Yokuts). Unknown to the padre and the soldiers, Tulamniu and Pohalin Tinliu were enemies. As the party approached the village, the residents fled to a nearby tule swamp. They returned a short time later, and Zalvidea negotiated a peace between the headmen of the two villages.[31]

A short distance from the village the priest visited an "old woman, in a little hut, who was at her last breath, destitute of all human assistance. After having labored very hard to revive her, so that I might make her a Christian, I finally attained my desire and named her Maria Gertrudis: two hours after baptism she surrendered her soul to its Creator."[32]

Moving southwards, the Spaniards arrived at the foothills of the Tehachapi Mountains, where they spent several days exploring the surrounding country. On July 29, Zalvidea and nine soldiers visited the village of Tecuya, located west of the Cañada de las Uvas. Zalvidea baptized two old men, whom he named Fernando and Ramón. On August 1, the entire party journeyed northwards, arriving at a village of the Yauelmani. According to Zalvidea, many volunteered to be baptized but only if missions were opened in their land. The following day, the Spaniards turned back and a few days later arrived at Santa Bárbara.[33]

Shortly after Zalvidea and his party left the Tulare Valley, another expedition entered the interior. Commander Gabriel Moraga, Father Pedro Muñoz, about twenty-five soldiers, and a few neophytes departed from Mission San Juan Bautista on September 21, 1806. Muñoz intended to spread the word of God and search for mission sites. On the San Joaquin River, the Spaniards met forty-two men of the Nupchenche (Yokuts) who presented them with fish. "I made them acquainted with the purpose of our visit," Muñoz recalled, "showing them an image of Our Lady of Sorrows. This they received with much satisfaction, appearing, according to their behavior, ready to enroll under the banner of the Divine Savior."[34]

The following day, the Indians escorted the Spaniards to their village, which was situated on the east side of the San Joaquin River. Governed by an individual called Choley, it numbered about 250 inhabitants. According to Muñoz, "they all received my talk with pleasure and, having listened silently to the Divine Word, they begged to become Christians." He baptized twenty-three old women and three old men, explaining to the rest that they must wait for a mission to be established in their territory.[35]

On the twenty-seventh, the Spaniards recrossed the San Joaquin and made camp in a spot infested with butterflies. They divided into three groups; one remained at camp, and the other two reconnoitered the areas to the north and northeast. Both parties encountered Indians on the Merced River, who fled at the first sight of the intruders. Found at one village, however, was a feeble and terrified old woman who managed the strength to plunge into the river. Rescued by one of the neophytes and treated kindly by the Spaniards, she overcame her fear. Muñoz gave "her as adequate a lesson as was permitted by the shortness of the time. I baptized her, she giving very clear evidence of the joy which filled her heart."[36]

On September 30, the Spaniards encountered terribly suspicious Indians. The few who approached were given food, presents, and instructions to bring in their relatives. To the thirty Indians who appeared, Muñoz explained the benefits of Christianity. They asked for a mission and to be baptized. Proceeding to the Tuolumne the next day, the Spaniards found deserted villages, heavily used trails, but no Indians.[37]

On the Stanislaus, and probably in the territory of the Siakumne (Yokuts), they discovered a village situated on steep cliffs. Between twelve and fifteen Indians descended to a narrow shelf but would not come closer because "soldiers killed and captured people." Muñoz explained the nature of his visit, but "it was not possible to achieve a single baptism, although there were a great many old women to whom baptism might be administered, because they would not come down from their hiding places and it was too difficult for me to go up."[38]

Continuing northwards to the Cosumnes River, the Spaniards met "affectionate and affable" Indians but could not communicate with them because they had entered Miwok territory. Lacking an interpreter, Muñoz was unable to offer baptism. But the potential of the area did not escape the priest: "This river has excellent land for agriculture and grazing and has a good oak forest. In the mountains there is pine. . . . It has also much ash, willow, torote, and wild vines."[39]

Returning to the Stanislaus, the Spaniards encountered forty armed Indians on the opposite bank. Carrying a flag made of feathers, three crossed to meet with the strangers, who convinced them their intentions were friendly. The main body of Indians would not cross the river, however. The Spaniards departed for the Tuolumne the next day, one party making a side trip to the mountains, where it located many Indians but no site for a mission.[40]

The expedition reached the Merced on October 7, terrifying twenty children, who "began to scream and throw themselves into the water to save themselves by flight." The party continued along the opposite bank and made camp in a meadow. Shortly, seventy-nine men from the village of Latelate arrived, presenting the Spaniards with seeds and fish. The Spanish reciprocated with food and presents.[41]

The following day, Indians and Spaniards met again:

On the morning of this day, carrying the image of Holy Mary of Sorrows (who was our patron Saint), we started out to pay a visit to the village, on account of the attention they had paid us. We were received with great joy. They laid out their mats on the ground for us to sit down upon. This matter attended to, we set forth the reason for our coming. They replied in a very pleased manner that they all sought baptism and the establishment of a mission. I baptized six old women and one old man who were present.

Near Latelate was the village of Lachio, where Muñoz thought a mission and a presidio might be established. The wide meadows were perfect for raising crops and grazing stock.[42]

The expedition moved eastwards before turning south. Traveling along the foothills of the Sierra Nevada, apparently it encountered no Indian settlements until arriving at the San Joaquin on October 11. Two days later a scouting party visited a village, Pizcache, of the Pitkachi (Yokuts). Its leader, Sujoyucomu, told the Spaniards about a fight between Indians and soldiers that had taken place on the east side of the mountains some twenty years before. The soldiers had killed many Indians, and the Pitkachi expected to be invaded from the east. Sujoyucomu was surprised the Spaniards had come from the west and demonstrated kindness. Muñoz baptized four old Indians, two men and two women.[43]

On October 16, the Spaniards arrived at the Kings River in the territory of the Wechihit (Yokuts). Upstream, a scouting party entered the village of Ayguiche, where it heard the same story about the fight on the east side of the mountains. The padre baptized eight women and one man at the village and twenty old women and two old men at three villages downstream.[44] A few days later the Spaniards reached the territory of the Telamni (Yokuts), and the missionary baptized twenty-two persons at the large village of Telame. On October 20, they visited another large village, Cohochs. Its residents welcomed the Spaniards, sought baptism, and asked for a mission. Returning to Telame, Muñoz baptized a little girl near death. He noted in his journal that "during the days which we spent at this place all the Indians showed themselves very much satisfied with having us in their midst, even to the extent of pointing out to us a spot appropriate for the establishment or foundation of a mission."[45]

On the twenty-seventh, the expedition penetrated the land of the Koyeti (Yokuts). The inhabitants of a small village sought baptism, but Muñoz could not perform the ritual because the Indians were too young. The party continued southwards, arriving at the Kern on the following day and passing through the Cañada de las Uvas on November 1. During the forty-three days spent in the interior, Muñoz baptized 141 persons, all *in extremis*.[46]

The following year, 1807, Gabriel Moraga, with twenty-five soldiers, returned to the Tulare Valley. Intending to round up runaway neophytes and "to bring in others for the Padres to make Christians," as one soldier put it, the Spaniards met stiff resistance. Yauelmani attacked the party when it entered the mountains, killing two soldiers and stealing one hundred horses.[47]

Also seeking fugitives, José Palomares and a few men departed from the presidio at Santa Bárbara in late October 1808. At Mission San Fernando, Palomares obtained a list of runaways and enlisted the service of three Indians and a Spaniard, all of whom were familiar with the southern interior. Indians in the San Gabriel Mountains informed Palomares that ten fugitives, five of whom were on his list, resided in the southeast corner of the Tulare Valley at a village led by an individual called Quipagui. Palomares traveled to the Antelope Valley, capturing on the way an Indian, Macal, who apparently had participated in the fight against Moraga the previous year.[48] The party crossed the Tehachapi Mountains, arriving near Quipagui's village. After a brief skirmish in which no one was hurt, Indians and Spaniards held a meeting. Quipagui told Palomares that the Christian Indians had fled either into the mountains or into the tule swamps. Palomares attempted to enlist the services of Quipagui in rounding up the fugitives. The Indian leader, obviously stalling for time, promised to help but only after it stopped raining. Before departing for Mission San Fernando, Palomares told Quipagui that the padres would pay him if he brought in the fugitives. Quipagui again promised his assistance, but the runaways never were delivered.[49]

In his report, Palomares recommended that Quipagui

be removed from that place with all his village for many reasons. The first is because he has killed many unconverted Indians and is still killing them. He is the most feared Indian in that entire country. The other reason is that he gives refuge to Christian fugitives, and they know that neither Christian nor heathen will go to look for them there on account of the terror which he inspires. I would have brought him back with his people but the weather did not permit me to do so without running the risk of injury in capturing and securing them.[50]

Expeditions searching for fugitive neophytes and mission sites also entered the northern reaches of the San Joaquin Valley. In mid-August 1810, Padre José Viader, six soldiers, and four neophytes departed from Mission San José. They journeyed north to Suisun Bay and then eastward to the San Joaquin River. Following the river into the territory of the Chulamni (Yokuts), Viader learned that fugitives from San José were in the vicinity. Unable to locate the Indians, the party continued upstream.[51]

On August 21, it arrived opposite a village led by Bozenats. Refusing to cross, the Indians informed Viader that they harbored no fugitive Christians. Traveling a short distance the following day, the intruders encountered about thirty armed Indians on the opposite bank who also refused to cross. They ordered the party to leave and demonstrated an eagerness to fight. Residing with them, they acknowledged, were fugitive neophytes from Missions Santa Clara and Santa Cruz.[52]

A short distance upriver, the party encountered hostile Indians on both banks. Six Indians on the near side fired arrows at a soldier and a neophyte interpreter. Those on the opposite bank also launched a volley of arrows, wounding a Spaniard. The soldiers returned fire, hitting at least one Indian. On August 24 the Spaniards headed back to the coast.[53]

Two months later Viader led another expedition into the interior. Consisting of twenty-four soldiers and about fifty neophyte auxiliaries, this party also invaded the territory of the Chulamni, secretly taking up positions near a village whose residents were conducting a ceremony. At dawn, October 21, they struck, capturing fifteen fugitives from San José and sixty-nine gentiles. Two of the runaways escaped, and fifty-one gentiles, all women, were released. The remainder were sent under guard to San José.[54]

Viader followed the San Joaquin upstream into the territory of the Mayem (Yokuts), where the residents denied sheltering fugitives from Mission Santa Clara. They promised never to allow Christian Indians in their village, but Viader did not believe them. Upriver the party halted near a village which Viader also suspected harbored fugitives. He sent word to the inhabitants that those Christians who gave themselves up would be pardoned. Shortly, six gentiles visited the priest, claiming that all the neophytes had returned to the mission and promising that henceforth none would be admitted to their village. Viader doubted the sincerity of the promise. The party reached the Merced River before turning back. At a village previously visited, Viader attempted to lure the residents into a trap, but "they refused to come out. . . . They guessed right for they would have been taken captive. From this point, considering that the people of Mayem would also refuse to come out, . . . we turned west." The party arrived at Mission Santa Clara on October 27, 1810.[55]

Many neophytes also resettled at several villages along the

lower Sacramento and San Joaquin rivers. In October 1811, Spaniards moving up a branch of the San Joaquin encountered at three villages neophytes who apparently resided there by permission of the padres at San José. A short distance upstream, the Spaniards arrived at a village of the Cholborn (Yokuts), where San José neophytes presented themselves. A padre baptized six old women and the baby boy of a neophyte. Crossing to the main branch of the San Joaquin, the expedition entered a village containing neophytes, and downstream, in the territory of the Coybos (Yokuts), encountered more neophytes from San José. The padre baptized a sick boy and an old woman.[56]

Continuing their journey, the Spaniards approached a village prepared for war. Its residents had been told that all the Coybos had been killed. The Spaniards quickly explained their peaceful intentions and moved on. Downstream they entered the Sacramento River and passed several large villages, including one which contained a few neophytes from San José. The expedition returned to San Francisco on the thirtieth.[57]

Seeking fugitives, Lieutenant Luís Argüello led ten soldiers from the presidio at San Francisco into the same region in 1813. At the mouth of the Cosumnes, three soldiers and one hundred neophyte auxiliaries from Mission San José joined his party. Shortly, Spaniards and auxiliaries confronted a fighting force of about one thousand men recruited from four villages. Apparently, the fugitives had warned their hosts that a Spanish military force soon would arrive.[58]

The Indians, as reported by Argüello,

attacked with such fury that all the valor of the soldiers was necessary in order to repulse them. This was accomplished by heavy fire, the hostile Indians maintaining their offensive for a long time and holding their position on all sides without perceiving the damage which their obstinacy caused then. They were confident perhaps in their own great number and the small number of soldiers and Indian auxiliaries with whom they were contending, as well as the advantages provided them by the terrain.

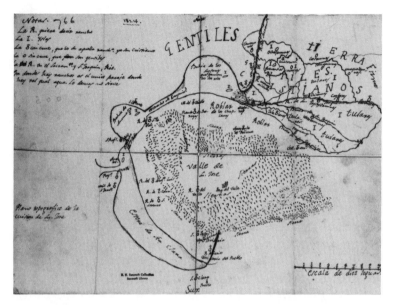

Map of Mission San José, neophyte and gentile villages, 1824. Courtesy of The Bancroft Library, University of California, Berkeley.

After three hours of fighting, the Indians abandoned their positions; most escaped capture by swimming to an island in the river or by hiding in the dense tule swamps. The intruders may have killed or wounded several Indians, but they failed to recover a single fugitive.[59] They also lost Julio, a neophyte leader at Mission San José, who was killed in the battle.[60]

A few years later, Argüello returned to the delta. With two priests and a contingent of soldiers, he sailed up the San Joaquin and into the territory of the Pasasime (Yokuts). According to Father Narciso Durán, these Indians "have been at the mission many times, and some of them have been baptized." Downstream, they met over one hundred Yachicumne (Yokuts) and Muqueleme (Miwok), "half of them painted and armed," but Durán convinced them he had come in peace. He noted in his diary that "most of these natives live on the mainland, and one may visit them on horseback, if, perchance, it should be necessary to do so." A few days later the party sailed out of the area.[61]

Increasingly, Spaniards rounded up stock as well as fugitives while in the interior. In November 1815, for example, Sergeant Juan Ortega led thirty men, including a priest, from Mission San Miguel to the Kings River. On the northern edge of Tulare Lake, in the territory of the Tachi, they encountered two mounted Indians driving four horses. The Indians abandoned their animals and swam to safety across the Kings River. A saddle on one of the horses was identified as that used by a neophyte called Antonio, a fugitive from Mission Soledad.[62]

Antonio had convinced the residents of a Tachi village that if captured by the soldiers, they would be killed. Thus, when the Spaniards arrived on November 10, they found the village deserted. Three horses, one from San Miguel and two from Soledad, were recovered, however. Later in the morning, eight or nine Indians appeared. They told the intruders that Antonio and his companions had fled up the Kings River to the Nutunutu (Yokuts).[63]

At the village where Antonio supposedly had taken shelter, the Spaniards found no fugitives. They proceeded to the territory occupied by the Telamni. In recent years the population of the area had declined drastically. The few Indians who remained at one village offered the Spaniards presents and allowed the padre to baptize four very old women and a terminally ill man.[64]

Venturing southwards, the party encountered fearful and suspicious Indians who had been told by fugitives from Mission Soledad that the Spaniards intended to kill them. When asked about the whereabouts of the runaways from Soledad, the Indians replied that two had gone to the village of Bubal of the Wowol to meet with two neophytes who were there by permission of their padre. Two other fugitives had joined the Tulamni. After instructing them to accept no more fugitives, Ortega departed for Bubal, where he and his men received a warm welcome. On November 15 they left Bubal to make contact with another expedition that recently had departed from Mission San Juan Bautista.[65]

The goal of that expedition also was to round up fugitive neophytes and to recover stolen horses. Commanded by Sergeant José Dolores Pico, the Spaniards had on November 7 made camp on the west side of the San Joaquin River in the territory of the Cheneche (Yokuts). They assaulted a settlement on the morning of the eighth, capturing over sixty fugitives and gentiles and recovering seven horses. The soldiers released four men and twelve old women; a padre baptized an infant girl on the brink of death. From their captives, the Spanish learned that upriver among the Nupchenche were many horses and four fugitives: Justo, Damian, Severo, and Pedro Pablo. A corporal and fourteen men departed immediately to the area; at a village they arrested the headman and a few companions. Most of the residents had fled into a tule swamp. The headman convinced the corporal that if released he would bring in the others. When the Indian failed to return, the corporal and his men rejoined Pico in Cheneche territory.[66]

Pico considered attacking a nearby village but concluded that "the Tulares were very much stirred up and it did not seem wise to do so until our return." He sent fifty-four neophytes and gentiles to the presidio at Monterey under a guard of nine men, while he and the others proceeded southwards to a settlement at the mouth of the Chowchilla River. The villagers launched arrows at the intruders, who returned fire and killed two. The Spaniards retreated to a safe position, where they made preparations to storm the village the following day.[67]

The Indians made their own preparations and at dawn formed near the Spaniards' camp. Pico described the confrontation:

I told the interpreter to ask them what they wanted and they answered, to fight. Even after we had said to them that the officer in charge did not wish to do them any harm, they gave no heed, but began to fight. Seeing this I ordered them be fired upon. They then retreated to the interior of the underbrush. The troops dismounted at my command and fell upon them, killing three and capturing one alive. Of the dead, one was found to be a Christian of Mission San Juan and a leader in stealing horses. Of those who escaped some were seen to be wounded, and, according to the quantity of blood visible along the river, I considered that most of them must have died.

A short time later, the Spaniards recovered one horse and captured two Indians, who told their captors that the dead Christian had been the most intent on killing them. That night Indians fired a few arrows into Pico's camp, none hitting its mark.[68]

The Spaniards followed the slough connecting the San Joaquin River with Tulare Lake into the territory of the Wimilchi (Yokuts). On one occasion, Pico warned several Indians not to "admit Christians or horses in their villages." On the fifteenth, he met the expedition led by Juan Ortega, and two days later the joint command visited a Nutunutu village, where Pico delivered another lecture about neophytes and animals.[69]

The Spaniards followed the slough back to its juncture with the San Joaquin. On the twenty-third, they entered a village but managed to capture only a neophyte from Santa Cruz and eleven elderly gentiles. They discovered the remains of 238 recently killed animals, a large amount of meat that had been quartered and dried, and sixteen horses, most belonging to Mission San Juan Bautista. Releasing all the prisoners except the neophyte, the Spaniards returned to Cheneche territory, where they found deserted villages. They arrived at San Juan Bautista on December 2 with nine Indian prisoners.[70]

Early the following year, 1816, another expedition, comprised entirely of neophytes from Mission Soledad and led·by an Indian called Socio, entered the Tulare Valley. Socio returned with several fugitives, but he left behind a woman because she had just given birth and two others because they were tending to sick children. Their husbands also were allowed to remain. Socio was unable to locate three fugitives—Marcos, Pastor, and Justo— who had taken up residence in a village containing numerous horses. He managed to recover thirty horses but lost twenty when Severo and Pedro Pablo, the fugitives Pico had sought, raided his camp.[71]

Neophytes largely comprised the expedition that entered the Tulare Valley in May 1816. Led by Father Luís Antonio Martínez, the force proceeded to a deserted Bubal. Although Chape, the headman, had taken most of his followers into the tule swamps, the neophytes managed to round up ten families. Shortly, Chape and seventy men appeared. He and Martínez exchanged gifts before the Spaniard departed. But upon his return from a visit to villages east of Tulare Lake, Martínez discovered Bubal had been relocated. He found the village but was met with a volley of arrows. The following day the neophytes entered the village and captured two women and a man. Martínez reported that "the village was burned and everything in it destroyed because the people in it had taken up arms against those who had treated them well."[72]

Loyal neophytes continued to penetrate the interior. In early December 1817, Odórico led a party from La Purísima to the Tulamni village of Tulamniu, located on the northwest bank of Buena Vista Lake. Odórico, called by Father Mariano Payeras "a worthy neophyte" who could be trusted, was to bring in his friend, Felipe Amuchu, a twenty-five-year-old fugitive.[73] Also to be apprehended were the parents of Amuchu, their second son, and two other men. Before the arrival of the neophytes, Taciats, the headman of Tulamniu, took his followers to safety across the slough connecting Tulare and Buena Vista lakes.[74] Evidently, the neophytes returned to La Purísima empty-handed.

In May 1818, Father Payeras informed Captain José de la Guerra, commandant at Santa Bárbara, that at Tulamniu were "many Christians of all the missions of this jurisdiction who are determined not to recognize their destiny." The Indians were establishing "a republic of Hell and a diabolical union which as a test has protected Amuchu and all of his companions."[75] By this time, at least thirty-three neophytes had resettled at Tulamniu.[76]

Guerra proposed to the governor that an expedition be mounted to round them up. He sought to recruit thirty men from Santa Bárbara and San Diego and to take with him Father Payeras. When some of the neophytes from Mission Santa Bárbara returned, however, the plan was cancelled.[77] In September, Payeras told Guerra that Indians from his mission remained with Taciats at Tulamniu and that the gentiles there no longer feared an expedition would be sent against them.[78]

That fugitives were spreading knowledge about horses to interior Indians also troubled Payeras. In early July 1819 he complained to Father Guardia Baldomero López that "any little altar boy . . . steals tame and castrated herds and takes and sells them in the *Tular*."[79] Later in the month, he sent a circular to the padres, noting that "in the Tulare (I am told by the Governor) both Christians and Gentiles make their journeys on horseback. Even the women are learning to ride. Fairs are held at which horses stolen from the missions are put up for sale."[80]

More despondent two months later, Payeras, in a letter to the governor, lamented that the spirit of insubordination

which is rampant in the world at large has reached the Christian Indians. A considerable number have withdrawn from the mild rule of the friars, and have become one body with the savages with whom they carry out whatever evil their heart and malevolent soul dictates. A contagion is general, and we must confess that the pagans are corrupted by the bad example and perverse suggestions of the apostates. . . . From day to day the danger of an attack from the united apostates and gentiles is growing.[81]

Of particular concern to the Spanish were the Muqueleme. In a letter to the governor, Father Narciso Durán claimed that the Muqueleme

give shelter to numerous Christian fugitives who are their friends and neighbors. We do not dare to demand their return, for the heathen are very refractory and according to the account of our Indians are disposed to fight and try to kill the Christians, the soldiers, the priests and others

who may go there. It is said to be the common refrain of the wild Indians
that they are still unbeaten, for they have many bows, arrows and
horses.[82]

In October the Spanish launched an expedition against the
Muqueleme but met stiff resistance. The Indians killed a neophyte auxiliary and wounded three or four soldiers. The Spanish
killed twenty-seven and wounded twenty Indians and recovered
forty-nine horses, but they returned to Mission San José without
a single fugitive. Durán admitted to the governor "that this business is not yet finished."[83]

The same month, the governor ordered Lieutenant José María
Estudillo to undertake a reconnaissance of the Tulare Valley.
Estudillo departed from Mission San Miguel on October 21 with
a few soldiers, two Yokuts guides, and forty-one neophyte auxiliaries. The expedition arrived a few days later at Bubal. According
to Estudillo, Bubal had provided more converts to Mission San
Miguel than any other village.[84] By 1819, the padres had baptized
at least thirty-seven Indians from this village.[85]

Estudillo found Bubal deserted. Apparently, in late September,
several residents had attended a fiesta at Mission San Miguel,
where they learned of Spanish intentions. They told the villagers
the Spanish sought to apprehend neophytes and gentiles and
would kill all who refused to return with them to the mission.
Certainly not forgotten was the fact that Father Martínez had
razed their village three years before. Estudillo, however, managed to capture forty-five persons, including a neophyte woman,
Liberata, who had been given permission to return to Bubal.
Understanding the importance of the village to Mission San
Miguel, the commander treated the captives "with the greatest
kindness." He dispatched five messengers into the swamp, and
soon many Indians appeared, including Chape, the headman of
the village. Estudillo released the captives and departed the following day.[86]

Proceeding east of Tulare Lake, the intruders entered the terri-

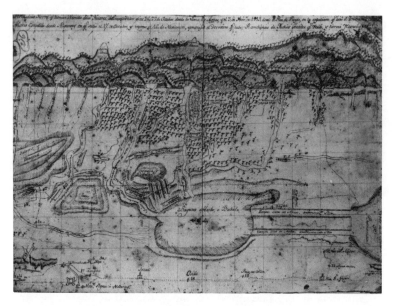

Map of the Tulare Valley, by José María Estudillo, 1830. Courtesy of The Bancroft Library, University of California, Berkeley.

tory of the Koyeti. Tuckal, a headman, told Estudillo that his people had known for several days that Spaniards were coming. At another village, Estudillo spoke with its headman, Joasps, and the leaders of seven villages who had arrived to attend a funeral ceremony. The Spaniard explained why he had come, and the headmen "assured me that they had among them no more Christians." Joasps told Estudillo that he and his people had never seen troops before, although they had heard about them. A few days later the expedition arrived in the territory of the Telamni, where Estudillo convinced the residents of a village to deliver two neophytes from San Miguel and to search for three more who were in hiding. "They begged me," he recalled, "to pardon them, for they were all either their sons or brothers. I exhorted them not to detain any Christian in the future even though he were a relative."[87]

Estudillo entered Tachi territory on November 1 but found a

village usually friendly to the Spanish deserted. Its residents had taken seriously a warning issued by neophytes from Mission Soledad that the Spaniards had hostile intentions. Estudillo proceeded to the Kings River, where a Nutunutu envoy told him to remain in place. The Indian would inquire if the several headmen assembled at a nearby village would speak with him. Estudillo dismissed the envoy and marched into the village. He lectured the headmen about harboring fugitives and then crossed the river into Wimilchi territory.[88]

Traveling north of Tulare Lake on November 9, the party reached a village of the Cheneche, where neophytes from Santa Cruz, Santa Clara, San Francisco, and Soledad resided. Recently three Indians—Pomponio, Baltazar, and Clareño—had arrived with twelve horses stolen from Mission Santa Clara. Estudillo found the settlement deserted and concluded that continuing to a village on the Merced River would be unproductive because "it would have been already abandoned for many days by both natives and the renegade Christians who live with them. They would be hidden in the tules and swamps whose inviolability is a complete certainty, the more so since they carry nothing with them, and get about easily with their knowledge of the country." Estudillo returned to Monterey on November 16.[89]

As the coastal neophyte population declined because of disease and fugitivism, Spaniards had little choice but to penetrate the interior on campaigns specifically designed to recruit gentiles and to round up runaways. The more they intruded into the affairs of independent Indian societies, however, the more difficult it became for them to achieve their goals. By chastising or punishing gentiles for harboring neophytes, they increasingly turned nominally friendly peoples into hostile adversaries. Moreover, by relying heavily on neophyte auxiliaries, the Spaniards fostered inter-Indian rivalry and hatred. Operating with their own objectives, the auxiliaries were no less intruders than those who led them into the interior.

Interethnic relations in the interior deteriorated further after Mexico gained its independence from Spain. Neophytes not only continued to withdraw from the missions, but in some cases they left en masse. The expeditions Mexicans launched to recover runaways differed little in intent from those undertaken by Spaniards, but the resistance they encountered intensified significantly. Determined to remain in the interior, many of the fugitives directly confronted those sent to take them back. While not always successful in these encounters, they demonstrated to the Mexicans that penetrating the interior came at great risk.

CHAPTER 5

Violent Confrontation

IN February 1824, three years after Mexico proclaimed its independence, the corporal of the guard at Mission Santa Inés flogged a neophyte visitor from Mission La Purísima, sparking an uprising in which the neophytes drove the missionaries and guards into a building at the rear of the church and set fire to several structures. The following day soldiers retook the mission, but many of the neophytes fled to La Purísima where the neophytes there also had risen.[1]

At La Purísima, rebels killed four Californios (Mexican residents of California), two of them travelers on their way to Los Angeles, but seven Indians may have lost their lives in the takeover. Subsequently, the rebels released all the prisoners they had taken, including Father Antonio Rodríguez, who chose to remain at the mission.[2] Mariano, Pacomio, Benito, and Bernabé commanded the rebels.[3] They built fortifications, cut loopholes in the walls of the church, and activated a cannon that had been used only for ceremonial purposes.[4]

Once the uprising began at Santa Inés, neophytes dispatched a messenger to Mission Santa Bárbara informing Andrés Sagimomatsse, an alcalde (neophyte officer appointed by the padres), that soldiers would arrive shortly to kill the Indians while they attended mass. The alcalde sent the women and children into the nearby foothills and a messenger to Mission San Buenaventura.[5] Indians at this mission, however, expressed no interest in participating in the uprising. Many years later, a Californio claimed the Indians at Santa Bárbara "were at odds with those of San Buenaventura. But for this circumstance the Indians of the latter Mission would have risen."[6] After a short battle with the Mexican guards, in which three Indians died, Sagimomatsse and his followers sacked the mission, appropriating money and clothing but disdaining wine, religious items, seeds, and furniture. They retreated to the foothills behind the mission.[7]

Troops arrived from the Santa Bárbara presidio the same day the neophytes fled, finding only four or five old women and a half-wit. They murdered an Indian wandering about on a mule and the following day killed four Indians who had played no part in the uprising. The soldiers also looted the houses of the Indians. When Father Antonio Ripoll sent messages to the rebels imploring them to return, they questioned why they would be treated differently than the four Indians the soldiers had murdered. They sought to know what they would do at the mission "since the soldiers have robbed all our belongings."[8]

When two Indian workers from the presidio joined the rebels, spreading the rumor that soldiers were intent upon killing all the Indians and abolishing the mission, Sagimomatsse departed for the Tulare Valley.[9] Before leaving, he sent three messengers, Hilarion Chaaj, José Venadero, and Luís Calala, to contact interior Yokuts.[10] Padre Juan Cabot of Mission Soledad also dispatched Indian messengers to the interior. They visited several villages, warning the occupants not to join the rebels.[11]

Seeking to enlist interior Indians to their cause, the Purísima rebels sent sacks of beads to several Yokuts societies. The Tachi and Telamni refused the presents; the Nutunutu took the presents but did not join. The residents of Bubal and another Wowol village accepted the presents, some departing for La Purísima. Upon learning that the rebels had been defeated, however, they turned back.[12]

On March 16 soldiers had surrounded Mission La Purísima. The Indian rebels opened fire with muskets and the cannon they had activated. The soldiers bombarded the mission with artillery. After a battle lasting two and a half hours and the intercession of Father Rodríguez, the rebels surrendered. Sixteen Indians and one Californio lost their lives.[13] Either before or after the attack, some of the Purísima neophytes escaped to the interior.[14]

In the meantime, Sagimomatsse attempted to spearhead a general revolt among the Indians of the Tulare Valley. Apparently, he intended to attack Mission Santa Bárbara and perhaps the nearby presidio as well. Largely unsuccessful in his recruiting efforts, he did receive the support of the leader of a village located northeast of Buena Vista and Kern Lakes in the territory of the Paleuyami (Yokuts). Half of the fighting men of this village joined the rebels at their camp at San Emigdio.[15]

Before the arrival of Sagimomatsse at San Emigdio, local Indians had captured an American and a greatly disliked Californio who resided at San Buenaventura. Coastal and interior Indians may have disagreed over the fate of the prisoners. According to Father Ripoll, the neophytes advocated leniency, the gentiles, execution. Be that as it may, Indians murdered both men.[16]

On the whole, amicable relations were forged between neophytes and gentiles at San Emigdio. On one occasion, Sagimomatsse had twenty-five steers butchered and evenly distributed the meat among members of both groups. Not terribly concerned about their fate, Indians spent much of each day gambling with money taken from Mission Santa Bárbara and bathing in sweat houses. Initially, neophyte and gentile males freely exchanged married and unmarried females.[17] Sagimomatsse put a stop to this practice, however.[18]

Mexican civil and religious authorities greatly exaggerated the threat the rebels posed to the missions and pueblos. Padre Blas Ordaz, for example, believed the Indians were well armed and led by a Russian. He was convinced that neophytes from Mission San Fernando had joined the rebels and that those at San Gabriel were in a state of agitation.[19]

In April the Californios sent a military force into the interior. An indecisive battle took place on the eleventh in which soldiers killed four Indians and recovered thirteen horses.[20] A short time later, Padre Luís Antonio Martínez and a few soldiers visited two abandoned villages near San Emigdio where they found a horse from La Purísima and evidence that a large herd recently had been in the area. Martínez feared that the rebels had gone to the edge of the Sierra Nevada from where they would raid the coast with impunity.[21]

Some of the rebels may have found sanctuary in Walker's Pass in the foothills of the Sierra Nevada. A decade after the uprising, a party of American trappers visited a village in the area. Zenas Leonard recalled:

> After we halted here we found that these people could talk the Spanish language, . . . and on inquiry ascertained that they were a tribe . . . , which . . . some eight or ten years since resided in the Spanish settlements at the missionary station near St. Barbara, on the coast, where they rebelled against the authority of the country, robbed the church of all its golden images & candle-sticks, and one of the Priests of several thousand dollars in gold and silver, when they retreated to the spot where we found them.[22]

Soldiers, accompanied by Padres Vicente Francisco de Sarría and Antonio Ripoll, contacted the Santa Bárbara rebels near Buena Vista Lake on June 10. Because the Indians had taken refuge in a tule marsh, it was clearly in the best interests of the Californios to negotiate. Pablo de la Portilla, commander of the force, promised Jaime, a spokesman for the rebels, that upon surrendering the Indians would be pardoned by the governor. Jaime conveyed this message to his superiors. A short time later he informed the commander that the Indians were ready to return to their missions. They were, however, reluctant to turn over their weapons. After two conferences, Portilla allayed their fears.[23]

The surrender was jeopardized when a gentile and a neophyte from San Miguel erroneously informed the Indians that more troops were on their way. Immediately, several rebels fled from the area, although most returned a short time later.[24] The surrender took place as scheduled. As recorded by an eyewitness, "Father Sarría said to them: 'Come along, come along for we have to sing the *Corpus* tomorrow.' . . . That afternoon a great number of mission rebels came over to us; on the following day the Indians put together an arbor for the function of the *Corpus* which was celebrated right there in camp."[25]

On the thirteenth, several Indians informed Portilla that their alcaldes had lost status during the uprising and suggested that new ones be appointed. The commander agreed, selecting Lazaro Huilamuit and Juan Pablo Aguilait. He allowed Andrés Sagimomatsse to retain his authority, however. The three Indian leaders joined twenty-five soldiers and a few vaqueros to search for horses and the Indians who had fled the previous day.[26]

The party proceeded north along the edge of Buena Vista Lake to the village of Tulamniu, where fifty armed Indians surrendered. The village was in a state of confusion, because three Indians from San Diego had told the residents the Californios intended to murder them. The party located eighteen neophytes from Santa Bárbara; fifteen were returned to the mission. The other three, along with seven neophytes from Missions San Diego, San Miguel, and San Luis Obispo, found sanctuary in a tule swamp.[27]

Portilla sent Lázaro Huilamuit and a few men back to Tulamniu, where four neophytes were found and brought to camp. And at the village of Halau, Jaime persuaded sixteen Indians from Santa Bárbara to surrender. Leaving Sagimomatsse and six other Indians in the interior to locate the neophytes still missing, the soldiers returned to the coast.[28] Portilla reported to the governor on June 28, acknowledging that 163 Indians remained unaccounted for.[29]

The military authorities executed seven Purísima neophytes for murdering the four Californios. They sentenced eight Indians to eight-year prison terms, and the ringleaders—Mariano, Pacomio, Benito, and Bernabé—received ten years each.[30] In July 1825, criminal charges were brought against these rebels because articles taken from the mission had not been returned.[31] If these were the same items Leonard later observed at the village in Walker's Pass, a case can be made that Purísima rebels founded the settlement.[32] According to the padres' annual report of 1827–28, some of the Purísima neophytes still were at large.[33]

Discontented neophytes from other missions continued to flee to the interior. In December 1825, José Pico led a force of twenty-nine soldiers from the presidio at Monterey to the San Joaquin River. On the way, Pico captured Rustico and Canuto, fugitives from Mission San Juan Bautista who long had eluded the authorities. He also located fourteen neophytes Father Felipe Arroyo de la Cuesta had sent to apprehend the fugitives and captured sixteen men and twenty-three women and children, all gentiles. The fugitives and the male gentiles were sent to Mission San Juan Bautista. Rustico, Canuto, and the gentiles were turned over to the corporal of the guard.[34]

Pico proceeded in an easterly direction, his destination being the Hoyima (Yokuts) who resided along the San Joaquin River just to the east of where it bends to the north. He sought a neophyte from Mission Soledad and another from San Juan Bautista. The Californios attacked a village on January 5, 1826, capturing forty Indians but failing to locate the two fugitives. An Indian from San Juan Bautista was arrested, however. He was married to a gentile and had a small child. Pico released all the women and children but kept seven men, including the married neophyte.[35]

In the vicinity of the village, Pico observed "fresh bones and hides of horses which the Indians had slaughtered." The following day he warned the Indians that if found again with "dead horses in their possession, they would be taken to a strange country and never see their own land again." On January 11, the soldiers overran a village of the Apiachi (Yokuts) and captured ten neophytes from Soledad. Pico accused the villagers of recently killing and eating a horse and warned them that they would be severely punished if horses were again found in their possession.[36]

The following day, the party arrived at the Kings River. A village, probably occupied by the Nutunutu (Yokuts), was situated on the opposite side. Pico persuaded an Indian leader to cross but only after considerable effort:

He stated that he had come only with great reluctance because he had never before seen any soldiers, but had only heard them talked about. I succeeded in winning his confidence and asked him if he had Christians in his village, to which he answered no. I asked if he had any horses and he said no. To this I could only reply that his own companions had told me that they had two horses. This argument he answered by saying that although it was true that there had been two horses, the latter had not belonged to his village but to some heathen at the village of Cauya. These individuals, on learning of our arrival, took flight and left the horses in their village.[37]

The Californios journeyed upstream, making camp a short distance from a village. Pico called upon its leaders to turn over all Christian fugitives, but none was delivered. The following day Pico met with several leaders of another village. Initially, all denied harboring neophytes, but later that afternoon they turned over three fugitives from Mission Soledad. Fearing for their safety, the Californios retreated to a safer area.[38]

On January 14, they continued upstream, searching for five animals lost the previous day. Near a Wimilchi (Yokuts) village, Pico divided his command into small parties to scour the area for the animals and the Indians who stole them. When the parties reassembled, the soldiers reported killing seven Indians. They also turned over to Pico six captives who denied stealing the stock, blaming the act on their enemies, the Nutunutu. The soldiers discounted any chance of recovering the animals.[39]

A few days later Pico sent eleven soldiers with twenty-two Indian prisoners to San Juan Bautista. Pico and eighteen men traveled downstream, arriving at a village on January 20. As recounted by Pico, the Indians "were all on the other side of the river and all armed, both Christian and heathen. The Christians belong to Mission Soledad. I talked to these Indians and called for the chief but he would not come. They said they would not come over to where I was because they were afraid and because they already knew how we had killed seven of the heathen Guimilches [Wimilchi]." Rebuffed and unable to cross the river at that point, the Californios continued downstream to a better crossing and proceeded along the eastern shore of Tulare Lake.[40]

On the twenty-second they arrived opposite the village of Bubal, now located on an island in the lake. Neophytes from Mission San Miguel presented papers from their padre giving them permission to be in the area. The headman of the village supplied the soldiers with food and offered assistance in fighting the Tachi, promising to drag them out of the tule swamps in the lake. Declining the offer, Pico departed the following day for San Miguel.[41]

Having traversed a wide area, killed a few Indians, and captured several fugitives and gentiles, Pico's expedition was one of the most successful undertaken by the Californios. Later in 1826, however, Cosomne (Miwok) routed a force of Californios and neophytes from Mission San José. Evidently, the neophyte auxiliaries initiated the attack and suffered as many as thirty-four dead. The intruders retreated, abandoning the cannon they had employed against the Cosomne.[42]

In November, José Antonio Sánchez of the presidio at San Francisco led a punitive expedition, consisting of 21 soldiers, 21 volunteers, and 150 neophytes, against the Cosomne.[43] A padre at Mission San José, apprehensive that the recent victory would instill in the Cosomne even more confidence and defiance, financed the campaign with money, arms, and horses. Victorious this time, the command killed forty-one Cosomne and returned to Mission San José with forty prisoners, mostly women and children who were enrolled in the mission. Because none of the prisoners was wounded, a visiting British naval officer "feared that the Christians, who could scarcely be prevented from revenging the death of their relations upon those who were brought to the mission, glutted their brutal passion on all the wounded who fell into their hands."[44] A subordinant reported that the mother of a boy of four or five was shot while attempting to save her son. This "furnished a subject of mirth of her executioners. Many such instances of wanton cruelty occurred, the blame of which we were told was to be imputed solely to the Tame Indians and their thirst of revenge."[45]

Not all the neophytes at Mission San José proved to be loyal supporters of the missionaries. In mid-May 1827, some four hundred neophytes fled to the interior.[46] Deeply troubled over such a large-scale defection, Father Narciso Durán confessed to Ignacio Martínez, commandant of the San Francisco presidio, that he could not "get over the surprise of such an unforeseen occurrence by a people that appeared to be so peaceful and docile."[47] An alcalde, Narciso, organized the mass desertion, and when sent to persuade the runaways to return, he remained with his followers. He sent messages to the neophytes at Missions Santa Clara, San Juan Bautista, and Santa Cruz to join him in the interior. Father Durán blamed American trappers then in the interior for the desertions. Neophytes informed him that the Americans had offered the Indians of San José protection if they would leave the mission.[48]

The trappers causing so much concern had arrived at Mission San Gabriel in late November 1826. Led by Jedediah Smith and guided by Spanish-speaking Indians, the twenty-man party crossed the Tehachapi Mountains early the following year and in February camped on the east side of Tulare Lake near a Wowol (Yokuts) village. "When I arrived," Smith recalled, "some mats were spread in front of the Lodges and I was invited to sit down. Grass seed was then brought in and poured on my head until I was nearly covered."[49]

Smith and his party trapped their way north, striking the San Joaquin where it exits the mountains and following it downstream to the Stanislaus. Smith saw few Indians along the river, noting in his journal that "the greater part of those that had once resided here . . . [have] gone into the missions of St Joseph and Santa Clara."[50] The Americans experienced no difficulties with Indians until they arrived at the Cosumnes, where they were attacked by a party of Muqueleme (Miwok). No injuries were inflicted, but the trappers were forced to withdraw to safe ground. The following day the Americans discovered the Indians had taken some of their traps and had formed on the opposite bank. Unable to cross to do battle, they remained helpless until an Indian ventured too close to the bank and was shot dead.[51]

Smith led his men north to the American River and, seeking a route across the Sierra Nevada, followed the south fork deep into

Nisenan territory. When Indians (perhaps Yalesumne) pressed too close, Smith "tried to convince them of my friendly disposition but to no purpose. Their preparations were still going forward and their parties were occupying favorable points around me." Smith ordered two of his best marksmen to fire at long range so "it might give them the idea that we could kill at any distance. At the report of the guns . . . two indians fell."[52] Unable to cross the mountains, the trappers returned to the Stanislaus.[53]

When word reached the coast that Americans were in the adjacent interior, Father Durán formulated his theory regarding the desertion of the four hundred neophytes. Writing to Lieutenant Ignacio Martínez on May 16, the priest claimed that "the Anglo-Americans sent several communications to people in that part of the country, offering them protection to abandon the mission and Christian obligations and return to their villages to live and die gentiles." Americans had visited the villages of the Muqueleme and Cosomne "and their stay brought about this inconvenience to this mission."[54] Durán may have been particularly concerned about the Cosomne joining the Americans because recently they had suffered greatly from a Mexican military invasion.

Regarding the Muqueleme attack on the trappers, Martínez claimed in a letter to Governor José María Echeandía that once the Indians realized the Americans were not Mexican soldiers they made peace.[55] His assessment was correct, because shortly after the encounter, Te-Mi, a Muqueleme leader, returned a horse and seven or eight traps the Indians had taken, and on a regular basis delivered to the Americans meal, raspberries, and other food in exchange for meat.[56]

Receiving information from a neophyte that Father Duran was troubled by the presence of Americans in the interior, Smith wrote to the priest on May 19, informing him that he and his trappers had attempted to leave California by crossing the Sierra Nevada but were forced to remain in the interior until the snow melted.[57] The following day, Smith and two companions departed up the Stanislaus and successfully traversed the mountains. The rest of the party, under the command of Harrison Rogers, were to remain in camp until Smith returned with supplies.[58] In the meantime, Governor Echeandía instructed Martínez to locate the Americans and order them to leave the province. Martínez turned the task over to Sergeant Francisco Soto, who with about a dozen soldiers arrived at the trappers' camp in early June. Soto delivered to Rogers a letter from Luís Antonio Argüello, commandant of the San Francisco presidio.[59] Argüello chastized Rogers for remaining in Mexican territory and for attempting

to win the goodwill of these natives, while at the same time you survey the land and rivers. Moreover, you give notice to these same natives that all that Territory, as far as the Columbia River, is yours. You point out to them boundaries on the San Joaquin River and appoint captains with insignias, over whom you have asserted civil and political authority. The actions are too insolent, and in no way will our Mexican government view them with indifference.[60]

Rogers penned a reply to Argüello. He insisted that neither he nor the United States had any designs on California, that he had not communicated with Indians except those who came to his camp, and that he was willing to give himself up if so ordered.[61]

On his return journey, Soto rounded up the neophytes who had fled from Mission San José and visited several villages of gentiles to ascertain if the Americans had attempted to influence them in any way. Soto told Argüello he had found no evidence the trappers had encouraged the neophytes to leave the mission. In a letter to Governor Echeandía, Argüello admitted there was little evidence to implicate the Americans but insisted they had come to California not to trap but to explore.[62]

In August, Smith returned to California. On the Colorado River, Mohave Indians killed ten of the eighteen members of his party, and when he reached the Stanislaus in September he found his trappers in a destitute condition. With three men he departed immediately for Mission San José where he was promptly arrested. He was later taken to Monterey. In November, however,

Echeandía issued him a passport to leave the province, and at the end of December 1827 he headed north.[63]

Smith took with him a large herd of horses an Englishman, William Garner, had purchased for him in Monterey.[64] Twenty years later, Garner recalled that Smith "bought three hundred and ninety seven head of horses and mules, of the best kind that could be found in the country; and only one horse amongst them cost as high as fifteen dollars—the average price he paid for them was about nine dollars."[65]

With the departure of Smith and his trappers, Mexican authorities could better concentrate on a much more serious problem— Indian stock raiders. In April 1828, a party of Californios and neophyte auxiliaries traveled to the San Joaquin River where it exits the foothills. On the twenty-sixth, ten soldiers and fifteen auxiliaries crossed the San Joaquin and attacked a Hoyima village, killing three and capturing twenty-six Indians. According to the commander of the expedition, Sebastian Rodríguez, "we found 27 horses, . . . the flesh of which the Indians had been eating for three days, after the animals had been killed with arrows. In the brush there may have been 60 to 80 more horses." The Californios burned all the remaining horse meat, "not leaving the Indians as much as a quarter to eat."[66]

Upstream the intruders found deserted villages. Rodríguez noted that "these three villages are all part of the tribe of Joyimas [Hoyima], and when horses are brought in they are divided up among the Indians who caught them, to be eaten at leisure." A scouting party discovered some Indians in hiding, and in the ensuing fight the Hoyima killed an interpreter and five other neophytes. The intruders captured five men, nineteen women, and thirteen boys and girls. Later, several other Indians also were taken, including two neophytes from San Juan Bautista and two gentiles, Selli and Salmi, apparently well-known horse thieves.[67]

The command then ventured north into the territory of the Heuchi (Yokuts). Before its arrival, Delfino, a neophyte from San José, had spread the word that a military force was in the area, but Rodríguez managed to capture eight gentiles and three neophytes from San Juan Bautista. On April 30, he sent a contingent into the territory of the Chauchila (Yokuts) to "catch either Christians or heathen, for these people are also horse eaters." No Indians were found. A few days later, the Californios arrived at Mission San Juan Bautista with fifty-two horses and eighty-five neophytes and gentiles.[68]

In late May, Rodríguez again penetrated the interior, this time to Buena Vista Lake. The village of Tulamniu, located on the north shore, was deserted, its residents having been warned by a neophyte from Mission San Miguel that Californios intended to kill them. Shortly, however, the headman appeared; he told Rodríguez that the six Christians living in his village had fled to a tule swamp.[69]

The contingent that entered the swamp returned with a few Indians; one informed Rodríguez that he would find horses and saddles at a village in the mountains near Santa Bárbara. When Rodríguez and fifteen men arrived at the village, they confronted the headman, who presented a document stating that he had authorization from a padre at Mission La Purísima to recover horses belonging to the mission. Unconvinced, Rodríguez confiscated eight saddles, five mules, and fifteen horses. On the way back to Buena Vista Lake, the Californios collected eleven more horses.[70]

While Rodríguez was absent, the headman of Tulamniu turned over four of the six neophytes who had fled from the village; upon the return of Rodríguez, he delivered the other two. And a leader of the Yauelmani (Yokuts), who resided on the east side of the lake, presented the Californios with twelve horses. Admitting that Christians resided in his village, he surrendered them a short time later.[71]

Rodríguez proceeded to the village of Bubal. He demanded from the headman sixteen neophytes and apprehended nine gentiles to ensure delivery. The headman located only two fugitives, however. Rodríguez then departed for Mission San Miguel, where he turned over to Father Juan Cabot forty-seven animals from Missions San Luís Obispo, La Purísima, Santa Bárbara, Buenaventura, San Fernando, and San Gabriel. Thirty-one neophytes and gentiles were taken to the Monterey presidio.[72]

Judged by the number of neophytes and animals recovered, the two expeditions conducted by Rodríguez were highly successful. But the Californios had little time for self-congratulation. Late in 1828, a party of neophytes departed from Mission San José, apparently with permission from the resident priests, to visit relatives. On November 9, Father Durán reported that most of the neophytes had returned except for the Lakisamne (Yokuts), whose natal villages were on the Stanislaus River. Durán identified Estanislao as the ringleader.[73]

According to a contemporary, Estanislao was "about six feet in height, with a skin nearer white than bronze. He was of slender build and an excellent horseman. His face was nearly covered by a beard." Born at the mission, he became a vaquero and mule trainer.[74] He also served as an alcalde.[75] From the Stanislaus River, Estanislao sent a message to Father Durán announcing that his people were rising in revolt. He had no fear of the soldiers because they "are few in number, are very young, and do not shoot well." Durán notified the presidio commander that the rebels expected to be joined by neophytes from Missions Santa Clara, Santa Cruz, and San Juan Bautista. He emphasized that "everything depends upon capturing dead or alive a certain Estanislao from this mission and a person from Santa Clara called Cipriano."[76]

Sometime in late 1828 or early 1829, a sergeant and fifteen soldiers confronted the rebels in a dense thicket, where they received a barrage of insults. In the skirmish that fóllowed, the Indians killed two and wounded six soldiers, including a sergeant who subsequently died in the pueblo of San José. Several Indians also may have died.[77] A short time later, Estanislao and six followers apprehended two neophytes fishing on the San Joaquin River. As related by Father Durán, "Macario was relieved of the horses, his saddle, harness and clothing. An even more lamentable circumstance was that the companion, named Benigno[,] went over to the enemy." Estanislao sent Macario back to the mission with a message that soon the rebels would attack coastal settlements.[78]

In early May the Californios organized another military force. Commanded by José Antonio Sánchez and initially comprising nine cavalrymen and three artillerymen from the presidio at San Francisco, it was augmented at Mission San José with more cavalry, a few civilians, and seventy neophyte auxiliaries. The intruders sought to dislodge the Indians by bombardment, but the artillery piece was rendered useless when one of its wheels broke. The soldiers opened fire with their carbines, but to no effect.[79]

The command made camp a short distance from the Indian stockade. Later in the day, when Estanislao appeared in the distance, Sánchez ventured out to talk with him. He promised the rebel that no harm would come to him if he returned to the mission. The following day, Sánchez again called upon Estanislao to surrender, but the rebel replied that he would prefer to die in the underbrush. Thirteen leaders, all gentiles, came forward and told Sánchez they were afraid of Estanislao and Cipriano. The commander encouraged them to return to their villages, but they remained with the rebels.[80]

From several directions, Californios and auxiliaries attacked but withdrew after about three hours of fighting. The rebels killed two and wounded eight Californios. Eleven auxiliaries also were wounded. The Californios counted eight rebels killed. Concluding that further assault was foolhardy, Sánchez broke camp later in the day, arriving at Mission San José on May 10.[81]

Left behind and in the hands of the Indians was Andrés Mesa. Estanislao summoned Indians from nearby villages to celebrate the victory and to witness the execution of the Californio. They hung him by one foot from the branch of an oak tree and riddled him with arrows. His body and that of another soldier were then burned.[82]

Upon receiving a report of the campaign, the commandant of the San Francisco presidio ordered M. G. Vallejo to organize yet another expedition against Estanislao and Cipriano. He informed

Vallejo that "The Indian rebels from Mission San José and Santa Clara have gathered together at the rivers, resolved to die rather than surrender. They are extremely insolent, committing murders and stealing horses, . . . seducing other Christians to accompany them in their evil and diabolical schemes, openly insulting our troops. . . . They are relying upon the manpower of the wild Indians, on the terrain and positions which they are occupying." Vallejo was "to administer a total defeat to the Christian rebels and to the wild Indians who are aiding them, leaving them completely crushed."[83]

Vallejo departed from San José on May 26 with over one hundred soldiers and civilians and some fifty Indian auxiliaries from Missions Santa Clara and San José. At the site of the previous battle, he found the charred bones of the murdered soldiers but no Indians. When he set the thicket on fire, however, he received a volley of arrows. The Californios then opened up with their muskets and artillery. Vallejo ordered his cavalrymen to dismount and to probe the dense underbrush on foot. Waiting until the soldiers were nearly on them, the Indians launched their arrows, wounding three corporals. Before the Indians could cut them off from their mounts, the soldiers beat a hasty retreat. Probing the thicket the next day, the intruders discovered the Indians had fled during the night. Before withdrawing, the rebels may have buried some of the dead in the trenches they had dug for defense.[84]

The command followed the Indians to the Tuolumne River and on May 31 surrounded a village of the Tauhalame (Yokuts). A resident of the village, who was captured the previous day, was sent to implore the rebels to surrender. Instead, he told them to retreat into a nearby thicket, because once captured they would be killed. The Indian returned to the Californios' camp and was immediately executed. A neophyte, Matias, however, went over to the Californios. As recalled by Joaquin Piña, "Matias was told to speak to his compatriots and say to them that the troops were about to close in on them and that they should come out. Their reply was that they would not do this, they would prefer to die on the spot." The Californios and the neophyte auxiliaries then

attacked. The rebels, protected in trenches, responded with volleys of arrows that forced the intruders to retreat. After the battle
most of the Indians withdrew from the area.[85]

The following day the Californios captured three women,
including a neophyte called Agustina. Enlisting her and Matias as
guides, Californios and auxiliaries entered the thicket and discovered several bodies near the trenches. They also captured three
more women, who were shot on the spot. The civilian entrusted
with guarding Matias shot him as well. Except for the timely intercession of the commander of the expedition, Agustina and her
two companions also would have been murdered.[86]

As recounted by Piña, the retribution inflicted on the rebel
Indians continued:

> The Indian auxiliaries . . . managed to find a Christian Indian from
> Santa Clara. After capture he confessed that he had been the one who
> had burned the bodies of the two dead soldiers who had been killed on
> the previous expedition under Don José Sánchez. On learning this the
> Indian auxiliaries . . . began to beg the Commander for permission to kill
> the prisoner. . . . They were given this permission. So the Indian auxilia-
> ries formed a semicircle, placed him in the middle, and four of them
> began to shoot arrows at him. . . . Finally seeing that he did not die a
> cavalry officer shot him in the head with his carbine. . . . From there
> they took him to an oak tree and hung him up.[87]

The expedition returned to San José with eighteen horses Indians
had stolen from the vicinity of Missions San José and Santa
Clara.[88]

Learning that Indian prisoners had been murdered, the governor of California ordered an inquiry.[89] The investigator determined that two males and three females had been killed by
arrows but only one had died from gunshot. He identified a soldier, Joaquin Alvarado, as the murderer of a defenseless old
woman and recommended he be sentenced to five years' additional service in Baja California.[90]

On the advice of Father Durán, the governor pardoned the
rebel Indians, provided they return to their missions and by
"Christian and industrious conduct" exhibit proof of their repen-

tance. The governor admitted that "it is easier to control them when they are present than when they are absent."[91] Estanislao and many of the other Indians returned to Missions San José and Santa Clara.[92] Apparently, Durán allowed Estanislao to resume his duties and responsibilities as a vaquero, because in July he was back in the Tulares rounding up horses.[93] An apostate to the end, Cipriano died and was buried in the interior before the end of 1829.[94]

Unlike their Spanish predecessors, who witnessed the withdrawal of individuals from the missions, Mexican officials had to contend with the defection of groups of neophytes often led by those the missionaries had appointed to positions of authority. More than an act of personal disobedience, fleeing from the missions became a collective expression of rebellion. Perceiving the rebels to be a threat to the mission system, Mexican officials launched expeditions specifically designed to punish, thus increasing dramatically the frequency and intensity of the violent confrontations in the interior.

When outsiders, representing several nationalities, penetrated the San Joaquin Valley, relations between interior and coastal peoples deteriorated further. Initially, most came to trap fur-bearing animals, but those from New Mexico quickly realized that California's real wealth lay in horses and mules. Wasting little time in taking advantage of a new economic opportunity, interior Indians provided the Nuevomexicanos with stock. A commercial union was formed that profoundly altered interethnic relations throughout central California.

CHAPTER 6

Economic Adaptation

COMMANDED by Antonio Armijo, a party of sixty traders from New Mexico arrived at Mission San Gabriel on January 31, 1830. Their purpose in coming to California was to obtain mules.[1] William Garner, who had settled in California a few years before, recalled that the Nuevomexicanos purchased many animals "at the low price of fifty cents each, and among them were some very splendid animals."[2] They lost some of their stock to Navajos on the return journey but arrived safely in Jémez, New Mexico, in late April, having been gone about five and a half months.[3]

Although the road to California (called The Old Spanish Trail) terminated at Los Angeles, sub-branches eventually extended over a wide area. As explained by J. J. Warner, who arrived in California in 1831, "Los Angeles was the central point in California of this New Mexican trade. . . . From thence they scattered themselves over the country from San Diego to San Jose, and across the Bay to Sonoma and San Rafael. Having bartered and disposed of the goods bought, and procured such as they wished to carry back, and what mules they could drive, they concentrated at Los Angeles for their yearly return."[4]

Following the Nuevomexicanos into California were individuals representing several nationalities. In mid-1830 a trapping party, comprised mainly of Americans and a few French Canadians, camped at San Gabriel. Led by Ewing Young, the foreigners proceeded immediately to the San Joaquin Valley to trap for beaver.[5] In July they became involved in a Californio-Indian dispute. Early that month Californios and neophyte auxiliaries from Mission San José traveled to the Cosumnes River, where they recruited Indian allies. From there the combined force proceeded into the territory of the Ochejamne (Miwok), who were suspected of harboring fugitive Christians. Their leader, Huyumegepa, admitted Christians were in his village but refused to turn them over. Fighting broke out, the Ochejamne wounding eleven of the Indian intruders.[6]

The Californios turned to the nearby Americans for help. Several volunteered, and in the ensuing fight, which lasted three hours, the combined force killed three and wounded nineteen Ochejamne. The Indian auxiliaries set fire to the village.[7] Kit Carson, a participant in the fight, recalled that "the next day we demanded the runaways and informed the Indians that if they were not immediately given up we would not leave one of them alive. They complied with our demands, and we turned our prisoners over to those from whom they had deserted."[8]

Shortly after this incident, Young purchased horses and mules in the pueblo of San José.[9] Guarding these animals proved to be a difficult task, however. "Indians came to our camp during the night," Carson remembered, "frightened our animals, and ran off with sixty head." Twelve trappers, including Carson, located the Indians in the Sierra Nevada, "feasting off some of our animals they had killed. We charged their camp, killed eight Indians, took three children prisoners and recovered all of our animals, with the exception of six that were eaten."[10]

In February 1831, an expedition commanded by William Wolfskill arrived at Mission San Gabriel.[11] As recounted by Warner, with the party were several Nuevomexicanos, "some of whom had taken *serapes* and *fresadas* [woolen blankets] with them for the purpose of trading them to the Indians." The Nuevomexicanos returned to Santa Fe in the summer of 1831, with mules "of very fine form." The "price at which they had been bought in barter for blankets, caused quite a sensation in New Mexico."[12]

Late in the year eleven Americans entered Los Angeles to purchase mules. Five of their seven pack mules carried silver coins. Two men remained in the pueblo, while the others journeyed to the southern end of San Francisco Bay. In April the following year they reappeared in Los Angeles with six hundred mules and one hundred horses. The animals were resold in New Mexico.[13] Initially, American merchants in Santa Fe paid between six and ten dollars for a California mule.[14] Over the years, however, the price for horses and mules increased dramatically.[15]

Although concerned about the intrusion of trappers, Mexican officials and missionaries concluded that the traders posed a greater threat. As early as March 1831, Governor Manuel Victoria informed his presidio commanders at Santa Bárbara and San Diego that "those who have been in the habit of coming to this territory from New Mexico are establishing trade relations with the wild Indians, Christian fugitives and actually some of the mission neophytes." The Indians rob the missions of horses and sell them to the traders, "who take the animals to their own country by various routes."[16]

William Garner claimed that the year following the arrival of the first caravan from New Mexico, "the wild Indians began to steal from the settlements."[17] Father Juan Vicente Cabot reported in February 1833 that his mission of San Miguel had lost 108 mules and many horses since the Nuevomexicanos first came to California.[18] The same month, Father Vicente Pasqual Oliva of Mission San Gabriel alerted Governor José Figueroa to what he perceived to be a deteriorating situation: "The introduction of articles of commerce into this territory by natives of New Mexico has caused extensive robberies, both open and concealed. They sell, they trade, they induce the Indians to steal animals to sell."[19]

Summing up the situation a few years later, a visitor to California wrote: "Many of these traders are honest men, but there are many who purchase a part of their horses at a fair rate from the owner, and then set out on the pretended return, when in fact, they only retire to the interior, where pasture, and game, is abundant; they, there, pitch their tents, and . . . prevail on the Indians to supply them with as many horses as they wish."[20]

Local authorities attempted to curtail the activities of the traders. In January 1833 the legislative assembly passed an act prohibiting Nuevomexicanos from buying mules and horses at prices other than those set by a justice of the peace. Receipts were required to document the legality of the purchase. Thereafter, officials in Los Angeles were to inspect the animals before the traders departed for New Mexico.[21]

When a party of Nuevomexicanos left Los Angeles in January before submitting to an inspection, six Californios set out to bring them back. They failed to overtake that party, but on the Mohave River east of Los Angeles they encountered another with two hundred animals, most of them stolen. The Californios took the leader, Juan Jesus Villapando, to Los Angeles; his followers were to remain in place, but the men who returned to the river found the camp deserted. The Californios overtook the Nuevomexicanos in Tulare Valley, where they confiscated many horses, including one hundred head from Mission San Luís Obispo.[22]

On February 26, Governor Figueroa ordered a detachment of soldiers from the presidio at Santa Bárbara and a party of civilians from Los Angeles into the interior "in order to break up a union of the New Mexicans who, with pernicious intentions on the property of this territory, are gathering in the Tulares." If found in possession of stolen animals, the traders were to be brought, by force if necessary, to Los Angeles.[23]

Figueroa instructed the soldiers to treat fairly the Indians encountered in the interior: "In passing through the villages of the Indians, find the chief of the region, win his confidence, so that he will not be afraid or anxious, and declare that they may live in peace devoted to their labors. Be scrupulously careful in punishing the men under your command who transgress moderation in their dealings with the gentiles." The soldiers were to defend themselves against hostile Indians, but they "should be generous to their enemies when conquered, for more comes from good treatment than severity."[24] The Californios experienced no difficulties with Indians; they apprehended three traders and confiscated 430 animals taken from Missions San Luís Obispo and San Fernando. Found guilty and imprisoned, two of the traders later escaped and fled back to New Mexico.[25]

Foreigners entering California from the north also troubled the governor. In April 1833 he reported to the minister of war and navy that

the British and Americans, established on the Columbia River, make frequent incursions into this country on the pretext of trapping beaver and other quadrupeds. Scattering over various regions they identify themselves with the wild natives, following the same kind of life. They live in a wandering fashion with them and in this way become familiar and gain their confidence. From this has come rapidly one positive evil, namely that, influenced by these adventurers, the natives have dedicated themselves with the greatest determination to the stealing of horses from all the missions and towns of this territory.[26]

The month Figueroa wrote the letter, a party of neophytes from Mission San Francisco de Solano ventured to the mouth of the Sacramento, where trappers of the Hudson's Bay Company were camped. John Work recalled the meeting:

Four Indians came to the camp with some horses to sell in the evening. It appears that Indians are not allowed to make bargains whatever but that all must be done by the Priest or some of his deputies. The Indians dont [sic] seem to understand this arrangement. They say that . . . these horses are their own and neither the Priest or the Spaniards have anything to do with them. However in order to avoid trouble we declined buying any of the horses but two.[27]

While trapping on the San Joaquin River, the foreigners increasingly lost horses to Indians, and Work predicted he would "be obliged to go to war with these daring scoundrels." On July 13, his prediction came true. Eight Indians on horseback and nine or ten afoot, led by a "Spanish talking Christian," visited the trappers, who presented them with food and tobacco. While some of the Indians engaged the whites in trade, others attempted to steal their horses. In the ensuing fight, the trappers killed two Indians and drove the rest into a nearby tule swamp.[28]

The Indians regrouped and before sunrise the following morning launched a counterattack. As Work described it, "the arrows were falling thick among us but it was so dark that the indians could not be seen." Although continuing their fire until after day-break, the Indians succeeded in injuring only a horse. Apparently, the large size of the trappers' party discouraged the Indians from rushing the encampment. The whites, however, departed for Campo de Los Franceses at the juncture of the Stanislaus and San Joaquin rivers.[29]

On July 24, Work wrote in his journal that "the Indians are becoming troublesome and we are very short of ammunition, scarcely enough to defend ourselves." The following day, he sent eighteen men to a village, where some of its eighty to ninety residents were identified as participants in the recent encounter. According to Work, "the Indians immediately turned out in hostile array, one who came ahead of the rest made signs that the chief was among those who were killed on the 13th.—After the first fire from our people they fled into a dry channel of the river . . . , yet some were killed and several wounded, and the people took 18 horses but they are so miserably lean that they will be of very little service to us."[30]

Another fight occurred the next day. Some of Work's men, searching for stolen horses near the Mokelumne River, encountered Indians who fired on them. The trappers chased the Indians back to their village and then into a swamp, killing and wounding a few. They razed the village of nearly forty houses and confiscated twenty-one horses, four of which were identified as theirs. A short time later, the trappers journeyed north into the Sacramento Valley.[31]

Not long after Work's departure, Joseph Walker led a group of Americans into California, ostensibly to trap for beaver but also to acquire stock. On one occasion, they exchanged a yard of scarlet cloth and two knives with some Indians for 5 branded horses.[32] Twenty-five horses also were purchased from two deserters from the Mexican army. All told, the Americans obtained 315 horses and 45 head of cattle.[33] Zenas Leonard, a trapper who wrote an account of the expedition, failed to mention where and how the animals were obtained, but he acknowledged that "stealing horses is practiced more than any other kind of theft."[34] Many years later, William Craig, another member of the expedition, admitted that stealing horses was their real purpose in going to California.[35] Late in 1833, Ewing Young again entered California. On November 1, a party of Californios from San José encountered the trappers on the west side of the San Joaquin River. The Americans possessed a large number of horses the Californios claimed had been stolen from Missions San Fernando, San Gabriel, Santa Bárbara, and San Miguel. Young turned over twenty-seven animals but refused to surrender the rest, insisting they had been legally acquired. The Californios then moved into the territory of the Muqueleme (Miwok) and stormed a village. They killed twenty-two Indians, captured two fugitives from Mission San José, and recovered twelve animals. Back on the San Joaquin River, they met some French Canadians, probably in the employ of the Hudson's Bay Company, and confiscated three animals.[36]

A short time later, Governor Figueroa ordered the military commanders of the presidios at Monterey, San Diego, and Santa Bárbara to launch monthly expeditions into the interior. Private citizens and missionaries were to provide the mounts for the soldiers. Stock was to be confiscated from anyone who could not prove ownership. Foreign trappers were to be ordered out of the province, and Mexican citizens were to be notified that they must obtain a license to hunt. Those in possession of stock in the interior would be regarded as thieves and would be held responsible for damage done by the Indians, "whom they incite to evil." Commerce was to be conducted in the towns and not in the interior with Indians. Those who disobeyed the order were to be regarded as smugglers and their goods confiscated.[37]

Figueroa also defined his Indian policy. Indians were to be treated with "gentleness and charity," but they were to understand that stealing stock would not be tolerated. Those who ignored these orders were to be taken to the presidios for punishment. All Indians were under the obligation to reveal the identity of the thieves, "it being understood that if they do not do so they will be punished as accessories." Military commanders and property owners were to pursue the stock raiders and turn over prisoners to the proper authorities.[38]

Figueroa's instructions that Indians be treated humanely were ignored. On January 28, 1834, the Walker expedition encountered a party of Californios tracking Indians who had driven off three hundred horses from Mission San Juan Bautista. With the assistance of a few Americans, the Californios located the Indians in some timber and opened fire with artillery. Upon entering the camp, they found only a few feeble men and some women and children. Outraged at losing their prey, the Californios slaughtered the Indians and cut off their ears. According to Zenas Leonard, "their object in taking off the ears, was to show the Priests and Alcaldes, that they had used every effort to regain the stolen property."[39]

The murdering of Indians was not limited to Californios. In the summer of 1834, Ewing Young returned to California to acquire horses.[40] Several men joined his party in San José. Two were former members of the Walker expedition; three, apparently, were runaway sailors. While camped on the San Joaquin River, three of the newcomers, discovering the absence of Indian males at a nearby village, raped some of the women and stole valuable property. The following day, fifty Indians from the village caught up with the trappers. Hall Kelley warned the leader not to seek revenge: "The chief gave a word of command, and they turned about and hastened from us; but he, himself, stood awhile, looking toward us as though he feared not death. Turning slowly upon his heel, he walked away. Two of the party started to follow. I begged they would not; they persisted, saying they would do him no harm. In fifteen or twenty minutes after this, I heard the reports of their rifles." The two men returned with the bow and quiver of the chief.[41]

For several days, ten or twelve Indians pursued the whites, and on the American River stole several animals, which they gave to the residents of a village. The day following the theft, seven Indians from the village crossed to speak with the trappers. Five approached the whites with fish and seeds. "Standing in a semicircle not more than ten feet distant from me," recalled Kelley, "their orator began to speak and explain as to their innocence." The Americans, however, were in no mood for explanations: "They seized their rifles and shot down those fine innocent, and to all appearances, upright and manly men. . . . I heard but a single groan. Two or three of the party, mounting their horses, hastened to murder in like manner the other two, and they were shot while fording the streams."[42]

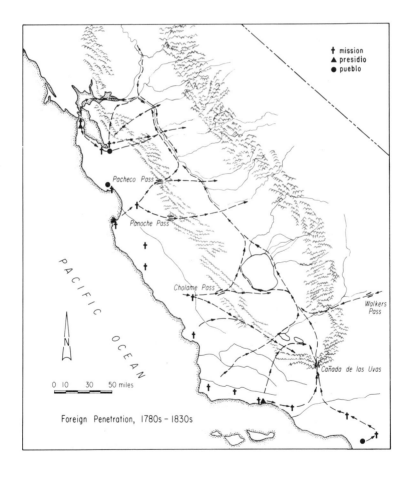

Foreign Penetration, 1780s – 1830s

Young and his men journeyed north through the Sacramento Valley with Mexican horses. Ninety-eight of them may have been purchased, but the fifty-six animals possessed by the newcomers may have been stolen.[43] Regarding the activities of Young, Governor Figueroa informed the head of the Hudson's Bay Company at Fort Vancouver that "these adventurers forgetting the hospitality with which they were treated by the inhabitants of this territory committed the crime of robbing upwards of two hundred head of horses belonging to various Mexican citizens."[44]

Also causing Figueroa considerable apprehension was the arrival at Los Angeles in January 1834 of 125 Nuevomexicanos. They brought with them a large quantity of woolen goods, including 1,645 serapes, 341 fresadas, and 171 colchas (bedspreads).[45] Their entrance into Santa Bárbara the following month prompted a local resident to predict that the mules they could not purchase "they mean to take by force."[46] Upon learning that members of the expedition had departed to the interior to encourage Indians to steal horses for them, the authorities in Los Angeles sent a military detachment to their camp. They were to be escorted to Los Angeles, where they would remain until all members of the caravan assembled for the journey home.[47]

Trappers and traders presented interior Indians with problems and possibilities. Largely unsuccessful in appropriating stock from Americans and Britons, they obtained highly prized manufactured goods from the Nuevomexicanos. Indeed, the commercial union forged between Indians and traders stands in sharp contrast to the often violent interaction of Indians and trappers. This economic bond, in turn, greatly affected intra-Mexican relations. Realizing the damage Indians could cause to the local economy if the traders' demand for stock remained unchecked, the Californios attempted to curtail contact with members of their own nation. At the time, they feared Nuevomexicanos more than Anglo-Americans.

The arrival of intruders from the east was only one of several forces of change emanating from outside of California. From the north came microbes which drastically reduced the populations of some Indian societies. From the south came instructions to abolish the mission system, which allowed large numbers of neophytes to move into the interior. The neophytes, in turn, spread aspects of Spanish culture over a wide area and exerted considerable influence over the less acculturated Indians with whom they established contact.

CHAPTER 7

Cultural Modification

IN 1829 or 1830, contaminated sailors introduced malaria to Fort Vancouver on the Columbia River. Three years later it had diffused to the interior of northern California, probably carried by trappers in the employ of the Hudson's Bay Company. The mosquito *Anopheles maculipennis freebornia* spread the disease throughout the Sacramento and into the San Joaquin valleys.[1]

J. J. Warner traveled up the San Joaquin River in 1833, and years later recounted the devastation.

> Around the naked villages, graves and the ashes of funeral pyres, the skeletons and swollen bodies told a tale of death such as to us no written record has ever revealed. From the head of the Sacramento valley to until we reached the mouth of the King's river, not exceeding five live Indians were seen. . . .
>
> As was evident to us from the signs which we saw, that at first the Indians buried their dead, but when the dead became so numerous that the living could not bury them, resort was had to the burning of the dead bodies, and when the living from diminished numbers were unable to do this, they abandoned their villages, the sick and the dying, and fled in dismay, only to die by the side of the springs and pools of water and beneath the shade of protecting trees.[2]

Apparently, the disease failed to diffuse into the Tulare Valley. While traveling along the eastern side of the valley in February 1834, Zenas Leonard made no mention of devastated villages. On the contrary, he observed "swarms of Indians scattered along in every direction."[3] Because those traveling in the northern San Joaquin Valley during the late 1830s and 1840s also failed to mention deserted villages and human remains, population recovery seems to have been rapid.[4] It resulted, however, not only from natural reproduction but also from political developments taking place in the coastal zone. In August 1833, the national Mexican government passed a law secularizing the missions of California. In theory the law, implemented the following year, required the padres to relinquish secular control over the neophytes and to perform only religious duties until replaced by parish priests. As quickly as possible, the missions were to be converted into pueblos and their lands distributed among the neophytes. Each family head or adult male over twenty years of age was to receive thirty-three acres of land. Half of the livestock, equipment, and seeds of each mission was to be divided among the neophytes. Remaining land, animals, and property would come under the jurisdiction of civil administrators who would oversee the missions until secularization was completed.[5] A few Indian pueblos were founded but functioned for only short periods, and most of the land promised to neophytes eventually fell into the hands of prominent Californios. From mission lands, private estates called ranchos were created. Throughout the 1830s and into the 1840s, however, most of the missions, although reduced in size, continued to operate.[6]

Secularization provided the neophytes with several options. They could remain at the missions and attempt to acquire the lands promised in the law, they could drift into the Mexican pueblos in search of work, they could seek employment on the ranchos, or they could trek into the interior. Those choosing the latter option participated in the repopulation of the San Joaquin Valley devastated by the malaria epidemic.[7]

Few would have left the coast without the belief they could find physical safety and social security in the interior. Rejoining kin probably was the goal of most, but given the population disruptions caused by disease and warfare, many had no choice but to seek residence among alien groups. This required the host societies to make social adjustments that allowed for the incorporation of persons based on criteria other than kinship.

Sixty-five years of colonization, however, had created loyalties and hatreds that often divided neophytes and gentiles. The English naval officer F. W. Beechey noted that the

wild Indians have a great contempt and dislike for those who have entered the missions, and they will frequently not only refuse to re-admit them to their tribe, but will sometimes even discover their retreat to their pursuers. This animosity between the wild and converted Indians is of great importance to the missions, as it checks desertion. . . . The Indians, besides, from political motives, are, I fear, frequently encouraged in a contemptuous feeling towards their unconverted country men, by hearing them constantly held up to them in the degrading light of *béstias!* and in hearing the Spaniards distinguished by the appellation *génte de razón.*[8]

Gentiles and neophytes, however, found ways to overcome this animosity. Writing in 1846, William Garner concluded that the Indians who left the San Luís Obispo area

would not be well received by their relatives and friends in the Tulares, if they went empty handed, and having nothing else to take with them as a peace offering, thought that taking a quantity of horses would serve a double purpose, which is this: instead of having to walk from 150 to 200 miles and meet with a cool reception, or something worse, they would be able to ride that distance and have wherewith to make themselves independent when they got there.[9]

The neophytes who moved inland entered a region that had undergone significant economic change. An extensive inter-Indian trade network long had been in place, but with the arrival of the trappers and especially the traders from New Mexico, Indians found new customers and therefore new opportunities to demonstrate their commercial expertise. Those located in Walker's Pass on the Kern River became especially active. Most likely Chumash refugees from Mission La Purísima, they traded with those entering and leaving the San Joaquin Valley. Zenas Leonard noted that they were "well acquainted with the rules of bartering for goods or any thing they wish to buy—much more so than any other tribe we met with."[10]

By the mid-1830s, they had become active stock raiders. According to Leonard, they have "the habit of making regular visits to the settlements for the purpose of stealing horses."[11] On occasion their neighbors stole from them the horses they had taken.[12] But so skilled were they in acquiring animals, they could easily sustain some loss of stock. Those undertaking the raids were divided into two bands, each comprising seven or eight young men and led by a neophyte. Raids were conducted on a monthly basis, one band operating at a time. Horses were eaten, traded with those coming through the pass, and exchanged with Paiutes residing north of Owens Lake on the east side of the Sierra Nevada.[13]

The economic change experienced by many interior peoples altered traditional political relationships. An Indian told an American military officer in 1848 that the stock raiders who resided at the southern end of Kern Lake "have certain chiefs who divide the horses among their followers at regular periods."[14] While passing through the Tulare Valley in 1850, Eugene Upton learned that "nothing can be bought or sold except by the chiefs."[15]

John Marvin commented on the complexity of Indian political organization: "The system of government which holds among the Indians, is far more complicated than would be generally supposed. In addition to the Alcaldes, Judges of the Peace, &., they elect Commissary, Generals, Chiefs of Divisions, &., &., to all of whom certain duties and certain honors pertain, which are eagerly sought after. In an Indian village of 500 persons, more officers would be found than in any Spanish or American town of thrice the number of inhabitants."[16]

That neophytes gained political power among some interior societies is evident from the accounts of non-Indians penetrating the interior. José Palomares recalled entering the village of José Jesús, "chief of the tribe on the Tuolumne River. He was a Christian Indian, but fled the missions, and since he had excellent qualifications . . . was named Chief."[17] Bennet Riley reported in 1849 that many "renegade *Christian* Indians who by their superior tack and intelligence have risen to a controlling influence among these Indians."[18] Marvin asserted that "a Mission Indian usually holds the office Alcalde in each tribe."[19] In 1850 a U.S. Army officer met a neophyte from Mission San Luís Obispo governing one hundred Tachi (Yokuts) at the southern end of Tulare Lake. To the east, a neophyte from San Miguel ruled another Tachi village. The officer also visited two large villages in the Four Creeks area. A gentile called De-e-jah controlled one; Francisco, a neophyte from San Luís Obispo, was in charge of the other.[20]

Further evidence of the political dominance of neophytes is presented in the treaties negotiated in 1851 between the United States government and Indians of the San Joaquin Valley. All twenty-nine leaders who signed the treaty conducted in the southern Tulare Valley used Spanish names. Of the fourteen who negotiated a few miles to the north, twelve employed Spanish names. Thirty-three leaders participated in the treaty on the Kings River, twenty-six "signing" in Spanish. The majority of those negotiating treaties in the northern reaches of the San Joaquin Valley used traditional names.[21]

Although fewer neophytes rose to influential positions in northern than in southern societies, continual pressure from Spanish and later Mexican military incursions dramatically altered Indian societies throughout the Central Valley. Beginning early in the nineteenth century, large numbers of Yokuts and Miwok were incorporated into the missions located directly west of the valley. Between 1805 and 1832, for example, nearly two thousand gentiles were baptized at Mission Santa Clara. Between 1811 and 1834 over five thousand were baptized at San José. Between 1816 and 1833, over one thousand received the sacraments at San Juan Bautista. Another one thousand gentiles were baptized at Santa Cruz, Soledad, and San Antonio between 1806 and 1838.[22] Areas most vulnerable to missionary influence became vacant. For example, it was reported in 1816 that the Mayem (Yokuts) had abandoned their lands along the San Joaquin River and had moved to Mission Santa Cruz.[23]

Most of the Indians baptized at these missions after 1805 came from the San Joaquin Valley. The population loss of this magnitude produced profound ramifications within interior societies. For example, before the arrival of the Spanish, the Miwok had been organized into patrilineages called *nena*. The male members of each nena, along with their wives and children, tended to reside in a single hamlet. The convergence of kinship organization and territory was the salient characteristic of the nena. The disruption caused by the intruders, however, forced members of different nena to amalgamate into new political units in areas offering better protection. Hamlets gave way to village communities comprised of individuals not necessarily related by kinship or marriage.[24] Similar readjustments took place among the more politically centralized southern Yokuts, such as the Tachi, Wowol, Wolasi, Telamni, Chunut, and Choinuk.[25]

Some villages, such as Bubal of the Wowol (Yokuts), were relocated several times.[26] Local terrain often determined where villages were reestablished. A French naval officer visiting California in the 1820s reported that the Indians usually construct their villages on "solid pieces of ground surrounded by marshes which the Spanish call *tulares,* from the great quantity of reeds . . . growing there. Thither the Californian riders cannot come with their horses."[27]

The fertility of the soil may have determined the location of some villages. Many of the neophytes fleeing into the Tulare Valley and adjacent mountains took up small-scale farming. At San Emigdio, for example, a Californio met in 1828 an Indian named Francisco and some old women cultivating a garden.[28] The Indians Zenas Leonard observed in Walker's Pass "follow agriculture pursuits to some extent, raising very good crops of corn, pumpkins, melons."[29] In 1841 Indian leaders at a village in the Tehachapi Mountains petitioned the prefect of Los Angeles to grow crops. Their request was granted.[30]

Early in the twentieth century, an Indian, Juan Coluco, told John P. Harrington that before the American takeover, Indians at the southern end of the Tulare Valley "cultivated plots of land, . . . and small ditches were used for irrigation. I saw the Indians cultivating with old-fashioned hoes such as were in use at the Missions of the coast. They had a good many horses and some cattle."[31] Documentary evidence corroborates Coluco's testimony. While passing through the Cañada de las Uvas in 1849, Benjamin Harris observed land "being prepared by the Indians for cultivation."[32] According to another visitor to the area, the Indians, "from what was taught them at the missions, were enabled to plant and raise grain before the Americans came among them."[33]

Neophytes carried into the interior other aspects of Spanish culture, the Spanish language being the most obvious. Whites penetrating the San Joaquin Valley during the 1830s and 1840s encountered Spanish-speaking Indians from one end to the other. An American settler noted that even "the wild ones learned Spanish, . . . that being the language of the country, and everybody had to learn something of it."[34] John Marvin mentioned that "the Indians in Tulare Valley, and those among the mountains adjoining speak Spanish tolerably well."[35] According to Eugene Upton, many of the chiefs in the Tulare Valley spoke fluent Spanish.[36]

Indians also incorporated Spanish words into their own languages. Terms for firearms and accessories such as *escopeta* (gun), *pólvora* (gunpowder), *balago* (lead) and *munición* (ammunition) were adopted by Nisenan-speakers.[37] The Southern Miwok borrowed *escopeta* and *pólvora* plus *puñal* (dagger), *cañón* (cannon), and *rifle* (rifle).[38] The Chukchansi (Yokuts) used *rifle* and *bala* (bullet), and the Monache (Paiute) *pistola* (pistol).[39] Words referring to animals and stock equipment were also employed by the Miwok, including *caballo* (horse), *garañón* (stallion), *jegua* (mare), *mula* (mule), *ganado* (cattle), *freno* (bridle), *silla* (saddle), *cincho* (cinch), *espuela* (spurs) and *jáquima* (hacamore).[40] The Nisenan adopted *mula, silla, espuela,* and *freno* as well as *reata* (lariat) and *corral*.[41] The Chukchansi and Monache borrowed *caballo, mula,* and *ganado*.[42] Religious terms such as *iglesia* (church), *dio* (God), *cruz* (cross), *misa* (Mass), and *diablo* (devil) were retained by the Miwok.[43] Nisenan used *alcalde* to signify an officer or official.[44] To the Nupchenche (Yokuts) *alcalde* referred to chief.[45] The Southern Miwok substituted *capitán* for chief.[46] *Vaquero* (cowboy) was adopted by the Southern Miwok, the Nisenan, and Monache.[47] The Miwok also borrowed *música* (music).[48]

Less obvious than the diffusion of the Spanish language was the introduction to the interior of European music and instruments. While visiting a village at the juncture of the American and Sacramento rivers in 1841, American naval officers heard songs suggesting a Spanish origin: "Their music was more in harmony than among the other tribes we have seen."[49] In 1855, at the southern end of the San Joaquin Valley, Americans witnessed the persistence of Spanish music. An army officer recalled that "while we were waiting for the dance, we were astonished as well as pleased by a band of Indian musicians. They were Mission Indians and had learned from the Priests to play. Three performed on the flute, one on the violin, one the triangle and another beat the drum."[50] An observer to the same event wrote that "some of the Indians, who had been at one time at the old Missions, were singing songs in a nasal tone very much like the intoning of the service by the old Padres, from whom they had undoubtedly acquired it."[51]

Many of the neophytes continued to dress in the style introduced by the missionaries. A British naval officer, while sailing up the lower Sacramento River in 1837, encountered Indians "clothed in shirts, jackets, trousers."[52] Edwin Bryant observed twenty or thirty Indians in the Sacramento Valley in 1846, some of whom were "dressed in white shirts and pantaloons, with the Mexican sombrero, or broad-brimmed hat."[53]

The Hispanicized Indians who took up residence in the interior also introduced newly acquired skills to the region. As early as 1780, Father Junípero Serra complained that an alcalde from Mission Santa Clara had fled into the interior "with considerable number of followers, among whom are those we most need, such as the blacksmith, a number of carpenters and day workmen."[54] In 1824 the Indian rebels from Mission Santa Bárbara sent word to Father Antonio Ripoll that "we shall maintain ourselves with what God will provide us in the open country. Moreover, we are soldiers, stonemasons, carpenters, etc., and we will provide for ourselves by our work."[55] Visiting the interior in 1842, a Swedish traveler observed Indians manufacturing "several little things." The neophytes "were all trades people, and exercised now their respective trades."[56] Another visitor, however, concluded that the neophytes "returned to their native plains and hills, vastly worse for all they have learned, since they have wants they cannot now satisfy, and are partially unfit for savage life."[57]

Some of their "wants" were satisfied by the traders from New Mexico, whose woolen goods they eagerly sought. Stock, of course, was the Indians' item of exchange and the raid their primary means of obtaining it. That neophytes planned and led many if not most of the raids is evident from the testimony of first-hand observers. Neophytes "are the leaders in the incursions for stealing horses and in all acts of hostility against the whites," declared an American in 1849.[58] John Marvin reported that mission Indians "commonly lead thieving parties to the ranches and towns for plunder."[59] According to an American naval officer, "many of those who were once the best of Indian Christians are now the very worst of horse-thieves."[60]

The techniques developed to acquire and control horses indicate the raiders became experts in animal behavior. As recalled by William Garner, the Indians would open the gates to a corral, allowing the animals to slowly walk out by themselves. About half a mile from the corral, they would mount up and drive the animals at full gallop until daybreak, herding them "through the worst thickets and most intricate roads they can find, and turning round several times, for the purpose of deceiving their pursuers." Resting in a secluded spot for the remainder of the day, they would continue the journey that night.[61]

The raiders controlled the animals by launching arrows at those that broke from the herd. Two sticks tied crossways about an inch above the point of the arrow prevented it from penetrating deeply. Apparently, this technique worked very well. When struck by one of these arrows "the horse immediately takes his place again in the band and it is very seldom that the Indians are obliged to punish one unruly horse twice for that offense."[62]

In the event Californios gave pursuit, the Indians were well prepared to protect their recently acquired property. In his composite picture of a raid, Garner has most of the raiders dismount at a location on the trail that provided cover and protection while the others continued with the horses. If the pursuers were few in number, the Indians would leave their cover "and dispute the pass with their adversaries." More often they would "shoot their arrows from their hiding place at the first horseman that presents himself within their range. This method invariably checks the ardor of the horsemen, who seldom have the courage to advance, rather choosing to lose their horses than risk their lives in the dangerous pursuit." In the meantime, those with the horses "are driving on as fast as they can, well aware that their companions will follow them on foot, and find them in a short time in some preconcerted spot."[63]

Ironically, the Indian raiders often had to drive the animals through areas teeming with wild horses. How many roamed the San Joaquin Valley is impossible to determine, but according to the descriptions of those entering the interior in the middle of the nineteenth century, the number was extraordinarily high. William Garner claimed to have seen "in the course of two days' travel, forty thousand wild horses and mares."[64] James Carson concluded that the valley probably "contains a larger portion of wild horses than any other part of the world of the same extent. On the western side of the San Joaquin, they are to be seen in bands of from two hundred to two thousand. These bands are to be met with at intervals from Mount Diablo to the Tulare Lake. The traveller, in going from the mouth of the lake slough to the head of the lake . . . can see the plains covered with these fine animals."[65] Apparently, horses did not diffuse south of Tulare Lake.[66]

The animals left a favorable impression on the observers. Garner said that some were "as noble looking animals as ever I saw in my life."[67] Carson bragged that "the wild horse of the Tulares ranks amongst the finest of his species. He, unlike the common mustang to be found in the southern portions of America, is of fine size, unparalleled proportions, and as fleet as the wild winds he breathes."[68]

Why Indians raided for horses when large numbers roamed the interior puzzled Zenas Leonard. He thought "it would be less trouble for them to catch wild horses."[69] Only by raiding, however, could Indians obtain domesticated mules and horses. Most likely, the traders from New Mexico demanded such stock. They were easier than wild animals to herd, and they probably brought a higher price. William Heath Davis, who arrived in California in 1831, asserted that the Indians raided the ranchos for domesticated horses.[70] John Sutter, an immigrant from Switzerland, suggested that "it was easier for the Indians when they wanted tame horses to steal them than to tame them."[71] But not all domesticated horses were exchanged. Garner pointed out that the Indians kept the fleetest horses "for the purpose of hunting the elk, which

Mounted Indian in the San Joaquin Valley, by Charles Koppel, 1853. Courtesy of The Bancroft Library, University of California, Berkeley.

abound in the Tulare Valley."[72] In 1830 members of a Mexican expedition spotted some thirty Indians chasing deer on horseback in the northern San Joaquin Valley.[73]

Many of those who did not engage in stock raiding hunted and trapped wild horses.[74] When stock owners were particularly vigilant or when fresh meat was in immediate demand, the raiders also hunted and trapped. In 1844 two American travelers reported that stock-raiding Indians residing on the San Joaquin River some thirty miles from its mouth subsist "upon horse-flesh; some which they procure from the wild bands."[75] Regarding the Nutunutu (Yokuts), Carson wrote that they "kill wild horses and jerk their flesh."[76]

Wherever and however acquired, horses were consumed in large numbers by some groups. While traveling near the Stanislaus River in 1841, John Bidwell and his men came upon a pile of bones: "We thought that an army must have perished there. They were of course horses that the Indians had driven there and slaughtered."[77] In 1845 a party led by John Frémont camped at a spot on the Mariposa River "whitened with the bones of many horses."[78] From the Mokelumne River to the source of the San Joaquin, a newspaper reported in 1847, Indians "have become so habituated to living on horseflesh, that it is now with them the principal means of subsistence."[79]

Obviously, the distribution of mission lands along the coast and the spread of malaria in the interior had unconnected origins, but they intersected in ways that altered the history of central California. Those who fled into the interior simultaneously participated in the breakdown of the mission system and in the repopulation of the San Joaquin Valley. Taking with them knowledge and skills acquired at the missions, they introduced horticulture, animal husbandry, Spanish crafts and language, and new political forms to the interior. The diffusion of Spanish culture throughout the San Joaquin Valley resulted, therefore, not from temporary Hispanic penetration but from permanent neophyte occupation.

The breakdown of the mission system also had a profound

effect on Mexican society. The private citizens who acquired mission lands may have become socially and politically prominent, but they also inherited the managerial problems long faced by the missionaries. With the land came the large herds of horses, mules, cattle, and other animals initially designated neophyte property. Protecting horses and mules from Indians became a primary task of the rancheros; appropriating these animals became a primary task of Indians who once resided in the missions.

CHAPTER 8

Counter Intrusion

THE secularization of the missions resulted in a massive land transaction which saw the rancho replace the mission as the basic social and economic institution in the coastal zone.[1] But the rancho lacked the precise programs and goals of the mission. Ostensibly organized to sell products and turn a profit, it produced little to sell. Hides and tallow were exported, but fundamentally the rancho generated only enough food and material items to support its Mexican and Indian residents and to display the wealth and status of its owner.[2]

As the locus of authority, the ranchero was employer, judge, and military commander to the Indians on his estate. Unlike the missionary who had attempted to regulate the social and spiritual lives of the neophytes, the ranchero cared little about the noneconomic activities of his Indian workers. However, by paying the Indians in kind and by controlling the land upon which they raised their crops and animals, the ranchero relegated them to a position of dependency and thus created a class of peons. Upon the twin foundations of private landownership and peonage was the new social order erected in coastal California.[3]

As acknowledged by a ranchero, the Indian peons were indispensable: "Our friendly Indians we relied on very much, for they tilled our soil, pastured our cattle, sheared our sheep, cut our lumber, built our houses, paddled our boats, made tiles for our homes, ground our grain, killed our cattle, dressed their hides for market, and built our unburnt bricks; while the Indian women made excellent servants, took care of our children, made every one of our meals."[4]

The wealth of the ranchero was measured largely in numbers of cattle and horses, and clearly the management of the former was dependent upon the availability of the latter. Although written in the mid-1850s, the following discussion is equally applicable to the late 1830s. The vast herds of cattle

require the ranchero to be constantly on horseback for the purpose of protecting and managing his stock; when we consider the great distance of the ranchos from the main settlements and the . . . exposed position of nearly one-half of them, we may readily understand how essential to the successful pursuit of stock-raising is an abundant supply of horses; and, so satisfied of this fact are our rancheros, that it is not uncommon that one rancho alone should have fifteen hundred, two thousand, and even as high as three thousand head of horses.[5]

William Garner also discussed the importance of the horse: "The grants of land which have been given by Mexico are very large, and it is often the case, that a man who lives on a farm [rancho] will have to travel one or two hundred miles to purchase the actual necessitous clothing, or to sell his produce, which has all, or for the most part to be carried to market on horseback, on account of the badness of the roads."[6]

The rancheros rarely fed their animals hay or grain.[7] As a consequence, horses began to lose weight in September, and by the end of November, Garner observed, they were "scarcely fit to travel at all; . . . a man who lives a hundred miles from town, will need at least ten horses to carry him the journey."[8] William Heath Davis recalled that "a large number of horses were needed on each rancho for herding stock, as they were used up very fast. They were numerous and cheap, and the owners placed no restraint upon the vaqueros, who rode without a particle of regard for the horses, till they soon became unfit for further use in this way."[9]

Most of the vaqueros referred to by Davis were California Indians who had learned their trade while residing at the missions. Least affected of all the neophytes by the breakup of the missions, the vaqueros continued their line of work by transferring their loyalty from the missionary to the ranchero.[10] Many were entrusted with defending the ranchos against the incursions of hostile Indians. Protecting stock, however, proved to be a nearly impossible task.[11]

Father Narciso Durán reported in late 1832 that the pueblo of San José and neighboring ranchos were "almost on the verge of ruin by reason of the incessant robberies of horses committed by apostate Christian Indians in league with gentiles. . . . Their unpunished insolence constrains us to foretell that, before many years, we shall see ourselves obliged to abandon our posts and reunite at one point for common defense."[12] So damaging had the raids become that Governor José Figueroa, beginning in November 1833, allowed civilians to capture stock thieves when encountering them "in the act or upon proof of crime."[13]

Civilians from San José entering the interior in late 1834 or early 1835, however, failed to distinguish between innocent and guilty Indians. They confiscated property and kidnapped seven boys. Fearful that abuses such as this would continue, Figueroa issued orders to the alcalde (mayor) of San José. When encountered on future campaigns, Indians "who are defenseless shall not be molested, nor shall weapons be used against those who offer no resistance." Indians were to be pursued only when caught in the act of stealing and no expedition was to be undertaken without his permission. Figueroa ordered the alcalde to place the captured children in the care of the padres at Mission Santa Clara "so that they may be educated there or returned to their parents as may seem appropriate."[14]

Indian raids continued. In February 1835, the alcalde reported that recently Chauchila and Hoyima (Yokuts) had stolen "the rest of the horses which belonged to the pueblo." San José "is in a lamentable condition, having no way to round up its cattle scattered in the fields."[15] Late the following year, local Californios complained to San José officials about the loss of horses. They were convinced that neophytes took the animals into the interior, sold them to gentiles, and then implored the padres to protect them from the civil authorities. As an example, they pointed to Mateo, a neophyte from Mission Santa Clara who had become an active stock raider. Recently he had turned himself over to the padres at Mission San José. They sent him to Santa Clara where he was protected from prosecution. The Californios also referred to Estanislao, the Indian rebel who in 1829 had returned to Mission San José after being defeated by a force of Californios.[16]

Estanislao, however, had become a loyal neophyte who provided important assistance to the Californios. In August 1837 he and another Indian, Borbon, led civilians and soldiers to a Muqueleme (Miwok) village. Their task was to apprehend eleven fugitives, led by Paisco and Nilo, who had fled from the mission in protest over the treatment received from the Indian alcaldes. The Muqueleme were then in a state of political disarray. Recently, two chiefs had been murdered and apparently to resolve the issue large numbers had gathered at the village where the fugitives found refuge. In the ensuing fight, the intruders evidently captured all the runaways except two who were killed and Nilo who, badly wounded, may have drowned in a tule swamp. The success of the campaign notwithstanding, the authorities at San José deemed it unwise to send another expedition against the Muqueleme.[17]

In mid-August, Indians stole one hundred horses from Rancho San Antonio, situated some twenty miles north of San José and adjacent to San Francisco Bay. Rancheros pursued the robbers to the San Joaquin River but recovered only thirty head.[18] Indians also targeted Rancho San Pablo, located just north of San Antonio. On August 15, two Indian vaqueros arrived at the rancho supposedly to visit relatives. When informed by loyal Indians that the visitors intended to steal horses, local rancheros located the men and another Indian on the Strait of Carquinez. All three managed to escape, one by jumping into the water. Safely on the opposite bank, the Indian broke into laughter while gesturing obscenely to his pursuers.[19]

Foreign immigrants, especially those who acquired grants in or adjacent to the San Joaquin Valley, also had to contend with Indian raiders. According to M. G. Vallejo, Governor Juan Bautista Alvarado believed the foreigners would "hold in check the vandal hordes who were threatening to wipe out all the wealth which had been accumulated in more than seventy years at the cost of great sacrifice of blood and money."[20] Burdened with the task of checking "the vandal hordes" was John Marsh. Originally from Massachusetts and recently converted to Catholicism, he purchased Rancho Los Meganos in 1837. Located about forty miles north of San José and near Mount Diablo, the rancho was extremely vulnerable to Indian raids. Its previous owner, José Noriega, had resided there only with the protection of between seven and ten vaqueros. Noriega never had received official possession of the property because the alcalde of San José feared to travel to the rancho where the transaction was to take place.[21]

In January 1838, Marsh drafted a plan, apparently for the governor, to halt the incursions of the Indian raiders, especially in the area where his rancho was located. He calculated that fifty men in the district were capable of bearing arms. They should be divided into two groups. Those over forty years of age would assemble twice a year, except in cases of emergency, to have their arms and equipment inspected. The younger men would undergo inspection on the first Monday of each month. Each militiaman would possess a weapon, one pound of powder, fifty balls, and two strong horses. The governor would appoint the captain, but the lieutenants would be elected.[22]

In late April, Marsh moved on to Los Meganos and began life as a Californio ranchero. Residing on the rancho were some thirty Indians, many of whom were suffering from malaria. Marsh, who had received a license to practice medicine in California, gave them quinine and quickly gained their trust.[23] Vallejo recalled that the local Indians did not trouble Marsh "because upon various occasions he had cured some of the Indian women who were suffering from illnesses which the Indian doctors did not know how to cure."[24]

As with all rancheros residing in isolated areas, Marsh must have carefully chosen the location of his house. William Heath Davis recalled that most houses were built on "open ground, devoid of trees, generally elevated, overlooking a wide stretch of the country." This allowed the residents to "notice if any intruders were about the Rancho for the purpose of stealing cattle or horses."[25] Marsh constructed his house to withstand attack, cutting loopholes beneath the eaves to fire at Indian raiders. Two of his Indian vaqueros always slept in the attic to assist him in case of a raid.[26]

In the fall of 1838, upon returning from a visit to San José, Marsh found his house ransacked and most of his horses driven off. Later, he and several rancheros located the Indians in the Sierra Nevada; they killed eleven and recovered five hundred animals, many bearing Marsh's brand.[27] For their part in the campaign, John Marsh and seven other Americans gained the trust and respect of the Californios. Vallejo wrote in his memoirs that "aside from the pleasure I experienced upon receiving word of the defeat of the band of outlaw Indians headed by the neophyte Telmo, I was also very glad to see that American citizens whom the majority of Californians used to look upon with suspicion had shown themselves so inclined to make common cause with us against the Indians of the Tulare region."[28]

Joint efforts such as this, however, failed to deter the stock raiders. In mid-August 1838, a band of Muqueleme hit Rancho las Borregas, located near Marsh's settlement. Led by Ambrosio, a former neophyte, the Indians killed one and wounded several Californios. A party of Californios pursued the raiders into the interior and captured Ambrosio. Brought back to Mission San José, he was given last rites by a priest and shot to death.[29]

In January 1839, six Indians led by Yóscolo struck a rancho near San José, killing two persons and fleeing with, according to José Francisco Palomares, "much booty." Four or five soldiers, a few civilians, and one hundred Indian auxiliaries overtook the raiders a few miles from the rancho. As Palomares reported, the commander of the force, Manuel Peña, allowed the Indian auxiliaries to do all the fighting:

So it was that the followers of Yóscolo succumbed to the many arrows that assailed them from all sides. Yóscolo died fighting, and, while he had the strength, he did not cease to do damage to his enemy.

Peña's Indians had some wounded. . . . The soldiers had not fired a single shot. . . . When everything was over, Peña ordered them to cut off Yóscolo's head. An Indian took this work upon himself and brought it, dripping with blood, to the captain who, with his own hands, fixed it on the iron of his lance and so carried it to the mission. He ordered it nailed on a pole and put in front of the church, where it remained for two or three months. The bodies of the thieves remained unburied on the site of the battle.

Only one neophyte, Pedro, lost his life.[30]

Palomares insisted that thereafter thefts of horses were less frequent in the jurisdiction of San José.[31] And for a short time the Californios took the offensive. In early July 1839, a force of eighty men, led by Captain Antonio Buelna, assaulted two villages on the Kings River. The Californios captured seventy-seven Indians, mostly women and children, one of whom was identified as a thief.[32] The prisoners were turned over to José Castro who put them to work on his rancho.[33]

Indian raids soon resumed. In late July, Indians stole animals from Mission Santa Clara, killing one person and wounding three others in the process. A few Californios and neophyte auxiliaries caught the raiders in nearby mountains. They killed one Indian and wounded two others.[34] In December, Indians struck twice in the vicinity of San José, carrying off considerable numbers of horses.[35] The pursuit party that formed consisted of fifteen soldiers and civilians and fifty-five neophytes. The expedition overtook the raiders, but sustained heavy casualties. The Indians wounded the commander and six soldiers and killed three civilians.[36]

In January 1840, Indians raided Rancho Pinole, situated adjacent to San Pablo Bay, and appropriated nearly all the saddle horses belonging to the owner, Ignacio Martínez. A party of Californios overtook the raiders, killed several, and recovered the stock.[37] But the Indians forced the rancheros to retreat, leaving behind a dead comrade, Felipe Briones. His body was recovered a short time later.[38]

Terribly concerned over the incessant attacks, Governor Alvarado ordered in July the formation of a force of twenty men to police the areas most frequently visited by the stock raiders. The men were to be divided into two squads. One was to be stationed at San Juan Bautista; it would patrol the region from La Panocha to Las Garzas. The other was to reside at San José; it would guard the area from Las Garzas to Mission San José. The commanders of each squad were to apprehend Indians suspected of wrongdoing and prevent those lacking passports from crossing the line they guarded. The volunteers would serve for three months; the program would then be reviewed.[39]

If ever activated, the militia failed to curtail the raids. Indians attacked Mission San Juan Bautista in January 1841.[40] In March, stock raiders drove off two hundred head of horses within six miles of Monterey.[41] Indians struck Santa Clara the same month, killing an Indian vaquero but losing two men.[42] And in July, Indians ran off three hundred animals from the vicinity of San José. Regarding this last raid, Charles Wilkes, an American naval officer, reported that the pursuing party "came to a village, and without any inquiry whether its dwellers had been the aggressors, it was set on fire, and reduced to ashes; some of the defenseless old men, who from their infirmities could not escape, were put to death, and forty or fifty women and children carried off as prisoners. This was not all: these prisoners were apportioned as slaves to various families, with whom they still remain in servitude, and receive very harsh treatment."[43]

The alcalde of San José told Wilkes that Indian stock raiders remained within striking distance of the pueblo, but pursuit was impossible because no troops were available.[44] For vastly different reasons, the American also sought an end to Indian raiding: "This constant foray on one side or the other keeps up a continual embitterment, and as long as the present imbecile government lasts, this state of things must every day grow worse, and will undoubtedly tend to affect the value of property, as well as to prevent [American] immigration, and settlement in the country."[45]

One kind of property already was affected. William Dane Phelps, visiting California in 1841, noted that once "the best horses were then to be had for 50 cents a piece. But there is now

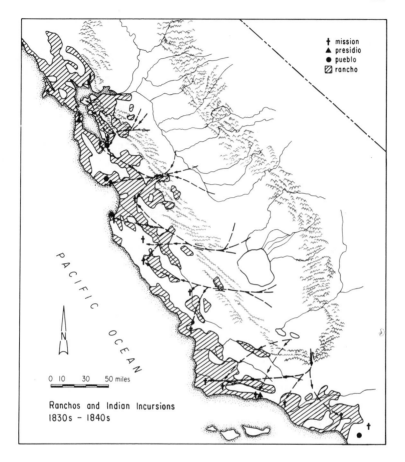

† mission
▲ presidio
● pueblo
▨ rancho

PACIFIC OCEAN

N

0 10   30   50 miles

Ranchos and Indian Incursions
1830s – 1840s

a scarcity, as the Indians on the frontiers for a number of years back have stole all the horses they could lay hands on."[46] The following year a French naval officer, M. Duflot de Mofras, wrote that "the supply of horses is now diminishing in California, for the Indians carry on endless raids, and almost every night hundreds are carried off to the Tulare Valley. . . . The value of horses has materially increased since these Indian depredations. At one time horses were sold like cattle; but today even a mule is valued as 10 or 15 piasters."[47]

Indian raids damaged the ranchos in other ways as well. In early June 1843, three Californios from the Monterey area petitioned the governor for assistance. Soon they would be forced "to abandon the *ranchos* . . . since the overseers and those charged with running the *ranchos* no longer desire to remain upon them, because they no longer have any security of life." Even the campaigns the government launched against the raiders caused them economic harm. The horses and saddles the soldiers requisitioned often were not returned.[48]

Although Indians began stealing stock shortly after the Spanish first settled in California, their attacks increased dramatically after mission lands were turned into private estates. The raids seriously harmed the rancheros, because the loss of horses deprived them of animals crucial to the management of other stock. The animal so vital to the rancheros was the same animal Indians depended on for food, transportation, and trade. The establishment of the ranchos, therefore, resulted in an intensification of violence between coastal Californios and interior Indians.

As increasing numbers of immigrants arrived in California, they, too, experienced Indian raids. Because native-born Mexican citizens had preempted most of the lands once controlled by the missionaries, many of the immigrants were forced to settle deep in the interior. There they confronted powerful Indian leaders governing societies that had undergone significant political and economic change. Whether or not a settlement took hold depended on the diplomatic skills and military strengths of the intruders and on the policies and strategies initiated by the Indians.

CHAPTER 9

Foreign Infiltration

IN late 1837 smallpox struck northern California. The disease spread from Fort Ross, a Russian trading post established on the coast north of San Francisco Bay in 1812, to Sonoma and then into the interior, decimating Indian societies in the northern San Joaquin and southern Sacramento valleys.[1] The disease may have accelerated the breakup of the northern missions and the diffusion of neophytes into the interior. An American naval officer, Charles Wilkes, claimed that "the ravages of the small-pox . . . completed the destruction of these establishments; for it swept off one-half of the Indians, and served to dispirit the rest. Many of them have joined the wild Indians, and are now committing acts of violence on the whites."[2]

In August 1839, John Sutter, a Swiss immigrant, led nine white men, ten Hawaiians (including two women), a young Indian boy, and boat crews up the Sacramento River and into the area recently devastated by the disease.[3] About ten miles below the mouth of the American River, the party encountered members of the Gualacomne (Miwok). Late in his life, Sutter recounted the meeting: "The Chief Anashe . . . was present with his people . . . when I came up. . . . A few runaways from San Jose came forward, who understood Spanish well enough to interpret between us. Anashe, from the beginning, was inclined to be in favor of peace, and to make terms of friendship with me; the others, for some time remained treacherous." Sutter also mentioned that the Gualacomne "had become very much reduced by various diseases, and particularly have they suffered from the small pox, which had made terrible destructions amongst them prior to my arrival."[4]

Sutter and his men continued upstream to the juncture of the

American and Sacramento rivers, where, recalled William Heath Davis, they encountered "seven or eight hundred Indians, men, women and children. We prepared ourselves for an attack, but our fears proved groundless. They came off to our anchorage in large numbers in canoes made of tule."[5]

On the north bank of the American resided the Pusune (Nisenan), enemies of Miwok groups occupying the territory south of the river.[6] A large village comprised of remnants of the Ochejamne, Chucumne, Gualacomne, and four other societies was located on the south bank.[7] Known to the Californios as the Ochejamne *ranchería* (village), it was governed by Narciso, a former resident of Mission San José. Narciso took a liking to Sutter and assisted him in building the settlement called New Helvetia.[8] Sutter, in turn, employed the Indian as his alcalde.[9]

Evidently, Narciso was the Ochejamne chief Huyumegepa, who had repulsed a combined force of Californios and neophyte auxiliaries in mid-1830 only to be defeated a short time later when the Californios enlisted the aid of Ewing Young and his party of American trappers.[10] Not long after the battle, large numbers of Ochejamne entered Mission San José. Huyumegepa was baptized "Narciso" on January 18, 1831.[11] He was one of 268 Ochejamne baptized that year.[12] By the end of 1831, a total of 514 gentiles, the second highest number for any year, had received the sacraments at San José.[13]

In 1838, when smallpox struck the mission, 252 Indians were buried at San José.[14] Obviously, not all died from the disease, but the former rebel Estanislao was one of its victims.[15] Perhaps fleeing from the disease, Narciso and his Ochejamne followers may have removed to the juncture of the American and Sacramento rivers sometime during the year. According to Juan Bautista Alvarado, neophyte fugitives were moving up the Sacramento River about the time Sutter arrived.[16]

Situated near a large village of neophytes and in the midst of several Indian societies, Sutter survived by practicing astute diplomacy. As recalled by Heinrich Lienhard, Sutter took gay-colored handkerchiefs, bags of Hawaiian sugar, and glass beads and left them near their camps where they could not fail to find them. In this way the resourceful captain gained the Indians' confidence and friendship; soon crowds of them appeared at his headquarters, now actually begging for gifts. Day after day, the dusky visitors grew more numerous, and by giving them presents for running errands it was not long before they were even bribed to work.[17]

Sutter, however, had to maintain constant vigilance and occasionally fired his cannon to impress his neighbors.[18]

In the spring of 1840, Indians stole horses and cattle from New Helvetia, forcing Sutter to launch a retaliatory raid. A battle took place where the Feather River joins the Sacramento. Wilkes reported that a village had once existed at the juncture of the two rivers, but it "was destroyed by Captain Suter [sic] and his trappers, because its inhabitants had stolen cattle. . . . The affair resulted in one of the Indians being killed, twenty-seven made captive, and the removal of the remainder beyond the limits of his territory."[19]

During the summer of 1840, Indians residing near New Helvetia withdrew en masse to an area about twenty miles away on the Cosumnes River.[20] From their new position, they raided Sutter's settlement, killing cattle and stealing horses. In a punitive raid, Sutter employed his cannon against the raiders, who numbered between two and three hundred. "The fighting was a little hard," he remembered, "but after having lost about 30 men, they was [sic] willing to make a treaty with me."[21] Many of the Indians returned to New Helvetia and became the nucleus of Sutter's work force.[22] The remainder abandoned their villages and joined neighboring groups.[23]

Sutter relocated Indians from several villages to his post, including the Pusune, who proved to be some of his most capable workers.[24] Indian prisoners, many of them children whose parents he had killed on his campaigns, also were brought to New Helvetia. According to a neighbor, Theodor Cordua, Sutter claimed the children "as payment for the cost of the war."[25]

On one occasion Sutter had to contend with Indians still attached to a mission. In early October 1840, a party of neophytes arrived at New Helvetia. The leader, Acacio, possessed a passport issued by José de Jesús Vallejo, the alcalde of the Pueblo of San José. Acacio sought permission from Sutter to trade with the Sakayakumne (Miwok) on the Mokelumne River. Granting the Indian's request, Sutter warned him not to take anything by force.[26]

Instead of proceeding to the Mokelumne, Acacio's Indians visited a village of the Yalesumne (Nisenan) located on the American River, where they killed five men and captured all the women and children. Most of the men were absent, many working for Sutter. Pulpule, the leader of the Yalesumne, initially suspected that Sutter was somehow involved, but Sutter convinced him that the kidnappers would be apprehended and the captives returned to their husbands and fathers.[27]

The following day, Sutter, twenty white men, and numerous Indians overtook the neophytes on the lower Sacramento River and rescued most of the prisoners. A neophyte, Gerato, escaped with four women, however.[28] Sutter executed fourteen of the kidnappers on the spot.[29] He informed Vallejo about the affair, recommending that mission Indians not be allowed to journey into his region.[30]

Sutter could legally undertake military operations against Indians because he had been granted Mexican citizenship and endowed with civil authority for the administration of local justice, which included subduing hostile Indians.[31] In June 1841, he officially received a land grant of eleven square leagues, or nearly forty-nine thousand acres.[32] As did all Mexican grants, his contained provisions regarding the treatment of Indians: "He shall maintain the native Indians of different tribes on those places in the free enjoyment of their possessions without troubling them, and he may only reduce them to civilization through prudent measures and a friendly intercourse; he shall not cause them hostilities of any kind without previously obtaining authority from the Government."[33]

One of Sutter's "prudent measures" was to provide goods and services to neighboring groups. The gunsmith Sutter hired to repair his weapons also serviced those owned by Indians. On a regular basis, Indians brought to New Helvetia animal skins to trade for gunpowder and other items such as handkerchiefs, blankets, and liquor.[34] Sutter acquired powder, lead, shot, beaver traps, and clothing from the Hudson's Bay Company located on the Columbia River.[35]

Not all visitors came to trade. In late 1840 or early 1841, three Indians—Antonio, Sixto, and Angel—offered to take Sutter to an American supposedly living somewhere in the Sierra Nevada. Sutter declined, writing instead a letter to the American and entrusting Angel to deliver it. A few days later Angel returned, claiming the individual was nowhere to be found. Sutter's suspicion that Sixto and Angel intended to kill him once they had lured him away from New Helvetia was thus confirmed.[36]

On March 1, 1841, Antonio and fifty armed Indians arrived at New Helvetia. Antonio sought from Sutter some of his Indian workers for an attack on an enemy group. Suspecting that their real intent was to kill him and destroy his property, Sutter disarmed the Indians and sent them away. But later in the month, Antonio and nine companions returned to New Helvetia. Evidently, they attempted to persuade Sutter's Indian workers to join them in an attack on the settlement, but they changed their plans upon learning that Sutter had discovered their intent.[37]

Eventually, Sutter arrested four Indians. Interrogated by Narciso, Sutter's alcalde, one of the captives accused Margin, Camilo, and Julian of plotting to attack New Helvetia. Speaking on behalf of his comrades, Margin claimed they were incapable of doing harm because they had been raised in the missions. When Sutter threatened to kill them unless they told the truth, they admitted joining the conspirators but only under duress. They insisted that Antonio, Chupuhu, and Anashe had planned the attack.[38]

At the same time Sutter was punishing hostile Indians, he was trading with peaceful ones. In March 1841, he purchased forty horses from Indian stock raiders. Because every animal was branded, Sutter knew he had acquired stolen property.[39] Concerned about Sutter's activities, late in the year M. G. Vallejo, commandant general of the northern frontier, sent Rudesindo Berreyesa to New Helvetia to gather information. He reported that Sutter had gathered around him many Indians, all of whom posessed good horses, and had issued numerous passports to foreigners, especially to trappers of the Hudson's Bay Company.[40]

By the beginning of 1842, Sutter had extended his jurisdiction down the Sacramento ten to twenty miles. At the village governed by Anashe, he employed thirty Indians to catch and cure fish for his settlement.[41] Sutter bestowed upon Anashe the title of El Capitan de los Pescadores.[42] A few years later these Indians were observed growing beans, melons, and corn.[43]

Horticultural Indians also established a settlement on the south side of the lower Cosumnes River, an area left vacant by Sutter's military campaigns.[44] Some thirty adult neophytes and twenty children occupied the area in 1841. They spoke Spanish, several being literate; they professed the Catholic faith, some wearing the cross and rosary.[45] Included in the group were a weaver, shoemaker, carpenter, and a tanner.[46]

Within fenced fields they planted beans, corn, and melons and raised poultry and stock. And beginning in 1844, they grew wheat, mainly to trade to Sutter, who loaned them horses at harvest time to thrash the crop.[47] He also furnished oxen and ploughs.[48] On a regular basis Sutter sent his own wheat to the settlement to be ground.[49] Ox-drawn carts transported produce and supplies to and from the settlement.[50]

Sutter also was dependent upon local Indian labor. He acknowledged that the Indians, working for very little, "make slavery wholly unnecessary here, and may be employed for all field and house work."[51] Visitors to New Helvetia described how Sutter recruited his Indian workers. According to William Dane Phelps, Sutter "tells the Chief how many hands he wants for the next week, and at daylight on Monday they are sure to be there."[52] John Frémont remarked that "on application to the chief of a village, he readily obtains as many boys and girls as he has any use for."[53] Lienhard recalled that the Indian workers "were furnished by the various chiefs, who acted as corporals, and to flatter their vanity he called them *capitanos*. They also received far better pay than the poor wretches who worked as common laborers, and had to slave two weeks for a plain muslin shirt, or the material for a pair of cotton trousers."[54]

A Swedish traveler observed a ceremony in which an Indian leader presented to Sutter a contingent of workers:

Only the Chief of these Indians came armed with bows and arrows. All others came unarmed, and after having gone through their customary graceful movements in file, in square, in flanges, and in body, the Chief made a long speech, which sounded very eloquent. At last he laid down his bow and arrows at the feet of Captain Sutter, saying, "Take these, and with them penetrate my heart if I or my tribe betray the trust you now put in us and which we now solemnly promise to keep."[55]

The way Indians were treated at New Helvetia drew comments from visitors and employees alike. Lienhard admitted that he

had to lock the Indian men and women together in a large room to prevent them from returning to their homes in the mountains at night, and as the room had neither beds nor straw, the inmates were forced to sleep on the bare floor. When I opened the door for them in the morning, the odor that greeted me was overwhelming, for no sanitary arrangements had been provided. What these rooms were like after ten days or two weeks can be imagined, and the fact that nocturnal confinement was not agreeable to the Indians was obvious.[56]

The Swede expressed outrage at the way the Indians were fed:

Several hundred Indians flocked in for their morning meal, before being led out for labor. . . . I must confess I could not reconcile my feelings to see these fellows being driven, as it were, around some narrow troughs made of hollow tree trunks, out of which, crouched on their haunches, they fed more like beasts than human beings, using their hands in hurried manner to convey to their mouths the thin porridge which was served to them.[57]

Sutter paid his Indian workers the equivalent of twenty-five cents a day in merchandise. Phelps noted that "the only articles they now want is cotton to make shirts, and beads to gamble with. . . . Those who have distinguished themselves during the week he rewards with an extra string of beads, or a few needles and some thread."[58] Frémont wrote that the Indians "receive a very moderate compensation—principally in shirts, blankets, and other articles of clothing."[59]

A kind of monetary system was designed for the Indian workers. Each received a tin coin through which a hole was punched for every day worked. The number of holes indicated the value of merchandise to which the worker was entitled. At Sutter's store the Indians exchanged the coins for blankets and other items. To prevent the "currency" from falling into the hands of white men, it was accepted only from Indians.[60]

Sutter's efforts to keep his Indian workers under strict control were not always successful. When cattle were slaughtered, Indians often appropriated the choicest cuts, and on occasion they stole bread from the bakery.[61] But Indians caught defying his authority were imprisoned and occasionally executed.[62] Wilkes reported that Sutter "has, according to his own belief, supreme power in his own district, condemning, acquitting, and punishing, as well as marrying . . . those who are under him."[63] He often exclaimed: "I, Sutter, am the law."[64]

Convinced that the chiefs had too many wives while the young men had too few, he performed on one occasion a mass marriage. He had the Indian men and women form separate lines. Each woman then stepped forward to select a husband. Obviously, this was an effort to stamp out polygamy practiced by the Indians in his jurisdiction.[65] But Sutter failed to apply this moral standard to himself. Having left his European wife in Switzerland, he "acquired" a native woman while in the Hawaiian Islands and brought her to California. Later, he "gave" her to one of his Hawaiian workers.[66]

Sutter also took advantage of Indian girls. Lienhard recalled that "everyone knew Sutter was a typical Don Juan with women.

In addition to the large number of young Indian girls who were constantly at his beck and call, there were also in the fort many young Indian loafers who rarely worked, but were fed and nicely clothed because their wives received special consideration from the master of the fort. . . . As he grew older Sutter seemed to prefer young Indian girls."[67] Sutter fathered several children, but evidently none lived for very long.[68]

Sutter also provided Indian children to several rancheros in northern California. In his memoirs, Juan Bautista Alvarado accused Sutter of giving to friends twenty Indian children shortly after the founding of New Helvetia.[69] Cordua was highly critical of this practice. Children taken by Sutter in his Indian campaigns "became regular commercial objects because the inhabitants of the coast preferred the Indians of the Sacramento Valley as servants, and paid good prices for them. In this way a regular trade of human beings developed."[70] Sutter also provided Indian workers to rancheros on short-term contracts.[71]

The expansion of Sutter's authority and the success of his enterprise caused the Mexican authorities concern. Wilkes reported that "the present governor of the district west of New Helvetia, felt jealous of the power and influence that Captain Suter [sic] was obtaining in the country; and it was thought that had it not been for the force which the latter could bring to oppose any attempt to dislodge him, it would have been tried. In the mean time Captain Suter is using all his energies to render himself impregnable." The wall Sutter constructed around his buildings was designed to protect him from Mexican as well as Indian attacks.[72] Not without reason was New Helvetia called Sutter's Fort.

Californios also suspected Sutter of providing a sanctuary for runaway Indians. On July 26, 1843, M. G. Vallejo wrote to Sutter:

Since the frequent desertions of the Indians of this district to yours are a fatal and all-powerful example for others, and inasmuch as this office has definite information that several deserters are at present in hiding in your settlement with stolen horses and goods, I have ordered

Lieutenant-Colonel Victor Prudon to set out to capture them. He will act under the instructions you have on the subject. I strongly recommend to you for the future not to continue protecting fugitives of any kind.[73]

Governor Juan Bautista Alvarado, however, thought that Sutter's activities might serve Mexican ends. If all the trails were guarded, he reasoned, thus preventing the horse thieves from robbing the settlements, then perhaps Sutter could persuade them to settle at New Helvetia.[74]

Sutter's authority in the interior remained largely autonomous. Shortly after establishing his rancho, he created an Indian military force; his infantry eventually expanded to one hundred men, his cavalry to fifty. Two white men commanded the infantry, but a literate neophyte, Homobono, served as ensign.[75] He was a member of the group of neophytes residing on the Cosumnes.[76] Armed Indians led by one who could read and write shocked the Californios who visited the fort.[77] When not on duty, the soldiers worked around the fort to help pay for their uniforms and food.[78] Sutter also maintained a personal bodyguard comprised of twelve to fifteen Indians, who assembled every Sunday morning to drill. Their uniforms consisted of blue pantaloons, white cotton shirts, and red handkerchiefs tied around their heads. An Indian sergeant commanded the unit.[79]

Sutter had to maintain a strong military force because hostile Indians resided in the vicinity of New Helvetia. Traveling south from the fort in mid-1844, Overton Johnson and William Winter entered dangerous territory:

We proceeded down the Sacramento, passed around the head of the Bay, and came to the St. Wakine [San Joaquin], River, thirty miles above its mouth. . . . This part of the country is inhabited, by a very troublesome tribe of Indians, called the Horse Thieves, and contains no white settlement. . . . They have long been hostile to the Spaniards, and a short time previous, had killed a white man; and it was therefore necessary for us to be very cautious, while we were passing through their country.

The two men may have skirted the territory of the Muqueleme (Miwok): "They have their Villages in the small valleys, and

Indian guard at Sutter's Fort, by Joseph Warren Revere, 1849. Courtesy of The Bancroft Library, University of California, Berkeley.

nooks, deep in the mountains; where they keep their women and children, and to which they fly, as soon as they have committed any depredation. Among these fastnesses, they enjoy their booty in quiet, the Spaniards not daring to follow them among the mountains. . . . Many of these Horse Thieves have been educated in the Catholic Missions."[80]

When Indians stole some of his horses in May 1844, John Marsh suspected the Muqueleme. Sutter doubted they were responsible but informed Marsh he would look into the matter. He thought their reputation as horse thieves was exaggerated.[81] But an American who traveled from Sutter's Fort to the San Joaquin the following year may have referred to the Muqueleme when he noted in his journal that the Indians who resided on the river "hold indisputable possession of the country and steal & kill."[82]

That New Helvetia, though well fortified and defended, remained a tiny, isolated outpost in a vast Indian territory is clearly evident in an incident occurring in the fall of 1844 when a party of Nez Percé, Cayuse, and Walla Walla Indians arrived from the

Columbia River to trade. Sutter warmly received the thirty-six men and their wives and children. He knew some of them from his travels through their territories and gave them passports and permission to hunt within the limits of his jurisdiction. He advised them not to visit Mexican settlements.[83]

Near the fort these Indians acquired several horses and mules from stock raiders. A white man, Grover Cook, identified a mule as his and demanded it be returned. Elijah, son of the Walla Walla chief, Yellow Serpent, challenged Cook to take the mule if he dared, leveling his rifle at him as he spoke. According to Sutter, Elijah was an arrogant young man who terrorized the older chiefs, including his father. While camped close to the fort, Elijah had killed a member of his own group and on the San Joaquin had attempted to murder another.[84]

Sutter ordered the Indians to bring their animals to his corral, where those identified as stolen would be confiscated. The Indians refused to comply, stating that what they had acquired was theirs. A conference, attended by fifteen Indians and several whites, including Elijah and Cook, was held in Sutter's house. When Sutter left the house to attend to another matter, the two men argued violently. Cook shot and killed the Indian.[85]

The Indians quickly departed to the north, leaving behind the exchange items they had brought, the cattle Sutter had traded to them, and the stolen horses.[86] Upon returning to the Columbia River, they recounted to the British at Fort Vancouver what had transpired in California, causing an employee of the Hudson's Bay Company to predict that they would return to Sutter's Fort the following summer "to rob, pillage and murder."[87]

Shortly, Sutter faced another crisis. As a Mexican citizen and governmental official, he could not remain unaffected by political intrigues. In late 1844, when General José Castro rebelled against the government, Sutter sided with Governor Manuel Micheltorena, who instructed him to raise a military force.[88] Sutter enlisted about one hundred immigrants and between sixty and seventy Indians.[89] Joining Micheltorena near Monterey, Sutter marched to Los Angeles in early 1845. As events turned out, he joined the losing side. Most of his white soldiers defected, and he was taken into custody.[90]

Those immigrants who changed sides gained the trust of Pío Pico, the new governor of California. In February, for example, John Marsh and John Gantt signed a contract with Pico allowing them to organize an expedition against the Indian stock raiders. If the governor deemed the campaign successful, Marsh and Gantt would receive five hundred head of cattle and half of all the horses taken from the Indians. The remaining horses and other property confiscated would be divided among the men recruited for the campaign.[91] General Castro informed Gantt that the Tachi, Nutunutu, Telamni, Heuchi, and three other Yokuts groups were friendly. Hostile Indians resided to the north on the Tuolumne and Merced rivers.[92] Marsh and Gantt failed to enlist the necessary number of volunteers for such a dangerous mission.[93]

Sutter, in the meantime, convinced his captors he had only followed orders and soon was reinstated as military commander of the northern frontier.[94] While traveling homeward through the San Joaquin Valley, he and his companions confiscated stolen horses from a party of Indians.[95] In April he informed Thomas Larkin, U.S. consul to California, that during the journey he had given a good deal of thought to the horse thieves and concluded that if tens of thousands of dollars were spent and thousands of Indians killed, the problem still would remain. If, however, the Mexican government allowed immigrants to freely occupy land in the interior, the Indian raiders would be brought under control. Sutter claimed the immigrants were an industrious, peaceful people.[96] By this time, their numbers had swelled to nearly seven hundred.[97]

One of these immigrants was William Culnac, who acquired in 1843 a land grant at Campo de Los Franceses near the juncture of the Stanislaus and San Joaquin rivers. His first attempt to occupy the area met with failure. Peter Lausen remembered passing "through the place called French Camp. William Culnac was with me and we had our cattle together. . . . He was looking for a place to settle. I would not stop there because the Indians were unruly. . . . Culnac was also afraid to stop there and I took his cattle on with me to the Cosumnes."[98]

A short time later, Culnac's partner, Charles Weber, departed for Sutter's Fort, apparently to make contact with José Jesús, chief of the Siakumne (Yokuts).[99] As described by a contemporary, José Jesús was "six foot tall, straight as an arrow, majestic forehead and deep, penetrating look."[100] Educated at Mission Santa Clara where he had served as alcalde, he dressed in the attire of a ranchero— cotton shirt and pants, sash, serape, and sombrero. He abandoned the mission for life in the interior and may have succeeded Estanislao as leader of all the Indians on the Stanislaus River, although the Siakumne were under his immediate authority. His principal village, Chaspaiseme, was located about thirty miles up the Stanislaus from its juncture with the San Joaquin. The influence of José Jesús extended from the Mokelumne River in the north to the Tuolumne in the south.[101]

At the meeting, Weber and José Jesús forged an alliance that lasted for several years.[102] And with the friendship of the region's most powerful Indian guaranteed, Culnac in August 1844 again attempted to establish a settlement at Campo de Los Franceses. He sent several persons, including a married couple with three daughters, to the rancho, but they soon fled because of smallpox. About two months later, Thomas Lindsay returned to guard the stock. Locolumne (Yokuts) struck early the following year, killing Lindsay, setting fire to the buildings, and driving off the stock.[103] When Sutter located the Indians a few days after the attack, he must have been shocked at the ferocity of their response. The Locolumne killed his clerk, Juan Vaca, and wounded several of his men.[104] Thirty-six Locolumne may have died in the engagement.[105]

Because campaigns such as this were time-consuming and expensive, Sutter made a determined effort to solve his difficulties with local Indians. In June 1845, he wrote to Antonio Suñol:

I am negotiating a treaty with the principal leaders of the horse thieves, the object of which will be to put an end to their thefts, and have them come here in person. They send word that they would come if I pardoned them, which I have promised to do, and I expect them here in a short time. You may rest assured, sir, that my manner of treating with these Indians will result in much good to the country, and will be more efficacious than costly and pretentious campaigns that never meet with success.[106]

Sutter's problems with Indians continued to mount, however. In July he received a letter from an American official in Oregon inquiring about the killing of Elijah. Upon returning to the

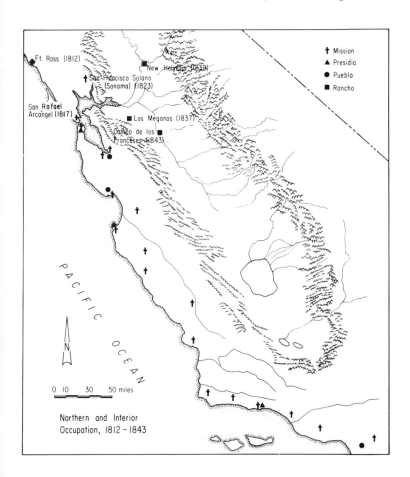

† Mission
▲ Presidio
● Pueblo
■ Rancho

Ft. Ross (1812)
New Helvetia (1839)
† San Francisco Solano
(Sonoma) (1823)
San Rafael
Arcángel (1817)
■ Los Meganos (1837)
Campo de los ■
Franceses (1843)

PACIFIC

N

OCEAN

0 10   30   50 miles

Northern and Interior
Occupation, 1812 – 1843

Columbia River, the Walla Walla told the American subagent for Indian affairs that they were willing to give up the horses not belonging to them on the condition that their property be returned and Grover Cook turned over to them or to the subagent.[107] Thomas Larkin wrote to the subagent, encouraging him to dissuade the Indians from returning to California. He feared the Indians would attack American settlers residing in the Sacramento Valley.[108]

The Mexican government became involved in the affair. In September the governor's secretary instructed the prefect of the district of Monterey to select a justice of the peace to investigate the killing and to bring those responsible to trial. The goods the Indians had left behind were to be secured and eventually returned to their owners. The justice could call upon the military for assistance. By this action, the foreigners would learn that regardless of origin or position whoever "treads the Mexican soil" is "under the protection of our Laws."[109]

Sutter continued to defy Mexican law. On September 16, 1845, he tried for murder and executed Rufino, the leader of the neophytes residing on the Cosumnes.[110] Heleno took command of this group.[111] He maintained the economic relationship his people had established with Sutter.[112]

If the execution was intended to cow local Indians, it did not succeed. Stock raiders drove off some of Sutter's cattle in late December; the pursuit party recovered only part of the herd.[113] The setback may have prompted Sutter to meet with the two most powerful chiefs in the region—José Jesús and Polo, the leader of the Locolumne. Early in 1846, Sutter gave them gifts and issued them passports in Spanish and English. They, in turn, promised to assist him in campaigns against Indians continuing to steal stock, in particular the Muqueleme.[114] Thereafter, José Jesús and Polo regularly visited New Helvetia, usually to deliver workers to Sutter.[115]

As Sutter's influence with local Indians grew, Mexican concerns increased. Sometime in May 1946, General José Castro encouraged the interior Indians to attack the immigrants. An American claimed the general had "made them promises of valuable presents if they would burn the crops and destroy the people."[116] Sutter was convinced that Castro had attempted "to revolutionize all the Indians against me."[117] He also suspected that a Muqueleme named Eusebio was in league with Castro. Apparently, the general addressed the Indian as "son" and "brother" and provided him with a gun.[118]

In late May, a party of Muqueleme made camp near New Helvetia. After meeting with local Indian leaders, who agreed not to interfere, the Muqueleme ran off a large herd of horses.[119] On June 1, Sutter wrote to M. G. Vallejo: "There has been another uprising among the Moquélumnes, and they have declared war against me. The roads are not safe for small parties from here to the pueblo of San José. In a few days I think of going out on a campaign, before they burn up our wheat, as some of the gentlemen at the pueblo of San José have advised them to do, and before Eusebio kills me with a firearm which he received at the pueblo from the said gentlemen."[120]

The campaign Sutter launched against the Muqueleme accomplished very little. One of the rafts capsized on the Mokelumne River; the whites lost ten rifles, six pistols, and a large supply of ammunition and clothing. An advance party located the Indians on the Calaveras River but suffered several casualties in the ensuing battle. When the remainder of Sutter's force arrived, the Indians retreated to the banks of the river, took cover among the dense brush, and continued the fight. Sutter claimed to have killed many Indians but acknowledged that "on account of having no more powder and balls, we found it very prudent to leave the Scene slowly, so that it appeared as [if] we wanted to Camp." Once out of sight of the Indians, the white men made a forced march back to New Helvetia.[121]

Sutter turned to Polo for help. He promised the Locolumne chief one hundred dollars in blankets, cotton twill, calico, and other items upon the delivery of Eusebio. In mid-June, Polo presented to Sutter the Indian's head.[122] An American who arrived at the fort a short time later observed that

the gateway to the fort was ornamented with the scalp of an Indian, the long black hair hanging dejectedly down, as if mourning for the death of its late proprietor. I speak lightly of this scalp because it had been the property of an Indian who had been sent since my last visit—it was said by Castro—to burn the wheat crop of New Helvetia, and if possible to kill Captain Sutter himself. In endeavoring to put his nefarious purposes into practice he had met with his death, and his scalp was nailed to the outer-wall to deter others from engaging in similar undertakings.[123]

Other Indians, however, may have been hired to assassinate Sutter and to destroy his wheat fields.[124]

The occupation by white men of land in the interior zone profoundly altered interethnic relations in central California. Some Indian leaders took advantage of the situation to ally themselves with the immigrants, but this put them at odds with those perceiving the settlers to be a distinct threat. The immigrants may have benefitted economically by employing Indian workers, but they suffered greatly from Indians who appropriated their stock. And as the Californios became concerned about relations established between immigrants and interior Indians, mistrust between the non-Indian residents of California increased dramatically.

When war between Mexico and the United States broke out, interior Indians were provided with unexpected opportunities. Preoccupied as they were with one another, Californios and Americans ignored the San Joaquin Valley, allowing the Indians to solidify their control over an area extending from the Tehachapi Mountains in the south to near Sutter's Fort in the north. Secure for the time being in their hidden villages in the foothills of the Sierra Nevada, the stock raiders took full advantage of the coastal conflict to plunder the ranchos with impunity.

CHAPTER 10

American Intervention

SO frequent and devastating had Indian raids become by the middle of the 1840s that many rancheros no longer believed their government capable of solving the problem. At least this was the view held by Thomas Larkin, U.S. consul to California, who reported in July 1845 that the Californios refused to improve their lands, because "the Indians tame & wild steal several thousand head of Horses yearly." Without the requisite number of horses, cattle raising was unprofitable.[1]

Early in 1846, Larkin complained that "the wild Indians are carrying off thousands of horses, and have shot with arrows, several people. Government appears to be doing nothing. If Mexico would command California as she ought to do, or let the people do it, . . . affairs would improve."[2] In April he claimed that "a considerable portion of the Californians are well aware, that their land and property would increase in value, by change of Flags! Some are quietly waiting the result. . . . The present deplorable state they are now in arising from the robbery of their Horses will hasten the result. They are convinced that a proper administration of affairs would put down the Indians."[3]

The following month the United States declared war on Mexico. In June, American settlers seized Sonoma, and in July, U.S. naval forces occupied Monterey and San Diego. Commodore Robert F. Stockton, commander of American military personnel in California, commissioned John Frémont a captain and placed him in command of the settlers. Eventually numbering over five hundred men, the California Battalion, in conjunction with U.S. Marines, occupied Los Angeles in August.[4]

By occupying the coastal zone, the American military assumed, inadvertently, the task of defending the pueblos, missions, and ranchos from Indian incursions. Always short of men, the military authorities called upon American settlers and even Californios for assistance. Many Californios, however, had become resigned to losing stock and, according to Larkin, "seldom follow them to regain their property."[5] While the foreigner invariably pursues the Indians, asserted an anonymous writer, the Californio informs the local authorities and then "quietly submits to his loss."[6]

In late July, when Indians raided Mission Santa Clara, only two or three Californios joined the pursuit party.[7] Comprised mainly of Company A of the California Battalion, the party located Indian horse thieves in the Santa Cruz Mountains. The Indians escaped, but the soldiers recovered one hundred horses, which were returned to the owners. The *Californian,* the territory's first newspaper, predicted that the action "will go far to gain the confidence and respect of the Californians."[8] But the newspaper was not convinced the raiders had been properly chastised. The following week it argued that "the only effectual means of stopping their inroads upon the property of the country, will be to attack them in their villages, in the California Mountains."[9]

About the first of September, a military force of some forty men moved against the stock raiders. Somewhere in the San Joaquin Valley the soldiers killed and wounded several Indians and recovered one hundred horses. They remained in the field for two weeks, venturing farther into the interior than had previous American military units.[10] But no sooner had this command returned when Indians stole fifteen or twenty horses from ranchos in the vicinity of Mission San Carlos. The American military commander at Monterey provided horses for the six civilians who pursued the Indians. The *Californian* reported that the well-armed men expected to overtake the raiders before they reached the Tulares.[11]

Causing the American authorities considerable apprehension in early September 1846 was the rumor that one thousand Walla Walla were approaching New Helvetia, where they intended to take revenge for the killing of Yellow Serpent's son nearly two years before. Soldiers and volunteers quickly took up positions in strategic passes, as Californios and Americans braced for a major confrontation.[12] About fifty Indian soldiers and ten or twelve white men, under the command of Edward Kern, guarded Sutter's Fort.[13] On September 12, Lieutenant Joseph Warren Revere of the U.S. Navy and twenty-five men reinforced the local contingent.[14]

About fifty Walla Walla arrived at the fort. Yellow Serpent spoke with Revere:

I have come from the forests of Oregon with no hostile intentions. You can see that I speak the truth, because I have brought with me only forty warriors, with their women and little children, and because I am here with few followers, and without arms. We have come to hunt the beasts of the field, and also to trade our horses for cattle; for my people require cattle, which are not so abundant in Oregon as in California. I have come, too, according to the custom of our tribes, to visit the grave of my poor son, Elijah, who was murdered by a white man. . . . When I came to California, I did not know that the Boston men had taken the country from the Spaniards. I am glad to hear it; for I have always been friendly to the Boston men, and have been kind to those who have passed through my territories. It must be plain to you that we did not set out on a hostile expedition against your countrymen.[15]

According to M. G. Vallejo, the Walla Walla professed peaceful intentions only after observing American military power.[16]

Once that crisis had been resolved, another developed. In September the Mexican inhabitants of Los Angeles, chafing under the arbitrary rule of their occupiers, rose in rebellion and drove the Americans from the pueblo.[17] The small U.S. contingent at Santa Bárbara abandoned its post a short time later.[18] Agustín Janssens recalled that the American garrison "crossed the mountains behind the mission to go down the Los Prietos Cañon. The cavalry went in pursuit, but could not catch them."[19]

Mexican rebels and American soldiers badly needed horses. In October a party of one hundred Californios rounded up all the animals they could find, even old, sore-back, broken-down mares, near Mission San Carlos. They also took with them the

Indian vaqueros in charge of the herds.[20] William Garner wrote in November that "the whole territory is now in a most pitiable state, both Americans and Californios having gathered into their possession all the horses they could find in the country. There is not a farm in the whole country at this present moment, that can boast of a horse or a saddle, unless they have secreted them in some place which has escaped the strictest searches of both parties."[21]

Entrusted with the task of crushing the uprising, John Frémont sought the assistance of immigrants and Indians.[22] John Sutter encouraged the Walla Walla to join the California Battalion and promised they would be paid for their services.[23] During a battle at Rancho Natividad, located a few miles northeast of Monterey, a contingent of thirty Californios attacked the Indians and a few Americans who had taken up positions in a grove of timber. As remembered by a participant in the fight, "the Walla Wallas were in their war dress and paint, which in itself was sufficient to strike terror to foes unused to such apparel; but when they jumped from behind the trees and scalped the one or two that they shot down, accompanied by their unearthly war-whoop, the Californians became utterly demoralized, and suddenly turned and never stopped running while in sight, not even to join their countrymen."[24]

Many years later, Sutter recalled that "the Walla Wallas brought back much spoils, trophies, clothing of the Mexicans they had killed."[25] After the battle, Frémont instructed Edward Kern to tell Yellow Serpent, who remained at Sutter's Fort, that his men had fought bravely and that he would need them for another two months. Kern was to provide beef and flour to the families of the Walla Walla who served with the Americans.[26]

In mid-November, a party of about twenty Americans departed from Sutter's Fort for San José. Thirteen Indians, commanded by Antonio, joined them on the Mokelumne River and eighteen more, led by José Jesús, chief of the Siakumne (Yokuts), on the San Joaquin. The Indians were on foot and armed only with bows and arrows.[27] Subsequently, they received on loan thirty-two horses.[28] Under the command of José Jesús, they formed a separate company of the California Battalion.[29]

Before departing from Monterey for Los Angeles, Frémont left in the care of several friendly Californios over one hundred head of horses, including ninety with Francisco Pacheco. As reported by the *Californian,*

> The Indians from the Tulares, who are always on the lookout, and besides, always get immediate information, when and where a quantity of horses may be found; could not resist the temptation, knowing as they do, that in this part of the country, at present, there is no force to follow them up, or otherwise injure them; accordingly in two or three days after Colonel Fremont had left these horses, and several others, which he had been kind enough to distribute amongst those individuals, who were most in need of them, they came down, and swept off every horse they could find, leaving the farmers entirely destitute of the means of carrying on their agricultural business.[30]

Had Frémont's battalion not been drawn south to quell the uprising, reasoned William Garner, it would have put an end to Indian depredations.[31] The *Californian* drew the same conclusion.[32] But the Indian raiders may have inadvertently assisted the Americans. Although the Californios in the San Luís Obispo area supported the uprising, they feared to leave their ranchos. "The Indians might come to steal, burn, and commit such other deviltries as might occur to them," reasoned Agustín Janssens.[33]

Los Angeles was retaken on January 10, 1847, and three days later the remaining Mexican forces surrendered to Frémont in the San Fernando Valley.[34] The coastal zones, from Sonoma in the north to San Diego in the south, came under the jurisdiction of an American military government. The military officials, however, had no governing experience and little precedent upon which to rule. Initially, the commander of U.S. forces served as governor. Appointed by the president and supported by the military, he possessed, at least in theory, enormous power and independence. But the laws and customs of war and orders from his superiors restricted his authority. Always short of financial support and military personnel and well aware that he would hold office only for a short time, the military governor of California ruled on an ad hoc basis.[35]

How to curtail the incursions of the Indian stock raiders became a major concern of the new government. In March 1847, Colonel Richard B. Mason wrote to General Stephen Watts Kearny, the military governor, claiming that there was no need to station troops at the pueblo of San José. They would be useless against the stock raiders who "come in small parties of two or three from different directions, meet at some preconcerted place & commence their operations, carrying off 200 or 300 hundred head of stock." Instead, he recommended that detachments be stationed on the west bank of the San Joaquin River and at the passes through which the raiders must travel with the stolen stock. Mason suggested that the soldiers guarding the pass near Mission San Juan Bautista be augmented with about thirty mounted Californios, who would serve for twelve months.[36]

Recently, Indians had raided ranchos in the area, not only stealing stock but also firing arrows at those who stood in their way. José María Sanchez, alcalde of San Juan Bautista, informed the governor about the attacks, pointing out that his people were without arms and ammunition and requesting that Kearny "put a remedy to the affair."[37] Kearny outlined his "remedy" in a letter to the Secretary of War: "I am of the opinion that much good might be done by making a few presents to them." He requested that medals, red flannels, colored handkerchiefs, tobacco, and a few colored blankets be shipped to him.[38]

Because of the incessant Indian raids, most Americans and many Californios must have welcomed the one thousand soldiers who sailed into San Francisco Bay in March. Known as the New York Volunteers and commanded by Colonel Jonathan D. Stevenson, the unit arrived too late to participate in the California campaign. Subsequently, one of the companies was stationed at Sonoma, two at the Presidio of San Francisco, two at Monterey, three at Santa Bárbara, and two at Los Angeles.[39]

Stationing most of the companies at coastal localities made no sense to many residents, and in April the *California Star* lashed out at the government's policy:

> Cannot the authorities do something for the protection of the frontier, and will they not do something? Will the government not listen to the complaints of the citizens; and will the large number of government troops now here, be kept idle along the coast, without any prospect of being either of territorial or national benefit, when the Indians are continually committing depredations along the whole line of the eastern frontier, and when they are penetrating the settlements to almost within sight of the Capital of the territory, plundering and killing the inhabitants.[40]

A member of the New York Volunteers echoed this criticism: "The present disposition of the troops is of no real service to the country. They are stationed in comfortable and quiet quarters in towns where they are least wanted, and the thieving Indians are allowed to make nightly excursions into the settlements, and to infest the roads."[41]

As the stock raiders became more aggressive, the size of their raiding parties increased, sometimes numbering between one and two hundred men.[42] John Marsh believed the Indians had become more daring because the numbers of animals on the ranchos had decreased. Writing to the *California Star* in early April under the nom de plume Agricola, Marsh recounted that during the past month the Indians had

> shot and dangerously wounded four persons employed on the farm of Mr. Webber near the Pueblo of St. Joseph, and at the same time stole the horses of the farm, and those also from the farm of Capt Fisher and Mr. Burnal in the same vicinity; in all above two hundred head. Within the last ten days, numerous parties of them have been committing depredations on many of the farms in the jurisdiction of the Contra Costa, and scarcely a night passes but we hear of their having stolen horses from some one.[43]

In another letter to the *Star,* Marsh predicted that if the raids were not curtailed, the economic ramifications would be disastrous. He questioned whether the rancheros could honor their accounts to merchants "when the horse thieves are taking away the last of the miserable remnant of broken down horses, that the wars and revolutions have left behind." He acknowledged that "the people of San Francisco will take little or no interest in this subject, as they may think themselves and their property safe in their shops and on board their ships." But they will look in vain "for hides and tallow, or other produce of the country, if the farmers have no horses with which to manage their cattle."[44]

Marsh also reported that six white men from Los Angeles soon would take up residence with José Jesús and his ally, Felipe, Indians he considered to be horse raiders. Apparently, the Indians had invited the men to join them while serving together in the California Battalion. The whites possessed trade goods they intended to exchange for horses.[45] The editor of the *Star,* however, challenged Marsh's conclusions:

We feel entirely certain that those Indians who marched to the Pueblo de los Angeles in the battalion of Col. Fremont, have been concerned in none of the thefts and outrages recently committed. . . . We have indubitable proof of this assertion, and therefore speak positively. They are entirely and wholly friendly to the Americans, and with proper treatment, will render most efficient service in ferreting out and bringing to punishment the wild, hostile, and thieving tribes which inhabit the western slope of the Sierra Nevada.[46]

Under increasing pressure to extend its authority to the interior, the military government attempted to regulate Indian activity through diplomatic means. In early April, upon the recommendation of Thomas Larkin, Governor Kearny appointed John Sutter Indian subagent for the Indians residing near the Sacramento and San Joaquin rivers. Kearny instructed Sutter to

explain to the Indians the change in the administration of public affairs in this Territory; that they must now look to the President of the United States as their great father; that he takes good care of his good children; that the officers now here are acting under his orders and instructions; that the Americans and Californians are now one people, and any offenses which they may commit against the latter will be punished in the same way as if committed against the former.[47]

A week later Kearny appointed M. G. Vallejo subagent for the Indians residing north of San Francisco Bay.[48] Sutter wrote to Kearny in mid-May. The Indians residing in the vicinity of his fort long ago had ceased raiding and had taken up farming. He predicted that shortly local Indians would harvest fine crops of corn, pumpkins, and melons. Some had planted wheat. Soon he would invite distant chiefs to visit his fort, where they would learn about the intentions of the new government. Sutter promised to punish those who failed to appear.[49]

On May 22, Cornelio and Carlos, who were chiefs of the Tauhalame (Yokuts), and the leaders of three other groups arrived at New Helvetia. Sutter gave them provisions and passports.[50] Cornelio and Carlos promised to cease stealing stock and trading with horse thieves. Aware that a military expedition soon was to enter the interior, Sutter cautioned the government against attacking the Tauhalame. He thought they would be useful in subduing the Chauchila and Pitkachi (Yokuts).[51] On May 27, he wrote to Kearny, recommending that force be used against these Indians.[52]

The previous month, Kearny had made preparations to send a contingent of the New York Volunteers, under Captain Henry Naglee, into the interior to punish the stock raiders. He also sought to recruit thirty Californios for the campaign.[53] Kearny turned to M. G. Vallejo for help in this matter, and the prominent Californio recruited twelve men in Sonoma. At Santa Clara, Vallejo encouraged local Californios to join, but only ten volunteered. He informed Kearny that many could not participate because the Americans had not returned their weapons and because they had no horses.[54]

Naglee and sixteen men arrived at Mission San Juan Bautista on May 24, where they were joined by Lieutenant Philip Burton and a few Californios.[55] Following the advice of John Sutter, they entered Tauhulame territory and met Carlos, who escorted them south to the Merced. Captain Naglee sent Carlos, a lieutenant, and eight men to make contact with the Chauchila. When the party returned, the lieutenant accused Carlos of deliberately leading him in circles.[56]

Naglee and his men followed the San Joaquin River upstream to the mountains, where they contacted Tomquit, leader of the Pitkachi, and thirty of his followers. The Indians sought to trade horses and bows and arrows for what items the soldiers and volunteers possessed. When Tomquit offered Naglee three very fine animals, the captain, suspecting they had been stolen, declined. Offended by the refusal, the Indian was mollified somewhat when presented with a shirt and a pair of pantaloons. On June 18 the party headed back to Monterey. Although he gained some geographical knowledge and met a few Indians, Naglee accomplished very little. No Indians were punished; no animals were recovered.[57]

Shortly before Naglee returned to the coast, Yellow Serpent and several Walla Walla visited New Helvetia. They had yet to be paid for their services during the Mexican-American War and sought a meeting with John Frémont. Kearny, Frémont, and a large party were then passing through the area on their way to Washington, D.C. After visiting the camp of the Americans, the Walla Walla returned to Sutter's Fort, delivering to Edward Kern orders from Frémont to pay them in horses.[58] Evidently, they received about one hundred head.[59]

While Kearny and Frémont were in the interior, a rumor reached Monterey that they had lost horses to Indian raiders. The *Californian* regretted the loss but suggested that

it may be productive of much good; for if those two officers, both experienced in Indian character, with forty of the best mountaineers, could not prevent the Indians from stealing their horses, it is not to be expected that the Rancher's [sic] on a border of six hundred miles can protect their Ranches. . . . It is to be hoped, if Gen. Kearny had been robbed, that it will show the authorities the propriety of establishing military posts along the Tulare Valley in such a manner as to prevent this band of thieves from entering the settlements and carrying off such bands of horses as they have been in the habit of doing heretofore.[60]

Kearny's party, consisting of sixty-four persons, had lost no animals to Indians.[61] By commenting on the rumor, perhaps the *Californian* sought to goad Colonel Richard B. Mason, the new military governor, into taking a more active role in curtailing Indian incursions.[62] In early June, William Dana pleaded with Mason to send troops to San Luís Obispo. Local citizens were helpless against Indian raiders, who were carrying off droves of horses. If the government failed to act promptly, Dana feared the rancheros would be forced to abandon their lands.[63]

A single company of the New York Volunteers was then stationed in the northern interior: one platoon at Sonoma, another at New Helvetia.[64] But the soldiers stationed at the fort failed in any appreciable way to reinforce Sutter's authority as Indian subagent. As two incidents clearly indicate, Sutter was virtually helpless in preventing disputes between Indians and whites. On July 10 two Californios entered a Yalesumne (Nisenan) village on Webber Creek, located about twenty miles northeast of the fort, appropriated a band of horses a military officer had left there, and whipped the headman, Shulule. Sutter issued orders for the arrest of the two men, but they were never apprehended.[65]

Shortly before this incident occurred, Antonio María Armijo, John Eggar, and Robert Smith massacred thirteen Indians at a village located some sixty miles north of the fort; they also took thirty-seven captives.[66] As recounted by a resident of New Helvetia, the captives, mostly women and children, were "tied together and driven to the settlements. Young children who were unable to proceed, were murdered on the road. In one instance an infant was taken from its mother, and killed in her presence, and that too in the most brutal manner."[67]

In a letter to the governor, Sutter asked how he was to act in this case.[68] Mason replied on July 21:

I beg that you will use every exertion to cause the guilty persons to be arrested, for which purpose you will call on the military officer near you for all the assistance in his power to afford. . . . When arrested, I will organize a tribunal for their trial; and if sentence of death is passed upon them, will have it executed. . . . The Indians that have been captured you must at once seize, by any means in your power, and restore them to their people: tell them that these atrocious acts have been committed by lawless scoundrels, . . . and that the perpetrators of the outrages shall be made a public example of.[69]

Mason also wrote to Lieutenant Charles Anderson, commander of the military force at New Helvetia, ordering him to give Sutter whatever assistance he needed in apprehending the murderers.[70]

Fearing, perhaps, that Indians would impose their own justice, a short time later the military government, in a letter to Sutter, further defined its Indian policy:

Let them understand that while the government will punish them for their depredations, it will also protect them and their property from injury by the whites. Tell them that if any ill disposed person should do them injury they must complain of it to you, and not themselves attempt to inflict punishment, or to retaliate upon the offenders. The government will always be ready to do ample justice to the Indians, and will redress all their wrongs; but it cannot permit them to take this matter into their own hands.[71]

Governor Mason appointed Sutter and M. G. Vallejo special judges to try, at or near New Helvetia, Armijo, Eggar, and Smith for the murder and enslavement of Indians.[72] Mason, however, moved the venue to Sonoma and appointed Lilburn W. Boggs to also serve as judge.[73] Sutter failed to attend the trial, which was held in October. The accused were acquitted.[74]

As Indian agent, Sutter was encouraged to write frequently to the governor regarding "the best measures to be adopted for the government of the Indians and for the security of their quiet and happiness." Sutter was to collect information about the Indian societies within his district. Of particular interest to the authorities were means of subsistence, forms of government, and modes of warfare.[75] In December Sutter responded to the request, transmitting statistical information concerning Indians located east of the San Joaquin and Sacramento rivers. He calculated that in his jurisdiction resided 478 neophytes and 21,873 gentiles.[76]

The limited number of neophytes was reflected in the labor shortage then affecting New Helvetia. In September, Sutter complained to William Leidesdorff that he had work for two hundred Indians, but sometimes only twenty or twenty-five were available. The time had passed, he lamented, when he could depend on Indians.[77] Sutter later informed his friend that soon he would lose a large quantity of wheat.[78]

While Sutter lost workers, other rancheros lost stock. In late August Indians stole horses from the ranchos in the vicinity of San José. The following month a military officer informed the alcalde of the pueblo that "an expedition will start for the Tulares as soon as it can be fitted out, to look after these thieving Indians, and to adopt such measures as may check for a time their depredations."[79] Captain Henry Naglee of the New York Volunteers was given command of the expedition. He was to search to the very limits of the territory controlled by the stock raiders. Indians found with stolen horses were to be brought to the coast, where they would be properly punished. His command was to travel light and, if necessary, remain in the field for fifty days.[80]

In a gorge in the Sierra Nevada, Naglee confronted Indians, who denied participating in recent raids. They claimed another group was responsible. Located a few days later, its leaders also professed innocence. One of the soldiers recounted to William Redmond Ryan what transpired. Naglee told the chiefs that

he did not believe them; they were all of the same colour, and, therefore, all thieves and murderers alike; and he should insist upon the culprits being given up. Again the chiefs remonstrated and protested against the injustice that had been done them; it was in vain: for the Captain commanded some of the men to take the chiefs into custody.... "Black Jack" [Naglee] pointed to a small space that had been recently cleared, and a firing-party took up its position there.... The two chiefs then folded their arms, and deliberately stalked to the place of execution— of murder, rather—exhibiting the greatest unconcern, whilst the few men of the tribe looked on in the same impassive manner. In less than another minute all was over, and the two chiefs lay stretched on the ground stone dead.[81]

Before his execution, one of the chiefs instructed his son, Chechee, to avenge his death.[82]

Indians harassed Naglee's command as it departed from the area, firing volleys of arrows but causing no harm.[83] When the soldiers arrived at Monterey, Governor Mason placed Naglee under arrest for murdering Indians. He was released early the following year for military duty with the volunteers in Baja California.[84]

Naglee's expedition failed to deter the stock raiders. In December 1847, Locolumne (Yokuts) struck at ranchos in the Livermore Valley and in the Mount Diablo area.[85] John Marsh lost most of his animals.[86] A short time later, Charles Weber received permission from the alcalde of San José to raise a party to punish the thieves.[87] Weber turned to his ally, José Jesús, for assistance, the Siakumne leader providing most of the two hundred men who formed the expedition. In February 1848, Weber and José Jesús located the raiders on the Calveras River, killed a few, and rounded up the stolen horses.[88] The fight may have turned José Jesús and Polo, chief of the Locolumne, into bitter enemies. Polo insisted on stealing horses from the immigrants; José Jesús sought to remain at peace with them.[89]

In January 1848, Mexico ceded California (and the rest of the Southwest) to the United States, and the military authorities now had to protect American territory. Commanding badly undermanned and poorly equipped troops, they increasingly turned to their former enemies, the Californios, for assistance. In mid-February 1848, Colonel Jonathan Stevenson placed Andrés Pico in charge of defending the ranchos between Los Angeles and Santa Bárbara. He ordered Pico to identify those men at each rancho capable of fighting Indians and to list the number of weapons they possessed. Those who refused to comply were to be fined ten to twenty-five dollars.[90]

This hastily formed alliance of rancheros and soldiers soon was tested. On the night of February 20, Indians struck at several ranchos in the Santa Bárbara area, including one only two miles from the military barracks. The following day ten soldiers and a few

Californios, who received ammunition from the Americans, went in pursuit.[91] They recovered some thirty horses, and on a ridge in the nearby mountains discovered a few huts and a corral the Indians had constructed. The leader of the Californios considered it unwise to pursue the Indians farther, and they returned to Santa Bárbara.[92] While they were gone, another band of Indians attacked two parties of whites only a few miles from Santa Bárbara, wounding one or two persons.[93]

By supplying ammunition to the Californios, the military authorities took considerable risk. Needing their support but fearing treachery, the Americans proceeded cautiously. In March 1848 the alcalde of San Luís Obispo, John Price, reported to Governor Mason that because they lacked ammunition, local citizens were helpless against the Indians who recently had stolen stock from the area. Mason suggested that the alcalde organize a party of thirty men to move against the Indians on a moment's notice. He promised to deliver twenty-five or thirty pounds of powder and a proportionate quantity of lead. But he cautioned Price to ensure "that this ammunition is not applied to improper purposes; that it is taken care of, and only used for the service for which it is intended."[94]

In late February, an Indian stock raider was captured near Santa Bárbara. Convinced that his life would be spared if he disclosed the whereabouts and strength of his band, he told Captain Francis J. Lippsitt, the local military commander, that three hundred to four hundred Indians resided on the margin of a small lake in the southern Tulare Valley. The corral they had built sometimes contained one thousand horses, but presently it held only two hundred. Some of the Indians were armed with rifles and pistols. Lippsitt identified the village as La Punta de la Laguna.[95]

Lippsitt and Pedro Carrillo, the alcalde of Santa Bárbara, attempted to form a joint command to attack the village. Lippsitt offered the alcalde ammunition to distribute to the Californios in exchange for the use of their horses. The Californios held two or three meetings, but those who belonged to one faction refused to contribute their quota of men as long as Carrillo commanded the party. Lippsitt decided to send thirty soldiers against the Indians if the Californios provided horses and guides. The horses could not be obtained, and the mission was cancelled.[96]

In early April, Colonel Stevenson authorized Francisco Noriega of Santa Bárbara to raise a volunteer force for a campaign against the Indians.[97] This may have been an unwise appointment, however, because Pedro Carrillo suspected Noriega of plotting to seize the American barracks. Supposedly, another party of Californios, organized in Los Angeles, either was to join Noriega's group or attack the local military post or the one at San Diego.[98] Whether the Californios actually conspired against the Americans or whether Carrillo issued his accusations for personal or political purposes is not known. The plan to assemble a force of volunteers evidently was cancelled.

Although the American military authorities attempted to recruit Californios in their campaigns against the Indian raiders, using friendly Indians for the same purpose was not considered. In late April 1848, José Jesús visited San José, seeking permission from Charles White, the alcalde, to attack some of his Indian neighbors who were constantly committing depredations. White told him the government would not sanction Indians waging war. If attacked, José Jesús had the right to defend himself, but all prisoners had to be brought to San José.[99] White issued him passports so he and his delegation could travel unmolested throughout the district, a decision that angered local Californios.[100]

Once he returned to the interior, José Jesús held two meetings with five or six Indian leaders and launched a campaign against an enemy group, probably the Muqueleme (Miwok). In July he informed White that he would arrive the following month with women and children captives. White reported this information to Governor Mason, suggesting that the friendship of José Jesús "may be used to advantage."[101]

At this juncture, Mason faced enormous problems. Gold had been discovered in January 1848, accelerating the occupation of California by Americans and others and intensifying the violence between Indians and whites. Because gold was found near New Helvetia but outside the boundaries of his grant, John Sutter immediately sought to acquire legal title from local Indians.[102] On February 4, Gesu and Pulpule (chiefs) and Colule and Sole (alcaldes) of the Yalesumne, leased to Sutter and his partner, James Marshall, a tract of land on Webber Creek near its entrance to the south branch of the American River. The lessees received the right to cut timber, erect a sawmill, cultivate the land, and open mines.[103]

In return, Sutter and Marshall promised to construct two millstones to grind the Indians' grain. Every year on the first day of January, Sutter and Marshall would present to the chiefs clothing and tools worth $150. At the end of twenty years, the land would revert to the Indians, who would pay a reasonable sum for the stones and other improvements.[104] Sutter may have used his position as Indian agent to convince the Yalesumne that all the provisions in the lease would be honored.[105] Apparently, the Indians agreed not to kill Sutter's horses, cattle, hogs, and sheep and not to burn the grass in the limits fixed by the lease.[106]

The lease was delivered to Governor Mason for approval. In an accompanying letter, Sutter claimed the Yalesumne would benefit greatly from the arrangement. They would be protected from their enemies to the north, furnished with food and clothing, and taught the "habits of industry." Moreover, by providing protection to immigrants, the settlement would advance the occupation of the foothills of the Sierra Nevada.[107] Mason, however, voided the contract because the United States did not recognize the right of Indians to sell or lease the lands on which they resided. Mason informed Sutter that should the federal government extinguish title to Indian land, it would become part of the public domain. Private claims made at the present time would only complicate matters.[108]

Word of the gold discovery quickly spread. By the end of May, half the eight hundred residents of San Francisco had departed for the gold mines; three-fourths had left by the middle of June.[109] Gold fever also spread to the military. By August, twenty-six soldiers at Sonoma, twenty-four at San Francisco, and the same number at Monterey had deserted.[110] In November, Governor Mason wrote to the adjutant general of the United States complaining that "so long as the gold mines continue to yield the great abundance of metal they now do, it will be impossible to keep soldiers in California, and it is of no use to send them here. Soldiers will not serve for seven and eight dollars per month when laborers and mechanics are getting from fifty to one hundred." Mason predicted that unless a civil government was organized at once, "anarchy and confusion will arise, and murder, robbery, and all sorts of crime will be committed with impunity in the heterogeneous and mixed community that now fills California."[111]

Mason did not exaggerate the problem. Unruly individuals from several nations took up residence not just in the mines but also in the coastal towns, where they caused difficulties for the local authorities. In mid-March 1849, William Garner informed Mason that San Lus Obispo had become a "refuge for criminals and vagabonds of every description, there existing no person here in authority to restrain or arrest them."[112]

Indian stock raiders contributed to the chaos. Garner told Mason that "Indian horse thieves have been hovering about the farms and plundering almost daily for the last seventeen days." Local rancheros were virtually defenseless because they had no ammunition.[113] And when many of its residents fled to the mines, San Lus Obispo became especially vulnerable. According to General Bennett Riley, the new governor of California, Indians took advantage of the absence of male inhabitants to "become more daring in their incursions. Depredations are more frequent than formerly."[114]

William Garner was one of those who left San Lus Obispo defenseless. In April he led a party of fifty Californios to the Kings River, where Indians reportedly had obtained large amounts of gold. For several days they camped on the south side of the river but found no evidence that local Indians possessed the metal.

Garner and five men ventured upstream to a village but were driven off. A few days later he returned with twenty men, but the Indians had burned their houses and were nowhere to be seen.[115]

The full contingent journeyed north, making camp on May 14 on the Fresno River in the territory of the Chauchila.[116] Garner wrote in his journal that "we have travelled about twenty miles today, the number of Indians around us have increased every hour for the last three days, and now number over a thousand— most of them have gold which is generally coarse, and to my enquiries of them where they obtained it, they pointed to the Eastward. There is a great stir among the Indians, and their squaws and children have left. I have now the greatest fears for my safety."[117]

On the fifteenth, Garner led seven men to a village in the mountains, where he was greeted by an Indian, Ventura, who had been raised in Monterey. While engaging him in conversation, Ventura shot and killed Garner; Indians also murdered six of the seven Californios. The one who escaped rejoined his companions, and they fled to the coast.[118]

On May 4, 1849, shortly before the murders, Assistant Adjutant General Edward R. S. Canby sent Major Anthony S. Miller and a battalion of the Second Infantry to the main crossing of the San Joaquin River. Miller was to select a site where a fort would be constructed.[119] A few days later, Canby issued further instructions:

Unauthorized interference with the Indians by the whites must, if possible, be prevented; and, on the other hand, the Indians will receive, through their agent, assurances of protection, if their conduct be such as to merit it; they will be advised to remain quiet in the pursuit of their ordinary occupations, and, when aggrieved, to make their complaints to the proper authorities; that any attempt to revenge themselves for fancied or real injuries will not be permitted, and that the offenders will in every instance be sought out and severely punished.

If any outrages are committed, you will require the offenders to be delivered up, and if this be not done promptly, you hold the tribe or rancheria to which they belong responsible for their conduct.

Suspecting that the Indians most likely to cause trouble resided on the Merced, Canby instructed Miller to send detachments to the river for the purpose of "overawing these Indians, or punishing them for any outrages they may commit."[120]

In response to the deaths of Garner and his companions, Canby ordered Lieutenant Clarendon Wilson and a detachment of dragoons to the Kings River, where the murders were thought to have taken place. He was to apprehend those responsible or "seize the chief or head men of the tribe or rancheria to which they belonged." With his prisoners, Wilson was to proceed to Major Miller's camp.[121]

Once aware that no murders had been committed on the Kings River, Wilson journeyed northwards, passing through the territories of the Tachi, Nutunutu, and Wimilchi (Yokuts) and speaking with several of their leaders. In his report, Wilson noted that the Indians "appear to be but little inclined to wander and have neither horses nor cattle at their Rancherias, but are said to have concealed in the Sierra Nevada large numbers of the former stolen from the settlements on the coast."[122]

At the encampment of Major Miller, Wilson learned that those responsible for the murders, the Chauchila, had withdrawn into the mountains. Wilson concluded that the Indians killed Garner and his men to deter others from entering an area rich in gold.[123] Governor Riley, however, theorized that Indians killed Garner "to revenge themselves for the aggressions committed by Americans upon the Indians of the Sacramento; indicating an evident understanding between different tribes speaking different languages, and separated by a distance of two hundred and fifty miles."[124]

Indian resistance already had begun in the gold-bearing regions. "The difficulties with the Indians are beginning to assume a more and more menacing character," exclaimed the *Alta California* in early May, "and sound policy would seem to dictate the propriety of sending bodies of troops into the disturbed districts. . . . This state of affairs is deeply to be regretted, and what is worse, it is believed generally, that it will to a great extent, prevent the successful working of the mines the present season."[125]

In early July 1849, Governor Riley led a few men into the interior, pausing for a time at Major Miller's camp on the San Joaquin River.[126] On the twenty-second, he wrote to the assistant adjutant general of U.S. forces in California recommending that a military post be established on the Kings River. He was alarmed that the miners prospecting on the Merced, Stanislaus, and Tuolumne rivers were driving the Indians southwards to the headwaters of the San Joaquin and Kings rivers. The Indians residing on the rivers,

with the exception of two or three tribes, have given evidence of the most friendly disposition towards the Americans. The country bordering on these rivers is rich in minerals, and the population now in the southern mines is moving to the south, and the close contact that must result will inevitably lead to many aggressions committed by one party upon the other. It is important that our own citizens be protected against Indian hostilities; and the dictates of policy, as well as humanity, require that the Indians should be secured against the aggressions of the whites.[127]

In mid-October, Riley wrote a long letter to the adjutant general of the U.S. Army pointing out the legal difficulties he faced in California. The laws of the United States regulating intercourse with Indians implied an Indian territory over which Congress exercised exclusive control, but no such territory existed in California. He feared that once California achieved statehood, federal and state authorities would compete over Indian jurisdiction.[128]

Riley recommended "that the title of the Indians to the lands which they are in actual occupancy be immediately recognized by Congress and that measures be taken to remove them from the immediate vicinity of the White Settlements and to establish them in some suitable location to the east of the *Sierra Nevada*." If such a location could not be found, he suggested the area between Buena Vista and Tulare lakes and the Sierra Nevada be set aside for a reservation. A site on the Russian River north of San Francisco Bay also was recommended. Indians would be confined at these two locations "until sufficient time has elapsed to make some permanent arrangement."[129]

The governor concluded his letter with a plea that the Indians be treated with humanity to prevent further demoralization and that "provision should also be made for their support until they are so far civilized as to be able to support themselves wholly or in great part . . . by the cultivations of the soil." Unless such efforts were undertaken immediately, Riley predicted that Indians soon would be surrounded by whites and would either starve to death or seize property. And "the commission of these depredations will be the pretence for the commencement of a war of extermination."[130]

Governor Riley's position that the federal government lacked a proper legal base to effectively deal with California Indians was well taken. His prediction that the State of California would vie with the federal government for Indian jurisdiction was remarkably prophetic. His call that Indians be removed to reservations was answered, although in terribly inefficient and harmful ways. His fear that whites would engage in a war of extermination was not exaggerated. In short, Riley identified the legal, military, and political factors that would shape Indian-white relations in the San Joaquin Valley during the 1850s and beyond.

CHAPTER 11

Historical Reconsiderations

FOR eighty years, Indians in the interior of central California interacted with Spanish missionaries, neophyte auxiliaries, Mexican soldiers, mission refugees, and American settlers penetrating their territories. While undergoing extensive social and economic change, they maintained their political independence and exhibited an aggressiveness that hindered foreign occupation and later damaged coastal settlements.

With a few exceptions, historians have overlooked these developments, largely because Indian behavior does not fit neatly into conventional periodization.[1] Each period—the Spanish, the Mexican, and the American—is associated with an important turning point: the initiation of Spanish colonization in 1769, the secularization of the missions in 1834, and the intrusion of American military forces in 1846. Historians acknowledge the presence of Indians in these periods but mainly as members of institutions established by the intruders: as neophytes in the missions, as workers on the ranchos, and as residents of the reservations. Indians thus appear in the historical literature mainly as a dominated, passive, and often tragically mistreated people. When applied to the coastal region after 1800 and to the interior after the beginning of the Gold Rush, this image has some validity. When applied to the interior before 1850, it badly distorts historical reality.

Considered to be of little historical importance until white settlement began with John Sutter, the San Joaquin Valley has been largely ignored by historians of the first two periods. As a consequence, they have overlooked important aspects of Spanish and Mexican colonialism and more importantly have failed to appreciate how Indian activity affected Hispanic institutions. The strategies interior Indians directed toward a mission or rancho sometimes affected the institution more profoundly than did the managerial policies initiated by the missionary or ranchero.

The importance of Indians in shaping aspects of California history can be truly appreciated only when the historical data are placed in a spatial and temporal framework that accounts for the processes of interaction. If the coast and interior of central California are viewed as two distinct but overlapping zones of interaction, the limitations of conventional periodization are, to a large degree, overcome.

The first phase in the history of the interior zone is characterized by a rather rapid shift from amicable to inimical interaction. As long as Spaniards sought ethnographical and geographical knowledge, Indians demonstrated curiosity and friendship. When Spaniards and later Californios sought human beings, Indians exhibited fear and hostility. By withdrawing into tule swamps or mountain retreats, by refusing to turn over children and runaways, and by violently opposing the penetration of their territories, Indians during this phase implemented strategies of *defensive resistance*.

The campaigns launched against Estanislao in 1829 brought the first phase to its conclusion. Although defeated militarily and reincorporated into Mission San José, Estanislao demonstrated to Mexican secular and religious authorities that discontented neophytes were prepared to fight to remain in the interior. Gone were the days when soldiers, civilians, and auxiliaries from the coast could penetrate the San Joaquin Valley with impunity.

The second phase began the following year when trappers and traders began arriving on a regular basis. The Nuevomexicanos provided interior Indians with opportunities and incentives that sent them to the coast on stock-raiding expeditions. Although Indian raiding had begun before 1830, it accelerated dramatically after this date. During this phase, Indians increasingly implemented strategies of *offensive resistance*.[2]

Dovetailing with the arrival of trappers and traders was the breakup of the missions. As a watershed in the history of the region, secularization is viewed mainly as the replacement of one Hispanic institution by another—the rancho for the mission. Californios, therefore, are perceived as the principal actors in the historical drama, and those most affected by secularization, the neophytes, are given no role to play. Most California historians regard the breakup of the missions as the coup de grace of the neophyte population. Driven from the missions by unscrupulous landgrabbers, the Indians became a marginal and thus historically insignificant people within Mexican society.[3]

This interpretation calls for substantial modification. The neophytes who drifted into the pueblos such as Los Angeles often experienced social disintegration and population decline, but those who trekked into the interior to join existing societies successfully reordered their lives.[4] Secularization provided interior Indian societies with informed and skilled individuals, many of whom rose to positions of authority. Rebel neophytes conducted most of the raids to obtain stock.

For some time, scholars have been aware that Indians raided the ranchos for animals, but few have understood the historical significance of this activity. During the 1930s and 1940s, for example, the anthropologist Anna Gayton produced a large body of first-rate scholarship but mentioned Indian raiding in her publications and research notes only on occasion. Concerned with reconstructing Yokuts society as it existed before white contact, probably she did not press her informants for this kind of information. On one occasion, when a Chukchansi told her about raiding the ranchos, she noted in her journal that "stealing horses sounds like lots of fun, to hear tell of it and see them look satisfied about the game."[5]

This view resembles that held by most anthropologists of the time. Regarding Indian warfare on the Great Plains, Robert Lowie insisted it was "an exciting pastime played according to established rules, the danger lending zest to the game."[6] Modern research has shown, however, that the acquisition of horses by trade and raid was a crucial activity in an extensive economic network that linked most Plains societies in ever-shifting relationships and which also connected them commercially to a succession of non-Indian nations.[7]

Sherburne F. Cook identified the aggressive behavior of interior California Indians but concluded the raids were conducted mainly to acquire food. Certainly, Indians stole stock for food, and this dietary adaption was crucial to their survival. Many interior peoples shifted from subsisting primarily on vegetable foods to relying heavily on meat.[8] But Indians had no need to continually raid the ranchos for this food source, because the San Joaquin Valley teemed with wild horses and other large game.

The commercial motive explains to a large degree why Indians raided the ranchos on such a regular basis. To acquire the woolen goods the Nuevomexicanos brought to California, Indians appropriated horses and mules from the Californios. Because it called for thorough planning and preparation, because it was largely undertaken by those who had acquired new skills and knowledge, and because it fulfilled commercial needs, the raid represents a "modern" economic enterprise. In this regard, the stock raiders performed a function similar to that of Indian trappers and hunters in the fur and hide trades in other regions of North America.[9] As "middlemen" in a long-distance trade network, they transferred a valuable product from Californios to Nuevomexicanos.

Throughout North America, trade either solidified or exacerbated relations between Indians and non-Indians. David Weber, for example, has shown that Americans undermined Indian-Mexican relations in the Southwest by trading illegally with a variety of groups during the 1830s and 1840s.[10] In California, however, most of the illegal trade with Indians was conducted not by Americans but by Nuevomexicanos. Americans never brought to California the quantity of trade goods that comprised the caravans from New Mexico. Moreover, because Nuevomexicanos encouraged interior Indians to steal stock from the coast, they, not Americans, were largely responsible for undermining Indian-Californio relations. The irony here is that Mexicans from New

Mexico damaged the economic foundations upon which Mexican society in California was constructed.

Because the variety of trade goods exchanged between California and New Mexico was limited, historians have concluded that the Old Spanish Trail was of limited commercial importance. Certainly, when compared to the variety of goods hauled over the Santa Fe Trail, the items taken to and from California suggest economic insignificance.[11] Volume, however, may be as important as variety. How many animals were taken from California is not known, but the evidence suggests many thousands.[12]

In the major study of the Old Spanish Trail, historians LeRoy and Ann Hafen claim that most of the animals illegally acquired were appropriated by traders and trappers. They acknowledge that Indians participated in the raids, but mainly in conjunction with Nuevomexicanos and Americans.[13] Most of the stock, however, was obtained not by outsiders, whose raids were limited and sporadic, but by Indians, whose raids were extensive and systematic.

Because of this economic motive, Indian offensive resistance in central California before 1850 shares little with that undertaken by Indians elsewhere in North America. And no better analysis of Indian raiding can be found than that presented by the *Alta California* in 1851:

Their depredations, wherever and whenever committed, were not aimed at human life, but levelled at the property of their white neighbors. . . . Instances of Indian cruelty were rarely heard. . . . "Horse-thief Indians," constituted the terror of the inhabitants of this sparsely settled region, and the tribes under the chieftainship of [Juan] Jose and [Jose] Jesus, in the San Joaquin valley, were the most formidable. These renowned leaders in the thieving excursions planned against the herds of the rancheros, were the escaped subjects of Spanish mission discipline. The Spanish owners of the country pursued a mode of warfare or chastisement little calculated to conciliate the hostile tribes, but even in return for the most wanton cruelties practiced by the parties of rancheros who went out against them, there were no deliberate night surprises, assassinations, or cold-blooded retaliatory deeds of barbarism.[14]

Because he experienced several attempts on his life, John Sutter probably disagreed with this assessment, but residing deep in the interior, he represents an exception. The subject of several full-length biographies, Sutter has been depicted as the pioneer who came to control much of the interior of northern California. "With the help of friendly tribes of his neighborhood," wrote James Peter Zollinger, "Sutter gradually made subservient the other Indians of the Sacramento and of the lower San Joaquin Valley."[15] Richard Dillon asserted that "by the fall of 1845, even with the Walla Walla war scares, Sutter had the northern California Indian situation very much in hand."[16] Interpretations such as these stem from the failure to understand the complexities and difficulties that came with residing in a vast Indian territory. The time and energy Sutter spent cultivating the friendship of Indian leaders and pursuing those he sought to dominate indicate the precariousness of his existence.

Failure to realize how vulnerable most of the rancheros were to Indian raids has also led to a misunderstanding of Mexican society. Living in a bountiful and beautiful land, residing on an estate the size of a principality, and exploiting a docile but hardworking Indian labor force, the ranchero has been pictured as an individual who mastered a life-style approaching pastoral perfection.[17] This romantic view, however, clashes with that held by the rancheros themselves. In 1876, Juan Bautista Alvarado called for an understanding of the plight of the Californios. "It is all very well for those who came to Alta California when there were no more Indians to fight," he wrote in his memoirs, "to make fun of us who for so many years did nothing . . . [except] to fight day and night against our eternal enemies, the heathen barbarians." Fearful that this aspect of life in Mexican California would be forgotten, he hoped "there might be found in the archives the reports concerning the many, many battles which the troops and militiamen . . . sustained against the mountain Indians."[18]

About the same time, an American, Edward Kemble, voiced similar concerns. Regarding the stock raiders, he noted that their fame and exploits are fast passing from the minds of California pioneers and are hardly known to later generations of Californians, having no special or appropriate mention in such modern books as I have seen of the country. They were the scourge of the eastern and middle portion of California in the period following the decadence of the missions and before the settlement of the Territory by Americans and other foreigners. . . . Those who arrived in California in 1845–46 heard much more of horse thief Indians than any other foe to civilization and settlement. They were much more dreaded when war broke out than the native Californians.[19]

Because historians only began to investigate the deleterious effects Indian raids had on Mexican society a century after he wrote, Kemble's concerns were well founded. In separate articles published in the 1970s, Sylvia Broadbent and Charles Hughes analyzed the ramifications of Indian raids near Monterey and San Diego, respectively. Although few immediately followed their lead, they pointed the way to further research on this subject.[20]

Recent historical studies of the Hispanic experience in California, however, have concentrated almost exclusively on developments transpiring after 1846. Leonard Pitt, for example, has investigated the dynamics of interethnic relations that evolved during the second half of the nineteenth century. By exposing the difficulties faced and analyzing the responses undertaken by Hispanics under American domination, Pitt has filled in important gaps in the historical record. His contribution to the historiography of California is not in question here.

Questioned, rather, are his particular views regarding the rancho system as it supposedly existed at the time of the American takeover. Because his focus is on the dramatic and often traumatic changes affecting Hispanics in California after 1846, he claims the rancho was a relatively stable, if hierarchical and inegalitarian, institution that provided its residents, Indian and Mexican, with a semblance of social and economic security. "Owing to the happy combination of good climate, ample land, and cheap Indian labor," he wrote, "the rancho order worked smoothly."[21]

According to Pitt, the social stability of the rancho was immediately shattered with the American occupation. Especially devastating to the rancheros was the Land Law of 1851, which forced them to prove title to their estates. The cost of traveling to San Francisco where the Board of Land Commissioners sat, hiring lawyers, producing documents, and locating witnesses forced many of them to sell sections of their lands or to go heavily into debt. Certainly, the law of 1851 and the exorbitant tax the state legislature placed on land contributed significantly to the demise of the rancho system.[22] But state and federal policies did not initiate the process of decline.

Nearly two decades of relentless Indian raiding preceded the American takeover, and by the time the Land Law was implemented, many ranchos were in a condition of economic ruin. The loss of large numbers of horses and mules deprived the rancheros of the means to effectively work their herds of cattle. This hampered their efforts to modernize their industry and thus to effectively compete with American farmers and ranchers.

It is apparent, therefore, that the rancho system did not work smoothly and that the dramatic changes affecting the Hispanic residents of California did not begin with the American conquest. This is not to suggest, however, that without Indian raiding the rancheros somehow would have overcome the pressures that came with the occupation. But with their estates intact, they would have been in a much better bargaining position to deal, at least initially, with the American intruders. And perhaps this would have cushioned to some degree the trauma of rapid change. The ramifications of Indian raiding thus extended far beyond the immediate economic losses suffered by the rancheros.

Consideration of Indian activity also generates a different perspective regarding the response of the Californios to the American military incursion. The conventional interpretation holds that many Californios failed to take up arms or did so reluctantly because they were disillusioned with their leaders, whose perpetual bickering had led to numerous bloodless "revolutions" between 1824 and 1846.[23] During that period, a dozen governors attempted to rule California. Certainly, political instability contributed to the discontent, but who occupied the governor's chair at a given moment was of less concern to the rancheros than the inability of any government to protect them from Indian raids. Although operating independently of the Americans, the Indian raiders inadvertently assisted them in their conquest of the coastal zone. For some Californios, protecting their ranchos from Indian raiders took precedent over defending their territory against American invaders. Others concluded that only with a change of government would Indian raiding be brought to an end. Realizing the hopelessness of their situation, many Californios thus accepted, if not welcomed, the American takeover.

Trained to fight a conventional war and burdened with the responsibility of occupying the coastal towns, the American military failed to protect the rancheros from Indian raids. By sending a few expeditions into the interior and by appointing a few civilians to serve as Indian agents, the new government established the outlines of an Indian policy. But the soldiers lacked the means and numbers to defeat hostile Indians, and the agents lacked the support and authority to protect peaceful ones.

Consequently, when historians claim that the conquest of California was achieved by U.S. military forces in 1846, they overlook an important dimension in the region's history. What they mean to say is that the coastal zone, from San Diego to San Francisco, was brought under military rule that year. The interior had yet to be conquered. Furthermore, the conquest would be achieved not by U.S. military forces but by civilians acting independently of state control and by volunteers serving in the state militia. The third phase in the history of the interior zone thus began when indigenous and intruding peoples competed, often violently, for the same land. It ended a few years later when the federal government imposed the reservation system upon the Indians of the Tulares.

Notes

CHAPTER 1

1. E. E. Evans-Pritchard, "Anthropology and History," in *Social Anthropology and Other Essays*, 176.
2. Ibid., 190.
3. For reviews of this literature, consult *The Journal of African History*, a British journal founded in 1960.
4. See I. Schapera, "Should Anthropologists Be Historians?", *Journal of the Royal Anthropological Institute of Great Britain and Ireland* 92 (July–December 1962): 143–56.
5. I. M. Lewis, "Introduction," in *History and Social Anthropology*, ed. I. M. Lewis, xiv.
6. Keith Thomas, "History and Anthropology," *Past and Present: A Journal of Historical Studies* no. 24 (April 1963): 10.
7. Ibid., 17.
8. William N. Fenton, "Ethnohistory and Its Problems," *Ethnohistory* 9 (Winter 1962): 3.
9. Alfred L. Kroeber, *An Anthropologist Looks at History*, ed. Theodora Kroeber, 183–84.
10. Robert T. Anderson, "Anthropology and History," *Bucknell Review* 15 (March 1967): 6.
11. Claude Lévi-Strauss, "Introduction: History and Anthropology," in *Structural Anthropology*, trans. Claire Jacobson and Brooke Grundfest Schoepf, 24–25.
12. Marshall Sahlins, "Other Times, Other Customs: The Anthropology of History," *American Anthropologist* 85 (September 1983): 534.
13. Kroeber, *An Anthropologist Looks at History*, 4.
14. Lévi-Strauss, "History and Anthropology," 18.
15. Evans-Pritchard, "Anthropology and History," 183.
16. *Ethnohistory*, an American journal, published its first issue in 1952.
17. Gregory Dening, *Islands and Beaches: Discourse on a Silent Land, Marquesas, 1774–1880*, 35. See also Gregory Dening, "Ethnohistory in Polynesia: The Value of Ethnohistorical Evidence," *Journal of Pacific History* 1 (1966): 23–42.
18. William C. Sturtevant, "Anthropology, History, and Ethnohistory," *Ethnohistory* 13 (Winter–Spring 1966): 1.

19. James Axtell, "Ethnohistory: An Historian's Viewpoint," in *The European and the Indian: Essays in the Ethnohistory of Colonial North America*, 6–7.

20. Bruce G. Trigger, *The Children of Aataentsic I: A History of the Huron People to 1660*, 12.

21. "The Significance of the Frontier in American History" has been reprinted many times; see George Rogers Taylor, ed., *The Turner Thesis Concerning the Role of the Frontier in American History*.

22. Francis Jennings, "A Growing Partnership: Historians, Anthropologists and American Indian History," *Ethnohistory* 29 (1982): 27. For a thorough critique of the frontier thesis, see Patricia Nelson Limerick, *The Legacy of Conquest: The Unbroken Past of the American West*, 17–32.

23. Robin F. Wells, "Frontier Systems as a Sociocultural Type," *Papers in Anthropology* 14 (Spring 1973): 6.

24. Jack D. Forbes, "Frontiers in American History and the Role of the Frontier Historian," *Ethnohistory* 15 (Spring 1968): 207.

25. Leonard Thompson and Howard Lamar, "Comparative Frontier History," in *The Frontier in History: North America and Southern Africa Compared*, ed. Howard Lamar and Leonard Thompson, 7. Thompson and Lamar argue that a zone closes with the end of the frontier phase. But this does not result in a static relationship developing between ethnic groups. Instead, a "new structural situation has been created. . . . Subsequent relationships are relations of ethnicity and class within a single society, not a frontier relationship between different societies" (p. 10).

26. Walker D. Wyman and Clifton B. Kroeber, "Introduction," in Walker D. Wyman and Clifton B. Kroeber, eds., *The Frontier in Perspective*, xiii.

27. Alfonso Ortiz, "Indian/White Relations: A View from the Other Side of the 'Frontier,' " in Frederick E. Hoxie, ed., *Indians in American History: An Introduction*, 9.

28. Bruce G. Trigger, "Ethnohistory: Problems and Prospects," *Ethnohistory* 29 (1982): 9.

29. Ibid., 15.

30. For a discussion of why the activities of whites should be deemphasized, see Robert F. Berkhofer, Jr., "The Political Context of a New Indian History," *Pacific Historical Review* 15 (August 1971): 357–82; and Calvin Martin, ed., *The American Indian and the Problem of History*.

31. Trigger, *Children of Aataentsic I*, 26.

32. Dening, *Islands and Beaches*, 43.

CHAPTER 2

1. Anna H. Gayton and Stanley S. Newman, "Yokuts and Western Mono Myths," *Anthropological Records* 5 (October 1940): 28.

2. William L. Preston, *Vanishing Landscapes: Land and Life in the Tulare Lake Basin*, 2.

3. Ibid., 2–3.

4. Gayton and Newman, "Yokuts," 28.

5. Joseph L. Chartkoff and Kerry Kona Chartkoff, *The Archaeology of California*, 37–38.

6. Ibid., 39–40.

7. Ibid., 68.

8. Gayton and Newman, "Yokuts," 28.

9. Chartkoff and Chartkoff, *Archaeology of California*, 75.

10. Ibid., 117.

11. Ibid.

12. Ibid., 120.

13. Ibid., 168–69.

14. Ibid., 186–93.

15. Ibid., 120–21.

16. William F. Shipley, "Native Languages of California," in *Handbook of North American Indians*, ed. William C. Sturtevant, vol. 8, *California*, ed. Robert F. Heizer, 81.

17. Robert F. Heizer and Albert B. Elsasser, *The Natural World of the California Indians*, 19.

18. See Mark Q. Sutton, "Some Aspects of Kitanemuk Prehistory," *Journal of California and Great Basin Anthropology* 2 (Winter 1980): 214–25.

19. James H. Carson, *Recollections of the California Mines*, 110.

20. *San Francisco Picayune*, November 15, 1851.

21. Ralph L. Beals and Joseph A. Hester, Jr., "A New Ecological Typology of the California Indians," in *Men and Cultures*, ed. Anthony F. C. Wallace, 414–17. This typology was adopted by Heizer and Elsasser in *Natural World*, 82–83.

22. Martin A. Baumhoff, "Ecological Determinants of Aboriginal California Populations," *University of California Publications in American Archaeology and Ethnology* 49 (May 1963): 162–65.

23. William J. Wallace, "Southern Valley Yokuts," in *Handbook of North American Indians*, ed. William Sturtevant, vol. 8, *California*, ed. Robert F. Heizer, 450.

24. Baumhoff, "Ecological Determinants," 163.

25. Ibid., 165.

26. Ibid., 165–66.

27. Ibid., 166–67.

28. Heizer and Elsasser, *Natural World*, 93.

29. Ibid.

30. Ibid., 100.

31. George W. Stewart, "The Yokut Indians of the Kaweah Region," *Sierra Club Bulletin* 12 (1927): 398.

32. *San Francisco Picayune*, November 15, 1851.

33. Stewart, "Yokut Indians," 393.

34. José Longinos Martínez, *California in 1792: The Expedition of José Longinos Martínez*, trans. Lesley Byrd Simpson, 33–34.

35. Jan Timbrook, "Virtuous Herbs: Plants in Chumash Medicine," *Journal of Ethnobiology* 7 (Winter 1987): 173.

36. Richard B. Applegate, "The Datura Cult among the Chumash," *Journal of California Anthropology* 2 (Summer 1975): 8–11. See also Travis Hudson and

Thomas Blackburn, "The Integration of Myth and Ritual in South-Central California: The 'Northern Complex,' " *Journal of California Anthropology* 5 (Winter 1978): 225–50; and Timbrook, "Virtuous Herbs," 174–75.

37. See Henry T. Lewis, *Patterns of Indian Burning in California: Ecology and Ethnohistory;* and Jan Timbrook, John R. Johnson, and David D. Earle, "Vegetation Burning by the Chumash," *Journal of California and Great Basin Anthropology* 4 (Winter 1982): 163–86.

38. Martínez, *California in 1792,* 51.

39. Stewart, "Yokut Indians," 397.

40. Stephen Powers, *Tribes of California,* 370.

41. Francisco Garcés, *On the Trail of a Spanish Pioneer: The Diary and Itinerary of Francisco Garcés in his Travels through Sonora, Arizona, and California, 1775–1776,* vol. 1, trans. and ed. Elliott Coues, 284.

42. Heizer and Elsasser, *Natural World,* 45.

43. Sherburne F. Cook, *The Population of the California Indians, 1769–1970,* 43.

44. [Juan Jose Warner], "Reminiscences of Early Life in California," unidentified newspaper article in Missions of Alta California, Benjamin Hayes Collection, C-C 21, pt. 1, Bancroft Library, Berkeley, Calif.

45. Sherburne F. Cook puts the figure at 83,820. See "The Aboriginal Population of the San Joaquin Valley, California," *Anthropological Records* 16 (July 1955): 70.

46. Walter Goldschmidt, "Social Organization in Native California and the Origin of Clans," *American Anthropologist* 50 (July–September 1948): 444–56. This theory is supported by Baumhoff in "Ecological Determinants," 228. For a more recent theoretical discussion of social organization, see P. H. Kunkel, "The Pomo Kin Group and the Political Unit in Aboriginal California," *Journal of California Anthropology* 1 (Spring 1974): 7–18.

47. Baumhoff, "Ecological Determinants," 228–29.

48. Edward Winslow Gifford, "Miwok Lineages and the Political Unit in Aboriginal California," *American Anthropologist* 28 (April 1926): 389–90.

49. Ibid., 390–91.

50. James A. Bennyhoff, *Ethnogeography of the Plains Miwok,* 15.

51. Anna H. Gayton, "Yokuts and Western Mono Social Organization," *American Anthropologist* 47 (July–September 1945): 423–25.

52. Ibid., 417–18. See also Powers, *Tribes of California,* 370–71.

53. Anna H. Gayton, "Yokuts-Mono Chiefs and Shamans," *University of California Publications in American Archaeology and Ethnology* 24 (October 1930): 388–89.

54. Stewart, "Yokut Indians," 393.

55. Antonio Ripoll, Statement to Daniel Hill, unidentified newspaper article in Indians of Santa Barbara, Benjamin Hayes Scrapbooks, vol. 39, Bancroft Library, Berkeley, Calif. See also Fernando Librado, *Breath of Sun: Life in Early California as Told by a Chumash Indian, Fernando Librado, to John P. Harrington,* ed. Travis Hudson, 4.

56. James T. Davis, *Trade Routes and Economic Exchange among the Indians of California,* 28.

57. Garcés, *On the Trail,* 278.
58. Davis, *Trade Routes,* 28.
59. Stewart, "Yokut Indians," 391.
60. Julian H. Steward, "Ethnography of the Owens Valley Paiute," *University of California Publications in American Archaeology and Ethnology* 33 (September 1933): 257–58.
61. Stewart, "Yokut Indians," 389.
62. Davis, *Trade Routes,* 31–32.
63. L. L. Sample, "Trade and Trails in Aboriginal California," *Reports of the University of California Archaeological Survey,* no. 8 (September 1950): 4.
64. Martínez, *California in 1792,* 50.
65. Steven R. James and Suzanne Graziani, "California Indian Warfare," *Contributions of the University of California Archaeological Research Facility,* no. 23 (March 1975): 95–97.
66. Stephen Bowers, "The Santa Barbara Indians," 1879, MS 532, Southwest Museum Library, Los Angeles, Calif.

CHAPTER 3

1. The establishment of Spanish institutions in California is thoroughly traced in Hubert Howe Bancroft, *History of California,* vol. 1. *1542–1800.*
2. The definitive, although biased, work on the missions is Zephyrin Engelhardt, *Missions and Missionaries of California,* 4 vols. For an in-depth discussion of Franciscan ideology, see Ramón A. Gutiérrez, *When Jesus Came, The Corn Mothers Went Away: Marriage, Sexuality, and Power in New Mexico, 1500–1846,* 66–94.
3. For a discussion of Spanish colonizing policy, see Daniel Garr, "Planning, Politics and Plunder: The Missions and Indian Pueblos of Hispanic California," *Southern California Quarterly* 54 (Winter 1972): 291–312. See also Francis F. Guest, "Junípero Serra and His Approach to the Indians," *Southern California Quarterly* 67 (Fall 1985): 223–61.
4. See Bancroft and Engelhardt for the details of the founding of the missions and presidios.
5. Herbert Eugene Bolton, "In the South San Joaquin Ahead of Garcés," *Quarterly of the Southern California Historical Society* 10 (September 1931): 211.
6. Pedro Fages, "Fages's Note to his Diary of 1772," in ibid., 218–19.
7. Juan Crespí, "Diary Kept during the Exploration That Was Made to the Harbor of Our Father San Francisco," in Herbert Eugene Bolton, *Fray Juan Crespí: Missionary Explorer on the Pacific Coast, 1769–1774,* 279, 293.
8. Ibid., 293–95.
9. Ibid., 295–98.
10. Pedro Font, *Font's Complete Diary: A Chronicle of the Founding of San Francisco,* trans. and ed. Herbert Eugene Bolton, 365.
11. Ibid., 366–67.
12. Ibid., 367–68.
13. Ibid., 372.

14. Ibid., 376.

15. Ibid., 383–84.

16. Donald Colgett Cutter, "Spanish Exploration of California's Central Valley," (Ph.D. diss., University of California, Berkeley, 1950), 23.

17. Ibid., 24–28.

18. Francisco Garcés, *On the Trail of a Spanish Pioneer: The Diary and Itinerary of Francisco Garcés in his Travels through Sonora, Arizona, and California, 1775–1776*, vol. 1, trans. and ed. Elliott Coues, 272–74.

19. Juan Bautista de Anza, "Anza's Diary of the Second Anza Expedition, 1775–1776," in *Anza's California Expeditions*, vol. 3, *The San Francisco Colony, Diaries of Anza, Font, and Eixarch, and Narratives of Palou and Moraga*, trans. and ed. Herbert Eugene Bolton, 1–3.

20. Bancroft, *History of California*, vol. 1, 269.

21. Garcés, *On the Trail*, 302–303.

22. Ibid., 275–77.

23. Ibid., 277–78.

24. Ibid., 278–82.

25. Ibid., 283–87.

26. Ibid., 288.

27. Ibid., 292–95.

28. Ibid., 297–300.

29. Ibid., 302–303.

CHAPTER 4

1. For a detailed account of the founding of these institutions, see Hubert Howe Bancroft, *History of California*, vol. 1, *1542–1800*.

2. Felipe de Goycochea to Pedro Fages, Santa Bárbara, December 14, 1790, in dossier regarding the killing of two soldiers by gentile Indians (1790 and 1791), trans. Maureen Campión de Necochea, Archivo General de la Nacion-Californias, vol. 46, Mexico City, transcript on file in U.S. Forest Service, Goleta, Calif.

3. Goycochea to Fages, Santa Bárbara, September 2, 1790, in ibid.

4. Ibid.

5. Goycochea to Fages, December 14, 1790, in ibid.

6. Señor Auditor Gava to Gen. Pedro de Neva, Chihuahua, April 23, 1792, in ibid.

7. Goycochea to Fages, September 2, 1790, in ibid.

8. Ibid.

9. Ibid.

10. Gava to Neva, April 23, 1792, in ibid.

11. Goycochea to Fages, Santa Bárbara, October 9, 1790, in ibid.

12. Goycochea to Fages, December 14, 1790, in ibid.

13. José Joaquín de Arrillaga to Gen. Pedro de Neva, Loreto, September 20, 1792, in ibid.

14. Marcos Briones to Hermenegildo Sal, San Luís Obispo, January 8, 1797,

in Sherburne F. Cook, trans. and ed., "Colonial Expeditions to the Interior of California: Central Valley, 1800–1820," *Anthropological Records* 16 (May 1960): 241.

15. Briones to Sal, San Luís Obispo, February 8, 1797, in ibid.

16. Briones to Sal, San Luís Obispo, January 14, 1797, in ibid.

17. Briones to Sal, February 8, 1797, in ibid.

18. Quoted in Sherburne F. Cook, "The Aboriginal Population of Alameda and Contra Costa Counties, California," *Anthropological Records* 16 (June 1957): 142.

19. Ibid., 142–43.

20. Regarding the origin of these institutions, see Bancroft, *History of California*, vol. 1.

21. J. N. Bowman, "The Resident Neophytes (*Existentes*) of the California Missions 1769–1834," *Historical Society of Southern California Quarterly* 40 (June 1958): 145–46.

22. Indian population decline is discussed by Sherburne F. Cook, "The Indian versus the Spanish Mission," in *The Conflict between the California Indian and White Civilization*, 3–34.

23. José de la Guerra to José Joaquín de Arrillaga, Monterey, January 29, 1804, in Cook, "Colonial Expeditions," 243.

24. Juan Martín to José Señan, San Miguel, April 26, 1815, ibid., 243.

25. Quoted in Zephyrin Engelhardt, *San Miguel, Arcangel: The Mission on the Highway*, 10.

26. Donald Colgett Cutter, "Spanish Exploration of California's Central Valley" (Ph.D. diss., University of California, Berkeley, 1950), 90–91.

27. Ibid., 91–92.

28. José María de Zalvidea, Report, July 19 to August 14, 1806, in Cook, "Colonial Expeditions," 245.

29. Because horses had multiplied so rapidly in parts of the coastal zone, Spaniards may have killed some thirty thousand in 1812. See Ross Cox, *The Columbia River*, 96n.

30. Zalvidea, Report, 245.

31. Ibid., 245–46.

32. Ibid., 246.

33. Ibid., 246–47.

34. Pedro Muñoz, Diary, September 21 to November 2, 1806, in Cook, "Colonial Expeditions," 248.

35. Ibid.

36. Ibid., 248–49.

37. Ibid., 249–50.

38. Ibid.

39. Ibid., 250.

40. Ibid.

41. Ibid.

42. Ibid.

43. Ibid., 251.

44. Ibid.

45. Ibid., 252.

46. Ibid., 252–53.

47. Felipe Santiago García, Account of Moraga's 1807 Expedition, in ibid., 255.

48. José Palomares, Report on the Expedition to the Tulares, October 25 to November 4, 1808, in ibid., 256.

49. Ibid., 256–57.

50. Ibid., 256–57.

51. José Viader, Report, August 15–28, 1810, in ibid., 258.

52. Ibid., 258–59.

53. Ibid., 259.

54. José Viader, Report, October 19–27, 1810, in ibid., 259. For an account of Indian auxilaries in the service of Spain in another area of the Southwest, see Oakah Jones, *Pueblo Warriors and Spanish Conquest.*

55. Viader, Report, October 19–27, 1810, in Cook, "Colonial Expeditions," 260.

56. Fr. Ramón Abella, Diary, October 15–31, 1811, in ibid., 260–65.

57. Ibid.

58. José Arguëllo to Gov. José Joaquin de Arrillaga, San Francisco, October 31, 1813, in ibid., 265.

59. Ibid., 265–66.

60. Narciso Duran, "Expedition on the Sacramento and San Joaquin Rivers in 1817: Diary of Fray Narciso Duran," ed. Charles Edward Chapman, *Publications of the Academy of Pacific Coast History* 2 (December 1911): 343.

61. Ibid., 345–49.

62. Juan Ortega, Diary, November 4–15, 1815, in Cook, "Colonial Expeditions," 267.

63. Ibid.

64. Ibid.

65. Ibid., 268.

66. José Dolores Pico, Diary, November 3 to December 3, 1815, in ibid., 268. Sherburne Cook claims that Cheneche and Nupchenche, along with Tape and Malin, were distinct villages within a large Nopchinchi political unit. See Sherburne F. Cook, "The Aboriginal Population of the San Joaquin Valley, California," *Anthropological Records* 16 (July 1955): 51–52.

67. Pico, Diary, in Cook, "Colonial Expeditions," 268–69.

68. Ibid., 269.

69. Ibid.

70. Ibid., 270–71.

71. Fr. Antonio Jaime to Gov. Pablo Vicente de Solá, La Soledad, March 30, 1816, in ibid., 273.

72. Fr. Luís Antonio Martínez to Fr. Vicente Francisco de Sarría, San Luís Obispo, May 29, 1816, in ibid., 271–72.

73. Fr. Mariano Payeras to Capt. José de la Guerra, La Purísima, December 24, 1817, in "Writings of Father Mariano Payeras," trans. and ed. Donald Colgett Cutter, unpublished manuscript.

74. Fr. Mariano Payeras, List of Neophytes Who Have Fled Mission La Purísima, 1818, in ibid.

75. Fr. Mariano Payeras to Capt. José de la Guerra, May 4, 1818, in ibid.

76. Fr. Juan Cabot to Capt. José de la Guerra, San Miguel, May 23, 1818, in Cook, "Colonial Expeditions," 280.

77. Joseph A. Thompson, *El Gran Capitan, Jose de la Guerra: A Historical Biographical Study*, 55–56.

78. Fr. Mariano Payeras to Capt. José de la Guerra, La Purísima, September 29, 1818, in Cutter, "Writings of Payeras."

79. Fr. Mariano Payeras to Fr. Guardia Baldomero López, La Soledad, July 4, 1819, in ibid.

80. Quoted in Irving Berdine Richman, *California under Spain and Mexico, 1535–1847*, 221.

81. Fr. Mariano Payeras to Gov. Pablo Vicente de Solá, n.p., September 20, 1819, quoted in Zephyrin Engelhardt, *The Missions and Missionaries of California*, vol. 3, 33–34.

82. Fr. Narciso Duran to Gov. Pablo Vicente de Solá, San José, June 2, 1819, in Sherburne F. Cook, ed., "Expeditions to the Interior of California: Central Valley, 1820–1840," *Anthropological Records* 20 (February 1962): 166.

83. Fr. Narciso Duran to Gov. Pablo Vicente de Solá, San José, October 28, 1819, in ibid.

84. José María Estudillo, "Estudillo among the Yokuts: 1819," trans. and ed. Anna H. Gayton, in *Essays in Anthropology*, ed. Robert H. Lowie, 68-71.

85. C. Hart Merriam, "California Mission Baptismal Records," in *Studies of California Indians*, 211.

86. Estudillo, "Estudillo among the Yokuts," 70–72.

87. Ibid., 72–76.

88. Ibid., 76–80.

89. Ibid., 81–85.

CHAPTER 5

1. Zephyrin Engelhardt, *The Missions and Missionaries of California*, vol. 3, 195–96. The causes of the uprising are discussed by James A. Sandos, "Levantamiento!: The 1824 Chumash Uprising Reconsidered," *Southern California Quarterly* 67 (Summer 1985): 109–33; and by Gary B. Coombs, "With What God Will Provide: A Reexamination of the Chumash Revolt of 1824," *Noticias* 26 (Summer 1980): 21–29.

2. Hubert Howe Bancroft, *History of California*, vol. 2, *1801–1824*, 529.

3. Ibid., 532. Two Californios claimed that José Pacomio masterminded the uprising and sought the elimination of all white men in California. See Juan Bautista Alvarado, "History of California," vol. 2, 1824–1834, trans. Earl R. Hewitt, C-D 2, pp. 42–52; and Mariano Guadalupe Vallejo, "Historical and Personal Memoirs Relating to Alta California," vol. 1, trans. Earl R. Hewitt, C-D 18, pp. 276–91, both in Bancroft Library, Berkeley, Calif. Bancroft disputes these claims. See his *History of California*, vol. 2, 527n.

4. Engelhardt, Missions, vol. 3, 196.

5. Fr. Antonio Ripoll, "Fray Antonio Ripoll's Description of the Chumash Revolt at Santa Barbara in 1824," trans. and ed. Maynard Geiger, Southern California Quarterly, 52 (December 1970): 347–48. For an account of the alcaldes, see George Harwood Phillips, "The Alcaldes: Indian Leadership in the Spanish Missions of California," in The Struggle for Political Autonomy: Papers and Comments from the Second Newberry Library Conference on Themes in American Indian History, 83–89.

6. Agustias de la Guerra Ord, Occurrences in Hispanic California, trans. and ed. Francis Price and William H. Ellison, 9–10.

7. Ripoll, "Fray Antonio Ripoll," 350.

8. Ibid., 350–52.

9. Ibid., 352.

10. John R. Johnson, "Indian History in the Santa Barbara Back Country," Los Padres Notes 3 (Spring 1984): 10.

11. Fr. Juan Cabot to Gov. Luís Arguëllo, February 28, 1824, in Sherburne F. Cook, ed., "Expeditions to the Interior of California: Central Valley, 1820–1840," Anthropological Records 20 (February 1962): 152.

12. Ibid.

13. Engelhardt, Missions, vol. 3, 203.

14. José Rafael Gonzales, "Experiencias de un Soldado de California," in Cook, "Expeditions," 157.

15. Interrogatorio, Santa Bárbara, June 1, 1824, in ibid., 153–54.

16. Ripoll, "Fray Antonio Ripoll," 349.

17. Interrogatorio, Santa Bárbara, June 1, 1824, in Cook, "Expeditions," 153–154.

18. Ripoll, "Fray Antonio Ripoll," 354.

19. Fr. Blas Ordaz to Gov. Luís Arguëllo, Mission Santa Inés, March 26, 1824, Doc. 2593, Archives of the Archdiocese of San Francisco, photostat copy on file at Mission Santa Barbara Archives, Santa Barbara, Calif.

20. Gov. Luís Argüello to Capt. José de la Guerra, Monterey, May 5, 1824, in Cook, "Expeditions," 152.

21. Fr. Luís Antonio Martínez to Gov. Luís Argüello, San Luís Obispo, April 30, 1824, Doc. 2609, Archives of the Archdiocese of San Francisco, photostat copy on file at Mission Santa Barbara Archives, Santa Barbara, Calif.

22. Zenas Leonard, Narrative of the Adventures of Zenas Leonard, ed. Milo Milton Quaife, 199–200.

23. Capt. Pablo de la Portilla, Report of the Expedition to the Tulares in Pursuit of the Rebel Mission Indians, Santa Bárbara, June 27, 1824, in Cook, "Expeditions," 155.

24. Ibid.

25. Gonzales, "Experiences," in ibid., 157.

26. Portilla, Report, in ibid., 155.

27. Ibid., 155–56.

28. Ibid., 156.

29. Pablo de la Portilla to Gov. Luís Argüello, Santa Bárbara, June 28, 1824, in ibid., 156.

30. Bancroft, *History of California,* vol. 2, 532.

31. Ibid., 536–37.

32. Robert F. Heizer, "The Direct-Historical Approach in California Archaeology," *American Antiquity* 7 (October 1941): 110.

33. Bancroft, *History of California,* vol. 2, 536–37, 537n. Between 1823 and 1825 the neophyte population of La Purísima declined from 722 to 532. Fugitivism may account for much of the loss. During the same period, Santa Bárbara and Santa Inés lost only 77 and 64 persons, respectively. See J. N. Bowman, "The Resident Neophytes (Existentes) of the California Missions, 1769–1834," *Southern California Quarterly* 40 (June 1958): 147.

34. Sergt. José Dolores Pico, Report, December 27, 1825, to January 31, 1826, in Cook, "Expeditions," 181.

35. Ibid., 181–82.

36. Ibid., 182.

37. Ibid.

38. Ibid., 183.

39. Ibid.

40. Ibid., 183–84.

41. Ibid., 184. Apparently Bubal had been moved from the west shore to Atwell's Island for security reasons. See Sherburne F. Cook, "The Aboriginal Population of the San Joaquin Valley, California," *Anthropological Records* 16 (July 1955): 43–44.

42. Capt. F. W. Beechey, *Narrative of a Voyage to the Pacific and Beering's Strait,* vol. 2, 24–25.

43. Lieut. George Peard, *To the Pacific and Arctic with Beechey: The Journal of Lieutenant George Peard of H.M.S. Blossom, 1825–1828,* ed. Barry M. Gough, 175.

44. Beechey, *Narrative,* vol. 2, 26–27.

45. Peard, *To the Pacific,* 175.

46. Hubert Howe Bancroft, *History of California,* vol. 3, *1825–1840,* 156n.

47. Quoted in Francis Florence McCarthy, *The History of Mission San Jose California, 1797–1835,* 187.

48. Ibid., 187–88. See also Lieut. Ignacio Martínez to Gov. José María Echeandía, San José, May 21, 1827, Doc. 3047, Archives of the Archdiocese of San Francisco, photostat copy on file at Mission Santa Barbara Archives, Santa Barbara, Calif.

49. Jedediah S. Smith, *The Southwest Expedition of Jedediah S. Smith: His Personal Account of the Journey to California, 1826–1827,* ed. George R. Brooks, 133–40.

50. Ibid., 146.

51. Ibid., 153–54.

52. Ibid., 156.

53. Dale L. Morgan, *Jedediah Smith and the Opening of the West,* 208.

54. Quoted in ibid., 208–209.

55. Lieut. Ignacio Martínez to Gov. José María Echeandía, San José, May 21, 1827, Doc. 3048, Archives of the Archdiocese of San Francisco, photostat copy on file at Mission Santa Barbara Archives, Santa Barbara, Calif.

56. Maurice S. Sullivan, *The Travels of Jedediah Smith: A Documentary Outline, Including the Journal of the Great American Pathfinder*, 35–36.

57. Morgan, *Jedediah Smith*, 209. The letter is published in Appendix A, p. 333.

58. Ibid., 209–10.

59. David J. Weber, *The Californios versus Jedediah Smith, 1826–1827: A New Cache of Documents*, 27–28.

60. Luís Antonio Argüello to Harrison G. Rogers, Mission San José, May 31, 1827, quoted in ibid., 28–29.

61. Harrison G. Rogers to Capt. Luís Antonio Argüello, n.p., June 3, 1827, quoted in ibid., 32–34.

62. Luís Antonio Argüello to Gov. José María Echeandía, quoted in ibid., 35–36.

63. Morgan, *Jedediah Smith*, 236–55.

64. Sullivan, *The Travels*, 45.

65. William Robert Garner, *Letters from California, 1846–1847*, ed. Donald Munro Craig, 103.

66. Sebastian Rodríguez, Diary, April 20 to May 6, 1828, in Cook, "Expeditions," 184–85.

67. Ibid., 185. The following year, Californios again attacked the Hoyima, killing forty men and eight women. See Gov. José María Echeandía to the Minister of War, San Diego, May 22, 1829, in Cook, "Expeditions," 187.

68. Rodríguez, Diary, 185.

69. Sebastian Rodríguez, Report, May 26 to June 9, 1828, in Cook, "Expeditions," 185–86.

70. Ibid., 186.

71. Ibid.

72. Ibid.

73. Fr. Narciso Duran to Ignacio Martínez, San José, November 9, 1828, in ibid., 169.

74. Quoted in Marion Lydia Lothrop, "The Indian Campaigns of General M. G. Vallejo, Defender of the Northern Frontier of California," *Quarterly of the Society of California Pioneers* 9 (September 1932): 165n.

75. Antonio María Osio, "Historia de California," in Cook, ed., "Expeditions," 169.

76. Duran to Martínez, November 9, 1828, in ibid., 169.

77. Osio, "Historia," in ibid., 170.

78. Fr. Narciso Duran to Ignacio Martínez, San José, March 1, 1829, in ibid., 169.

79. José Sánchez, Diary, May 1–10, 1829, in ibid., 173.

80. Ibid., 174.

81. Ibid.

82. Juan Bojorques, "Recuerdos sobre la Historia de California," in ibid., 172.

83. Ignacio Martínez to Mariano Guadalupe Vallejo, San Francisco, May 16, 1829, in ibid., 175–76.

84. Joaquin Piña, Diary, May 26 to June 1, in ibid., 177–78.

85. Ibid., 178–79.

86. Ibid., 179.

87. Ibid.

88. Mariano Guadalupe Vallejo to Commandant Ignacio Martínez, San José, June 4, 1829, in ibid., 176.

89. Gov. José María Echeandía to Commandant Ignacio Martínez, San Diego, August 7, 1829, in ibid., 180.

90. Commandant Ignacio Martínez, Report of the Fiscal, San Francisco, October 31, 1829, in ibid., 180.

91. Lothrop, "The Indian Campaigns," 170.

92. McCarthy, Mission San Jose, 217.

93. José Berreyesa, Statement, San José, July 15, 1830, in Cook, "Expeditions," 180.

94. Entry No. 6513, December 31, 1829, Mission Santa Clara Register of Burials, June 22, 1777–December 22, 1866, Orradre Library, University of Santa Clara, Santa Clara, Calif.

CHAPTER 6

1. Antonio Armijo, "Diary," in LeRoy R. Hafen and Ann W. Hafen, Old Spanish Trail: Santa Fe to Los Angeles, 159–65.

2. William Robert Garner, Letters from California, 1846–1847, ed. Donald Munro Craig, 103.

3. Armijo, "Diary," 165; Joseph J. Hill, "The Old Spanish Trail: A Study of Spanish and Mexican Trade and Exploration Northwest from New Mexico to the Great Basin and California," Hispanic American Historical Review 4 (August 1921): 464–66.

4. Juan José Warner, Benjamin Hayes, and J. P. Widney, An Historical Sketch of Los Angeles County, California, 34. Warner wrote chapter 1 which covers the years 1771 to 1847.

5. Ibid., 33.

6. José Berreyesa, Statement, San José, July 15, 1830, in Sherburne F. Cook, trans. and ed., "Expeditions to the Interior of California: Central Valley, 1820–1840," Anthropological Records 20 (February 1962): 187. Huyunhepa is mentioned in a list of chiefs compiled on October 1, 1828; see Documentos para la Historia de California, Archivo Particular de Sr Don Mariano Guadalupe Vallejo, C-B 14, no. 251, Bancroft Library, Berkeley, Calif.

7. Berreyesa, Statement, in Cook, "Expeditions," 187.

8. Kit Carson, Kit Carson's Autobiography, ed. Milo Milton Quaife, 15–16.

9. Joseph J. Hill, "Ewing Young in the Fur Trade of the Far Southwest, 1824–1834," Quarterly of the Oregon Historical Society 24 (March 1923): 25–26.

10. Carson, Autobiography, 16–17.

11. Hill, "The Old Spanish Trail," 468.

12. Warner, Hayes, and Widney, *Historical Sketch,* 33. For a history and analysis of the wool industry in New Mexico, see Nora Fisher, ed., *Spanish Textile Traditions of New Mexico and Colorado.*

13. Juan José Warner, "Reminiscences of Early California from 1831 to 1846," *Annual Publications of the Historical Society of Southern California* 7 (1907–1908): 178–79.

14. Zenas Leonard, *Narrative of the Adventures of Zenas Leonard,* ed. Milo Milton Quaife, 170.

15. M. Duflot de Mofras, *Duflot de Mofras' Travels on the Pacific Coast,* vol. 1, trans. and ed. Marguerite Eyer Wilbur, 254.

16. Gov. Manuel Victoria to Commanders at Santa Barbara and San Diego, Monterey, March 10, 1831, in Cook, "Expeditions," 162.

17. Garner, *Letters,* 103.

18. Eleanor Lawrence, "Mexican Trade between Santa Fe and Los Angeles, 1830–1848," *California Historical Society Quarterly* 10 (March 1931): 29.

19. Fr. Vicente Pasqual Oliva to Gov. José Figueroa, San Gabriel, February 17, 1833, in Cook, "Expeditions," 162–63.

20. *Honolulu Sandwich Island Gazette and Journal of Commerce,* December 2, 1837.

21. Lawrence, "Mexican Trade," 29–30.

22. Eleanor Lawrence, "The Old Spanish Trail from Santa Fe to Los Angeles" (M.A. thesis, University of California, Berkeley, 1930), 73–74. See also Oliva to Figueroa in Cook, "Expeditions," 162–63.

23. Gov. José Figueroa to Commandant of Santa Bárbara, February 26, 1833, appendix in Lawrence, "Old Spanish Trail," 133.

24. Ibid., 134–35.

25. Lawrence, "Old Spanish Trail," 75.

26. Gov. José Figueroa to Minister of War and Navy, Monterey, April 12, 1833, in Cook, "Expeditions," 188.

27. John Work, *Fur Brigade to Bonaventura: John Work's California Expedition of 1832–33 for the Hudson's Bay Company,* ed. Alice Bay Maloney, 42–43.

28. Ibid., 64.

29. Ibid., 65.

30. Ibid., 66–67.

31. Ibid., 68.

32. Leonard, *Narrative,* 142–43.

33. Ibid., 196, 197.

34. Ibid., 185.

35. Thomas Beall, "Recollections of Wm. Craig," *Lewiston Morning Tribune,* March 3, 1918.

36. Alcalde of San José to Political Chief of the Territory, San José, November 10, 1833, in Cook, "Expeditions," 188.

37. Gov. José Figueroa, Order and decree concerning robbers of horses and other livestock, Monterey, November 18, 1833, in ibid., 188–89.

38. Ibid.

39. Leonard, *Narrative,* 189–91.

40. Warner, "Reminiscences of Early California," 188.

41. Hall J. Kelley, *Hall J. Kelley on Oregon,* ed. Fred Wilbur Powell, 351–52.
42. Ibid., 352–53.
43. Kenneth L. Holmes, *Ewing Young: Master Trapper,* 97.
44. Gov. José Figueroa to John McLoughlin, n.p., n.d., quoted in ibid., 106–107.
45. Lawrence, "Mexican Trade," 30–31.
46. Robert E. Elwell to Jim _____, Santa Bárbara, February 4, 1834, Documentos Para la Historía de California, C-B 31, pt. 1, Bancroft Library, Berkeley, Calif.
47. Lawrence, "Mexican Trade," 30–31.

CHAPTER 7

1. For a detailed examination of the disease, see Sherburne F. Cook, "The Epidemic of 1830–1833 in California and Oregon," *University of California Publications in American Anthropology and Ethnology* 43 (1955): 303–25.
2. *Los Angeles Star,* August 23, 1874. Warner recounted this experience on two other occasions. See "Reminiscences of Early Life in California," unidentified newspaper article in Missions of Alta California, Benjamin Hayes Collection, C-C 21, pt. 1, Bancroft Library, Berkeley, Calif.; and Frank T. Gilbert, *History of San Joaquin County, California with Illustrations,* 11–12.
3. Zenas Leonard, *Narrative of the Adventures of Zenas Leonard,* ed. Milo Milton Quaife, 197.
4. Cook estimated that twenty thousand died; see his "Epidemic," 322. In light of the large numbers of Indians whites encountered in the Central Valley during the 1830s and 1840s, this figure seems too high.
5. The secularization of the missions is discussed by C. Alan Hutchinson, "The Mexican Government and the Mission Indians of Upper California, 1821–1835," *The Americas* 21 (April 1965): 335–62; Daniel Garr, "Planning, Politics and Plunder: The Missions and Indian Pueblos of Hispanic California," *Southern California Quarterly* 54 (Winter 1972): 291–312; and by George Harwood Phillips, "Indians and the Breakdown of the Spanish Mission System in California," *Ethnohistory* 21 (Fall 1974): 291–302.
6. Garr, "Planning, Politics and Plunder," 299–300.
7. Regarding these options see ibid.; Phillips, "Indians and the Breakdown"; George Harwood Phillips, "Indians in Los Angeles, 1781–1875: Economic Integration, Social Disintegration," *Pacific Historical Review* 49 (August 1980): 427–51; and Sherburne F. Cook, "The American Invasion, 1848–1870," in *The Conflict between the California Indian and White Civilization,* 300–29. Cook made no mention of population recovery, probably because his intent was to "prove" that the interior Indian population was in steep decline by the time of the American takeover. See Cook, "Epidemic," 322. For a study of Indian population persistence, see Albert L. Hurtado, *Indian Survival on the California Frontier.*
8. F. W. Beechey, *Narrative of a Voyage to the Pacific and Beering's Strait,* vol. 2, 19.

9. William Robert Garner, *Letters from California, 1846–1847*, ed. Donald Munro Craig, 171.

10. Leonard, *Narrative,* 200.

11. Ibid., 201.

12. Lieut. N. H. McLean to Maj. H. W. Wessels, Fort Miller, July 12, 1853, Letters Received by the Office of the Adjutant General, 1822–1860 (Main Series), RG 94, Microcopy 567, Roll 483, NA.

13. *Los Angeles Star,* May 7, 1853. For a discussion of post-contact trade relations established between California and other Indians, see Thomas N. Layton, "Traders and Raiders: Aspects of Trans-Basin and California-Plateau Commerce, 1800–1880," *Journal of California and Great Basin Anthropology* 3 (Summer 1981), 124–37.

14. Capt. Francis J. Lippsitt to Lieut. William T. Sherman, Santa Barbara, March 9, 1848, Pacific Division, Records of the 10th Military Department, Letters Received, 1846–1851, RG 98, Microcopy 210, NA.

15. Eugene Upton, "Letter from California," Merced River, June 12, 1850, unidentified newspaper article, Eugene Upton Scrapbook No. 7, California Historical Society Library, San Francisco, Calif.

16. *Daily Alta California,* December 9, 1851.

17. José Francisco Palomares, "Memoria," in Sherburne F. Cook, "Expeditions to the Interior of California: Central Valley, 1820–1840," *Anthropological Records* 20 (February 1962): 202.

18. Brig. Gen. Bennett Riley to Gen. R. Jones, Monterey, October 15, 1949, Pacific Division, Records of the 10th Military Department, Letters Received, 1846–1851, RG 98, Microcopy 210, Roll 1, NA.

19. John Marvin, "Some Account of the Tulare Valley, and the Indians from Fresno River to Tihone Pass," *San Francisco Morning Post,* July 28, 1851.

20. Lieut. George H. Derby to Maj. Edward R. S. Canby, Monterey, July 10, 1850, *Report of the Secretary of War,* U.S. Congress, Senate, 32d Cong., 1st sess., Exec. Doc. 110, 7–11.

21. Robert F. Heizer, ed., *The Eighteen Unratified Treaties of 1851–1852 Between the California Indians and the United States Government,* 26–56, 65–81. It should be noted that some of the signators may have been gentiles who used Spanish names for diplomatic purposes.

22. Robert H. Jackson, "Gentile Recruitment and Population Movement in the San Francisco Bay Area Missions," *Journal of California and Great Basin Anthropology* 6 (1984): 233–35. See also Sherburne F. Cook and Woodrow Borah, *Essays in Population History: Mexico and California,* vol. 3, 194–95.

23. Fr. Marcelino Marquinez to Gov. Pablo Vicente de Solá, Santa Cruz, December 13, 1816, in Sherburne Cook, "Colonial Expeditions to the Interior of California: Central Valley, 1800–1820," *Anthropological Records* 16 (May 1960): 273.

24. Edward Winslow Gifford, "Miwok Lineages and the Political Unit in Aboriginal California," *American Anthropologist* 28 (April 1926): 391–92.

25. Anna H. Gayton, "Yokuts-Mono Chiefs and Shamans," *University of California Publications in American Archaeology and Ethnology* 24 (October 1930): 401–402.

26. Cook, "Expeditions," 207n.

27. A. Duhaut-Cilly, "Duhaut-Cilly's Account of California in the Years 1827–28," trans. Charles Franklin Carter, *Quarterly of the California Historical Society* 8 (December 1929): 313.

28. Sebastian Rodríguez, Report, May 26 to June 9, 1828, in Cook, "Expeditions," 186.

29. Leonard, *Narrative,* 201.

30. Cook, "American Invasion," 322n.

31. Juan Coluco, Deposition, John P. Harrington Papers, 1916–1917, Anthropological Archives, Smithsonian Institution, Washington, D.C. Ditches discovered in 1900 near Tulare Lake may have been built by mission Indians for irrigation purposes; see I. Teilman and W. H. Shafer, *The Historical Story of Irrigation in Fresno and Kings Counties in Central California,* 5–6.

32. Benjamin Butler Harris, *The Gila Trail: The Texas Argonauts and the California Gold Rush,* ed. Richard H. Dillon, 100.

33. Extract of a letter, Tejon Valley, September 22, 1854, *Annual Report of the Commissioner of Indian Affairs,* 1854, 306. For an overview of Indian agriculture in California, see Jack D. Forbes, "Indian Horticulture West and Northwest of the Colorado River," *Journal of the West* 2 (January 1963): 1–14.

34. John Bidwell, *In California before the Gold Rush,* 65–66.

35. Marvin, "Some Account."

36. Upton, "Letter from California."

37. Hans Jørgen Uldall and William Shipley, *Nisenan Texts and Dictionary,* 247, 260, 263.

38. Sylvia M. Broadbent, *The Southern Sierra Miwok Language,* 242, 248, 260, 265, 266.

39. William Shipley, "Spanish Elements in the Indigenous Languages of Central California," *Romance Philology* 16 (August 1962): 17–21.

40. Broadbent, *Southern Sierra Miwok,* 229, 243, 258, 263, 269.

41. Uldall and Shipley, *Nisenan Texts,* 251, 257, 266, 271, 272, 275.

42. Shipley, "Spanish Elements," 17–21.

43. Broadbent, *Southern Sierra Miwok,* 231, 238, 240, 247, 248, 256.

44. Uldall and Shipley, *Nisenan Texts,* 267.

45. Madison S. Beeler, "Noptinte Yokuts," in Jesse Sawyer, ed., *Studies in American Indian Languages,* 35.

46. Broadbent, *Southern Sierra Miwok,* 243.

47. Ibid., 281; Uldall and Shipley, *Nisenan Texts,* 253; Shipley, "Spanish Elements," 17–21.

48. Broadbent, *Southern Sierra Miwok,* 258.

49. Charles Wilkes, *Narrative of the United States Exploring Expedition during the Years 1838, 1839, 1840, 1841, 1842,* vol. 5, 180.

50. Edward D. Townsend, *The California Diary of General E. D. Townsend,* ed. Malcolm Edwards, 129.

51. William Ingraham Kip, *The Early Days of My Episcopate,* 226.

52. Edward Belcher, *Narrative of a Voyage Round the World, performed in Her Majesty's Ship Sulphur during the Years 1836–1842,* vol. 1, 125–26.

53. Edwin Bryant, *What I Saw in California,* 239.

54. Fr. Junípero Serra to Fr. Fermín Francisco de Lasuén, Monterey, January 12, 1780, in *Writings of Junípero Serra*, trans. and ed. Antonine Tibesar, vol. 3, 421.

55. Fr. Antonio Ripoll, "Fray Antonio Ripoll's Description of the Chumash Revolt at Santa Barbara in 1824," trans. and ed. Maynard Geiger, *Southern California Quarterly* 52 (December 1970): 352.

56. G. M. Waseurtz af Sandels, *A Sojourn in California by the King's Orphan, The Travels and Sketches of G. M. Waseurtz af Sandels, a Swedish gentleman who visited California in 1842–1843*, ed. Helen Putnam Van Sicklen, 76–77.

57. T.F.W., "Letters from California," Yerba Buena, June 25, 1846, *Honolulu Friend*, December 1, 1846.

58. Bennett to Jones, October 15, 1849.

59. Marvin, "Some Account."

60. Joseph Warren Revere, *Tour of Duty in California*, 124.

61. Garner, *Letters from California*, 161–63. For another account of how Indians stole horses, see Ella S. Hartnell, "An Indian Ruse," *The Land of Sunshine* 6 (December 1896): 27.

62. Garner, *Letters from California*, 162.

63. Ibid., 163–64.

64. Ibid., 104.

65. James H. Carson, *Recollections of the California Mines*, 104. For other descriptions of the wild horses, see Harris, *Gila Trail*, 102, and Bryant, *What I Saw*, 302. The horse's impact on the environment is briefly discussed in William L. Preston, *Vanishing Landscapes: Land and Life in the Tulare Basin*, 59–60.

66. John A. Sutter, "Personal Reminiscences of General John Augustus Sutter," 1876, C-D 14, 126, Bancroft Library, Berkeley, Calif.

67. Garner, *Letters from California*, 104.

68. Carson, *Recollections*, 104–105.

69. Leonard, *Narrative*, 191.

70. William Heath Davis, *Seventy-five Years in California*, ed. Douglas S. Watson, 63.

71. Sutter, "Personal Reminiscences," 67.

72. Garner, *Letters from California*, 164.

73. José Berreyesa, Statement, San José, July 15, 1830, in Cook, "Expeditions," 187.

74. For a description of how Indians trapped horses, see John Baker, *San Joaquin Vignettes: The Reminiscences of Captain John Baker*, eds. William Harland Boyd and Glendon J. Rodgers, 41–42.

75. Overton Johnson and William H. Winter, *Route across the Rocky Mountains*, ed. Carl L. Cannon, 115–16.

76. James H. Carson, "Tulare Plains," *San Joaquin Republican*, March 17, 1852.

77. Bidwell, *In California*, 48.

78. John Charles Frémont, *Memoirs of My Life*, vol. 1, 445.

79. *San Francisco California Star*, April 10, 1847. For discussion of the dietary changes Indians underwent after white contact, see Sherburne F. Cook,

"The Mechanism and Extent of Dietary Adaptation Among Certain Groups of California and Nevada Indians," in *Conflict*, 447–507.

CHAPTER 8

1. The emergence of the rancho system is discussed in W. W. Robinson, *Land in California*, 45–90. See also David Hornbeck, "Land Tenure and Rancho Expansion in Alta California, 1784–1846," *Journal of Historical Geography* 4 (1978): 371–90.

2. Sherburne F. Cook, "The American Invasion, 1848–1870," in *The Conflict between the California Indian and White Civilization*, 304–305.

3. Ibid., 306–308.

4. Salvador Vallejo, "History of California," 1874, C-D 22, 46, Bancroft Library, Berkeley, Calif.

5. *Santa Barbara Gazette*, November 15, 1855.

6. William Robert Garner, *Letters from California 1846–1847*, ed. Donald Munro Craig, 106.

7. Joseph Belden, "Pastoral California through Gringo Eyes," *Touring Topics* 22 (August 1930): 46.

8. Garner, *Letters*, 106.

9. William Heath Davis, *Seventy-five Years in California*, ed. Douglas S. Watson, 36.

10. Cook, "American Invasion," 307–308.

11. For an account of Indians serving as guards, see George Harwood Phillips, *Chiefs and Challengers: Indian Resistance and Cooperation in Southern California*, 47–57.

12. Fr. Narciso Duran, "Notes on the Circular or Bando of Don Jos Mara Echeanda Addressed to the Missionaries of the Four Missions in the South on November 18th, 1832," quoted in Zephyrin Engelhardt, *The Missions and Missionaries of California*, vol. 3, 437.

13. Gov. José Figueroa, Order and decree concerning robbers of horses and other livestock, Monterey, November 18, 1833, in Sherburne F. Cook, "Expeditions to the Interior of California: Central Valley, 1820–1840," *Anthropological Records* 20 (February 1962): 189.

14. Gov. José Figueroa to Alcalde of San José, Monterey, January 24, 1835, in ibid.

15. Quoted in Oscar Osburn Winther, "The Story of San Jose, 1777–1869: California's First Pueblo," *California Historical Society Quarterly* 14 (1935): 23.

16. José Manuel Pinto, et al., to the Ayuntamiento of San José, August 21, 1836, Doc. 3616, Archives of the Archdiocese of San Francisco, photostat copy on file at Mission Santa Barbara Archives, Santa Barbara, Calif.

17. José de Jesús Vallejo to Mariano Guadalupe Vallejo, San José, August 21, 1837, in Cook, "Expeditions," 190.

18. Francisco Arucho to Mariano Guadalupe Vallejo, Valle de San Leandro, August 20, 1837, in ibid., 190.

19. Ignacio Martínez to Mariano Guadalupe Vallejo, San Francisco, September 9, 1837, in ibid., 190.

20. Mariano Guadalupe Vallejo, "Historical and Personal Memoirs Relating to Alta California," vol. 4, trans. Earl R. Hewitt, C-D 21, 117, Bancroft Library, Berkeley, Calif.

21. George D. Lyman, *John Marsh, Pioneer: The Life Story of a Trail-blazer on Six Frontiers,* 206–207, 213.

22. John Marsh, Draft of a Military Proposal, n.p., January 22, 1838, John Marsh Family Papers, C-B 879, Box 1, Bancroft Library, Berkeley, Calif.

23. Lyman, *John Marsh,* 213, 219–20.

24. Vallejo, "Historical and Personal Memoirs," 23.

25. Davis, *Seventy-five Years in California,* 45–46.

26. Lyman, *John Marsh,* 221, 228–29.

27. Ibid., 228–29.

28. Vallejo, "Historical and Personal Memoirs," 22.

29. José de Jesús Vallejo, Statement, San José, August 16, 1838, in Cook, "Expeditions," 191; Engelhardt, *The Missions,* vol. 4, 311–12.

30. José Francisco Palomares, "The Death of Yóscolo," ed. Robert L. Hoover, *Pacific Historical Review* 51 (August 1982): 313–14.

31. Ibid., 314.

32. Capt. Santiago Estrada to Prefect of the First District, San Juan de Castro, July 7, 1839, in Cook, "Expeditions," 191.

33. Mariano Guadalupe Vallejo to José Castro, July 7, 1839, Documentos para la Historia de California, Archivo Particular de Sr. Don Mariano Guadalupe Vallejo, C-B 7, 330–330b, Bancroft Library, Berkeley, Calif.

34. Prado Mesa to Mariano Guadalupe Vallejo, San José, August 1, 1839, in Cook, "Expeditions," 191.

35. José de Jesús Vallejo to Mariano Guadalupe Vallejo, San José, December 10, 1839, in ibid., 191.

36. Gov. Juan Bautista Alvarado to Mariano Guadalupe Vallejo, Monterey, December 13, 1839, in ibid., 191.

37. Davis, *Seventy-five Years,* 63–64. Davis's claim that the raid took place in 1839 is incorrect.

38. Juan José Vallejo to Mariano Guadalupe Vallejo, San José, January 15, 1840, in Cook, "Expeditions," 192.

39. Gov. Juan B. Alvarado, Decree, San Juan de Castro, July 4, 1840, in ibid., 192. This plan resembles that proposed by John Marsh in January 1838.

40. Manuel Jimeno to Secretary of Communications, San Juan de Castro, January 24, 1841, in ibid., 193.

41. William Dane Phelps, *Alta California, 1840–1842: The Journal and Observations of William Dane Phelps, Master of the Ship 'Alert,'* ed. Briton Cooper Busch, 142–43.

42. Ignacio Alviso to Justice of the Peace of San José, Santa Clara, March 12, 1841, Calendar and Catalogue, Archives of the Pueblo of San Jose, 266, San Jose Public Library, San José, Calif.

43. Charles Wilkes, *Narrative of the United States Exploring Expedition during the Years 1838, 1839, 1840, 1841, 1842,* vol. 5, 173–74.

44. Ibid., 208.

45. Ibid., 174.

46. Phelps, *Alta California*, 114.

47. M. Duflot de Mofras, *Duflot de Mofras' Travels on the Pacific Coast*, vol. 1, trans. and ed. Marguerite Eyer Wilbur, 254.

48. Esteban Munrás et al., Petition to Gov. Manuel Micheltorena, Monterey, June 4, 1843, in Vallejo, "Historical and Personal Memoirs," 271–72. Not all rancheros suffered from Indian raids; some gained financially from the losses of others. A German visiting Los Angeles in 1842 noted that "the rugged mountain ranges of the Sierra protect the valley from the Tulare Indians. . . . Horse raising . . . is more profitable here than in the North because the location offers better protection against Indian raids." See Edward Vischer, "Edward Vischer's First Visit to California," trans. and ed. Edwin Gustav Gudde, *California Historical Society Quarterly* 19 (September 1940): 203.

CHAPTER 9

1. Sherburne F. Cook, "Smallpox in Spanish and Mexican California, 1770–1845," *Bulletin of the History of Medicine* 7 (February 1939): 184–87.

2. Charles Wilkes, *Narrative of the United States Exploring Expedition during the Years 1838, 1839, 1840, 1841, 1842*, vol. 5, 172.

3. James Peter Zollinger, *Sutter: The Man and His Empire*, 66–67.

4. *Sacramento Daily Union*, September 29, 1862.

5. William Heath Davis, *Seventy-five Years in California*, ed. Douglas S. Watson, 19.

6. Heinrich Lienhard, *I Knew Sutter*, trans. George T. Smisor, 16–17.

7. William Dane Phelps, *Alta California, 1840–1842: The Journal and Observations of William Dane Phelps, Master of the Ship 'Alert,'* ed. Briton Cooper Busch, 210.

8. Mariano Guadalupe Vallejo, "Historical and Personal Memoirs Relating to Alta California," vol. 4, trans. Earl R. Hewitt, C-D 21, 28, Bancroft Library, Berkeley, Calif.; Zollinger, *Sutter*, 68–69.

9. John Sutter to Gov. Juan B. Alvarado, n.p., 1841, Departmental State Papers, vol. 17, CA-33, Bancroft Library, Berkeley, Calif.

10. See Chapter 6, 84.

11. Entry No. 6362, January 18, 1831, Mission San José Register of Baptisms, September 2, 1797–May 8, 1859, Chancery Office, Archdiocese of San Francisco, San Francisco, Calif. (I thank Randy Millikan for this source.)

12. C. Hart Merriam, "California Mission Baptismal Records," in *Studies of California Indians*, ed. staff of the Department of Anthropology, University of California, Berkeley, 222.

13. Robert H. Jackson, "Gentile Recruitment and Population Movements in the San Francisco Bay Area Missions," *Journal of California and Great Basin Anthropology* 6 (1984): 238.

14. Ibid.

15. Francis Florence McCarthy, *The History of Mission San Jose California, 1797–1835,* 217.

16. Juan Bautista Alvarado, "History of California," vol. 4, trans. Earl R. Hewitt, C-D 4, 211, Bancroft Library, Berkeley, Calif.

17. Heinrich Lienhard, *A Pioneer at Sutter's Fort, 1846–1850: The Adventures of Heinrich Lienhard,* trans. and ed. Marguerite Eyer Wilbur, 7.

18. John A. Sutter, *The Diary of Johann August Sutter,* 6.

19. Wilkes, *Narrative,* 182–83.

20. John A. Sutter, "Personal Reminiscences of General John Augustus Sutter," 1876, C-D 14, 40, Bancroft Library, Berkeley, Calif.

21. Sutter, *Diary,* 9.

22. Sutter, "Personal Reminiscences," 41.

23. John Charles Frémont, *Memoirs of My Life,* vol. 1, 442.

24. Lienhard, *Pioneer,* 7.

25. Theodor Cordua, "The Memoirs of Theodor Cordua, the Pioneer of New Mecklenburg in the Sacramento Valley," ed. Erwin G. Gudde, *Quarterly of the California Historical Society* 12 (December 1933): 309.

26. John A. Sutter to José de Jesús Vallejo, New Helvetia, October 15, 1840, Sutter Collection, 9 Letters, Misc. Box 312, California State Library, Sacramento.

27. Ibid.

28. Ibid.

29. Sutter, "Personal Reminiscences," 44–46.

30. Sutter to Vallejo, October 15, 1840.

31. Hubert Howe Bancroft, *History of California,* vol. 4, *1840–1895,* 136–37.

32. Zollinger, *Sutter,* 89.

33. Quoted in anonymous, *History of Sacramento County California,* 182.

34. Alvarado, "History of California," 213.

35. Sutter, *Diary,* 17.

36. Sutter to Alvarado, n.p., 1841.

37. Ibid.

38. Ibid.

39. Salvador Vallejo, "History of California," 1874, C-D 22, 112–13, Bancroft Library, Berkeley, Calif.

40. Zollinger, *Sutter,* 102.

41. Phelps, *Alta California,* 194.

42. Sutter to Alvarado, n.p., 1841.

43. Edwin Bryant, *What I Saw in California,* 344.

44. Frémont, *Memoirs,* vol. 1, 442.

45. Willard Buzzell, Deposition, San Francisco, California, September 6, 1853, Transcript of the Proceedings in Case No. 523, Hicks and Martin Claimants vs. the United States, Defendant, for the Place Named "Cosumnes," U.S. Land Claims 240 ND, 23, Bancroft Library, Berkeley, Calif. The Indians were Muqueleme Miwok.

46. John A. Sutter, Deposition, San Francisco, September 14, 1853, in ibid., 35.

47. George F. Wyman, Deposition, San Francisco, September 6, 1853, in ibid., 28.
48. Sutter, Deposition, in ibid., 34.
49. John A. Sutter et al., *New Helvetia Diary: A Record of Events Kept by John A. Sutter and His Clerks of New Helvetia, California, From September 9, 1845 to May 25, 1848,* 96, 98, 111, 124–25, 128.
50. Ibid., 25, 43, 61–62, 90.
51. John A. Sutter to _____, New Helvetia, May 18, 1845, published in the *San Francisco California Farmer,* March 13, 1857.
52. Phelps, *Alta California,* 208.
53. Frémont, *Memoirs,* 351.
54. Lienhard, *Pioneer,* 68.
55. G. M. Waseurtz af Sandels, *A Sojourn in California by the King's Orphan, The Travels and Sketches of G. M. Waseurtz af Sandels, a Swedish gentleman who visited California in 1842–1843,* ed. Helen Putnam van Sicklen, 72–73.
56. Lienhard, *Pioneer,* 68.
57. Waseurtz af Sandels, *Sojourn,* 58. Other visitors presented similar accounts; see Bryant, *What I Saw,* 267–68; Lienhard, *Pioneer,* 68; and Theodore T. Johnson, *Sights in the Gold Region and Scenes by the Way,* 143.
58. Phelps, *Alta California,* 208.
59. Frémont, *Memoirs,* 351.
60. Sutter, "Personal Reminiscences," 41; Bryant, *What I Saw,* 267–68.
61. Lienhard, *Pioneer,* 89.
62. Sutter et al., *New Helvetia Diary,* 2, 10; Lienhard, *Pioneer,* 89–90.
63. Wilkes, *Narrative,* 178.
64. Lienhard, *Pioneer,* 77.
65. Sutter, "Personal Reminiscences," 47.
66. Lienhard, *Pioneer,* 76–77.
67. Ibid., 76.
68. Ibid., 78.
69. Alvarado, "History of California," 214.
70. Cordua, "Memoirs," 309.
71. For a discussion of this aspect of Sutter's Indian labor policy, see Albert L. Hurtado, *Indian Survival on the California Frontier,* 55–71.
72. Wilkes, *Narrative,* 178, 180.
73. Quoted in Marion Lydia Lothrop, "The Indian Campaigns of General M.G. Vallejo, Defender of the Northern Frontier of California," *Quarterly of the Society of California Pioneers* 9 (September 1932): 194.
74. Alvarado, "History of California," 225.
75. Sutter, "Personal Reminiscences," 42.
76. Sutter, Deposition, U.S. Land Claims, 240 ND, 34.
77. Sutter, "Personal Reminiscences," 42.
78. Sutter, *Diary,* 18–19.
79. Sutter, "Personal Reminiscences," 77–78.
80. Overton Johnson and William H. Winter, *Route Across the Rocky Mountains,* ed. Carl L. Cannon, 115–16.

81. John A. Sutter to John Marsh, New Helvetia, June 28, 1844, John Marsh Collection, Box 240, California State Library, Sacramento.

82. James Clyman, *James Clyman: American Frontiersman, 1792–1881,* ed. Charles L. Camp, 174.

83. John A. Sutter to Thomas O. Larkin, New Helvetia, July 21, 1845, in George P. Hammond, ed., *The Larkin Papers: Personal, Business and Official Correspondence of Thomas Oliver Larkin, Merchant and United States Consul in California,* vol. 3, 278–80.

84. Ibid.

85. Ibid.

86. Ibid.

87. James Douglas to Sir George Simpson, Fort Vancouver, March 5, 1845, in E. E. Rich, ed., *The Letters of John McLoughlin from Fort Vancouver to the Governor of the Committee,* Third Series, 1844–46, 183. For an overview of this incident, see Robert F. Heizer, "Walla Walla Indian Expeditions to the Sacramento Valley," *California Historical Society Quarterly* 21 (March 1942): 1–7.

88. Sutter, *Diary,* 21–22.

89. Thomas O. Larkin to William Hooper, Monterey, March 22, 1845, in Hammond, *Larkin Papers,* 83.

90. Sutter, *Diary,* 24–25.

91. Contract between the Government and John Marsh and John Gantt in regard to the pursuit of the Indian Robbers, Los Angeles, February 27, 1845, John Marsh Family Papers, C-B 879, Bancroft Library, Berkeley, Calif.; Theodore H. Hittell, *History of California,* vol. 2, 388–89.

92. José Castro, Instructions to John Gantt, Los Angeles, February 27, 1845, in Sherburne Cook Papers, 79/21c, G-4, Bancroft Library, Berkeley, Calif.

93. John A. Sutter to Antonio Suñol, New Helvetia, June 14, 1845, John A. Sutter Collection, Misc. Box 311, California State Library, Sacramento.

94. Sutter, *Diary,* 25.

95. Sutter, "Personal Reminiscences," 127.

96. John A. Sutter to Thomas O. Larkin, New Helvetia, April 21, 1845, in Alvarado, "History of California," 215. Sutter's claim that only immigrants could conquer the horse thieves was repeated six months later. See John A. Sutter to Thomas O. Larkin, New Helvetia, October 8, 1845, in Hammond, *Larkin Papers,* vol. 4, 11.

97. Hubert Howe Bancroft, *History of California,* vol. 5, *1846–1848,* 524.

98. Peter Lausen, Deposition, San Francisco, September 1, 1853, Transcript of the Proceedings in Case No. 255, Charles M. Weber, Claimant, vs. the United States, Defendant, for the Place Named "Campo de los Franceses." U.S. Land Claims 298 ND, 24, Bancroft Library, Berkeley, Calif.

99. On August 16, 1843, a justice of the peace, Isadoro Guillen, granted Weber a safe-conduct passport to travel to New Helvetia. See Weber Family Papers, 1788–1981, C-B 829, Bancroft Library, Berkeley, Calif.

100. "California Indian Chiefs," *Sacramento Daily Union,* January 31, 1857.

101. Frank T. Gilbert, *History of San Joaquin County, California, with Illustrations Descriptive of its Scenery,* 12–13, 16.

102. *Stockton Daily Independent*, May 7, 1881; Gilbert, *History of San Joaquin County*, 16.

103. George H. Tinkham, *A History of Stockton*, 66–68.

104. Sutter, "Personal Reminiscences," 69–70.

105. Alpheces Flech, Deposition, San Francisco, September 1, 1853. Transcript of the Proceedings in Case No. 255 for the Place Named "Campo de los Franceses." U.S. Land Claims 298 ND, 19, Bancroft Library, Berkeley, Calif.

106. Sutter to Suñol, New Helvetia, June 14, 1845.

107. Sutter to Larkin, July 21, 1845, in Hammond, *Larkin Papers*, vol. 3, 278–80.

108. Thomas O. Larkin to Joseph B. Hull, Monterey, August 20, 1845, in ibid., 319.

109. José María Covarrubias to the Prefect of the District of Monterey, Monterey, September 24, 1845, in ibid., 363–64.

110. Sutter et al., *New Helvetia Diary*, 2.

111. Sutter, Deposition, U.S. Land Claims, 240 ND, 34–35.

112. On several occasions, Heleno visited New Helvetia; see Sutter et al., *New Helvetia Diary*, 53, 75, 134.

113. Ibid., 19.

114. John A. Sutter to John Marsh, New Helvetia, April 3, 1846, John Marsh Collection, Box 240, California State Library, Sacramento; John Marsh to ———, New Helvetia, March 2, 1846, in Mayo Elizabeth Wheeler, "John A. Sutter, a California Pioneer; an Historical Sketch and Collection of Correspondence" (M.A. thesis, University of California, Berkeley, 1924), 426.

115. Sutter et al., *New Helvetia Diary*, 52, 57, 62, 67, 68, 71, 73, 81, 105, 112, 117–18. Information about Polo is sketchy and not very reliable. A visitor to California claimed Polo had been educated at one of the missions and was fluent in Spanish. Supposedly, he took four wives but insisted his followers remain monogamous. See Joseph T. Downey, *Filings from an Old Saw: Reminiscences of San Francisco and California's Conquest*, ed. Fred Blackburn Rogers, 19.

116. "Letters from California, 1846," Yerba Buena, June 25, 1846, *Honolulu Friend*, December 1, 1846.

117. Sutter, *Diary*, 32.

118. John A. Sutter to William A. Leidesdorff, New Helvetia, July 22, 1846, Leidesdorff Papers, LE 164, Huntington Library, San Marino, Calif. The threat of attacks hindered Sutter's enterprise of providing Indian workers to various rancheros. He notified a friend he could not send him workers because they feared to leave their families unprotected. See John A. Sutter to William A. Leidesdorff, New Helvetia, June 1, 1846, Leidesdorff Papers, LE 137.

119. Sutter, *Diary*, 33–34.

120. John A. Sutter to Mariano Guadalupe Vallejo, New Helvetia, June 1, 1846, "Documentary, The Fremont Episode," *California Historical Society Quarterly* 6 (June 1927): 185.

121. Sutter, *Diary*, 33–34.

122. Sutter to Leidesdorff, July 22, 1846.

123. Joseph Warren Revere, *Tour of Duty in California*, 155.

124. Marius Duvall, *A Navy Surgeon in California, 1846–1847: The Journal of Marius Duvall,* ed. Fred Blackburn Rogers, 17.

CHAPTER 10

1. Thomas O. Larkin to *Journal of Commerce,* Monterey, July 1845, in George P. Hammond, ed., *The Larkin Papers: Personal, Business and Official Correspondence of Thomas Oliver Larkin, Merchant and United States Consul in California,* vol. 3, 294.
2. Thomas O. Larkin to F. M. Dimond, Monterey, March 1, 1846, in ibid., vol. 4, 216.
3. Thomas O. Larkin, "Description of California," Monterey, April 20, 1846, in ibid., 307–308.
4. The American conquest of coastal California is described in detail in Neal Harlow, *California Conquered: The Annexation of a Mexican Province, 1846–1850.*
5. Larkin, "Description," 306.
6. "Letters from California, 1846," Yerba Buena, June 25, 1846, *Honolulu Friend,* December 1, 1846.
7. Marius Duvall, *A Navy Surgeon in California, 1846–1847: The Journal of Marius Duvall,* ed. Fred Blackburn Rogers, 42.
8. *Monterey Californian,* August 15, 1846. Job. F. Dye, "Recollections of California," 1877, C-D 69, 18–19, Bancroft Library, Berkeley, Calif.
9. *Monterey Californian,* August 22, 1846.
10. Ibid., September 26, 1846.
11. Ibid., October 10, 1846.
12. John Adam Hussey and George Walcott Ames, Jr., "California Preparations to Meet the Walla Walla Invasion, 1846," *California Historical Society Quarterly* 21 (March 1942): 9–21.
13. Edwin Bryant, *What I Saw in California,* 267.
14. Ibid., 273–74.
15. Joseph Warren Revere, *Tour of Duty in California,* 157.
16. Mariano Guadalupe Vallejo to Thomas O. Larkin, Sonoma, September 15, 1846, in Hammond, *Larkin Papers,* vol. 5, 237.
17. Harlow, *California Conquered,* 159–73.
18. Bryant, *What I Saw,* 347n.
19. Agustín Janssens, *The Life and Adventures in California of Don Agustín Janssens, 1834–1856,* ed. William H. Ellison and Francis Price, 127.
20. William A. Maddox to Charles Weber, San Juan Bautista, October 28, 1846, Weber Family Papers, C-B 829, Bancroft Library, Berkeley, Calif.
21. William Robert Garner, *Letters from California, 1846–1847,* ed. Donald Munro Craig, 118.
22. Bryant, *What I Saw,* 347.
23. John Sutter, "Personal Reminiscences of General John Augustus Sutter," 1876, C-D 14, 153–54, Bancroft Library, Berkeley, Calif.
24. F. W. Swasey, *The Early Days and Men of California,* 70.

25. Sutter, "Personal Reminiscences," 153–54.

26. John Charles Frémont, *Memoirs of My Life,* vol. 2, 229–30.

27. Bryant, *What I Saw,* 359–60.

28. Jacob R. Snyder to Edward M. Kern, Los Angeles, February 11, 1847, in Mary Lee Spence and Donald Jackson, eds., *The Expeditions of John Charles Fremont,* vol. 2, *The Bear Flag Revolt and the Court Martial,* 302.

29. Sutter, "Personal Reminiscences," 153–54.

30. *Monterey Californian,* December 23, 1846.

31. Garner, *Letters from California,* 164.

32. *Monterey Californian,* December 23, 1846. Because Indian raiding continued long after the uprising had been crushed, Garner's and the *Californian's* claims lack merit.

33. Janssens, *Life and Adventures,* 127.

34. See Harlow, *California Conquered,* 193–218.

35. Theodore Grivas, *Military Governments in California 1846–1850,* 80–81.

36. Col. Richard B. Mason to Gen. Stephen Watts Kearny, n.p., March 20, 1847, Archives of California, Unbound Documents, CA-63, 146–47, Bancroft Library, Berkeley, Calif.

37. José María Sanchez to Gen. Stephen Watts Kearny, San Juan Bautista, March 19, 1847, Pacific Division, Records of the 10th Military Department, Letters Received, RG 98, Microcopy 210, Roll 2, NA.

38. Gen. Stephen Watts Kearny to W. L. Marcy, Monterey, California, April 28, 1847. U.S. Congress, House, 31st Cong., 1st sess., Exec. Doc. 17, 286.

39. William Heath Davis, *Seventy-five Years in California,* ed. Douglas S. Watson, 386. The history of the regiment is described in Donald C. Biggs, *Conquer and Colonize: Stevenson's Regiment and California.*

40. *San Francisco California Star,* April 10, 1847.

41. Felix Paul Wierzbicki, *California As It Is And As It May Be,* 16.

42. Garner, *Letters from California,* 164.

43. *San Francisco California Star,* April 10, 1847.

44. Ibid., May 1, 1847.

45. Ibid.

46. Ibid. Also challenging Marsh's contention that a party of whites intended to join the horse-thief Indians was an individual using the initials R. T. See ibid., August 14, 1847.

47. Gen. Stephen Watts Kearny to John A. Sutter, Monterey, April 7, 1847, U.S. Congress, House, 31st Cong., 1st sess., Exec. Doc. 17, 294.

48. Gen. Stephen Watts Kearny to Mariano Guadalupe Vallejo, Monterey, April 14, 1847, in ibid., 296–97.

49. John A. Sutter to Gen. Stephen Watts Kearny, New Helvetia, May 18, 1847, Archives of California, Unbound Documents, CA-63, Bancroft Library, Berkeley, Calif.

50. John A. Sutter et al., *New Helvetia Diary: A Record of Events Kept by John A. Sutter and his Clerks at New Helvetia, California, From September 9, 1845 to May 25, 1848,* 45.

51. John Sutter, Statement, New Helvetia, May 22, 1847, T. Perceval Ger-

son Collection, 100/51, Department of Special Collections, University of California, Los Angeles.

52. John A. Sutter to Gen. Stephen Watts Kearny, New Helvetia, May 27, 1847, Archives of California, Unbound Documents, CA-63, Bancroft Library, Berkeley, Calif.

53. Thomas O. Larkin to Robert Field Stockton, Monterey, April 26, 1847, in Hammond, *Larkin Papers,* vol. 6, 126.

54. Mariano Guadalupe Vallejo to Gen. Stephen Watts Kearny, Santa Clara, April 18, 1847, Pacific Division, RG 393, U.S. Army Continental Commands, 1821–1920, Microcopy 210, Roll 2, NA.

55. Capt. Henry Naglee, Journal, May 24–June 20, 1847, Naglee Family Collection, MR-116, 1, Bancroft Library, Berkeley, Calif.

56. Ibid., 9–13.

57. Ibid., 19–24.

58. Sutter et al., *New Helvetia Diary,* 49–51.

59. Frémont, *Memoirs,* 2, 231n.

60. *Monterey Californian,* June 19, 1847.

61. An individual who kept a journal of the journey made no mention of Indian raids. See Henry Smith Turner, *The Original Journals of Henry Smith Turner with Stephen Watts Kearny to New Mexico and California, 1846–1848,* ed. Dwight L. Clark, 126.

62. For an account of the transfer of power to Mason, see Harlow, *California Conquered,* 280–81.

63. William Dana to Gen. Stephen Watts Kearny, San Luis Obispo, June 6, 1847. Archives of California, Unbound Documents, CA-63, Bancroft Library, Berkeley, Calif.

64. Col. Richard B. Mason to Gen. R. Jones, Monterey, July 19, 1847, Pacific Division, Records of the 10th Military Department, Letters Received, 1846–1851, RG 98, Microcopy 210, Roll 1, NA.

65. John A. Sutter to Col. Richard B. Mason, New Helvetia, July 12, 1847, U.S. Congress, House, 31st Cong., 1st sess., Exec. Doc. 17, 374.

66. Ibid.

67. Extract from a letter, New Helvetia, July 10, 1847, in the *San Francisco California Star,* July 24, 1847.

68. Sutter to Mason, July 12, 1847.

69. Col. Richard B. Mason to John A. Sutter, Monterey, July.21, 1847, U.S. Congress, House, 31st Cong., 1st sess., Exec. Doc. 17, 376–77.

70. Col. Richard B. Mason to Lieut. Charles Anderson, Monterey, July 21, 1847, in ibid., 343–44.

71. Lieut. H. W. Halleck to John A. Sutter, Monterey, August 16, 1847, in ibid., 381–83.

72. Col. Richard B. Mason to Mariano Guadalupe Vallejo and John A. Sutter, August 19, 1847, in ibid., 384.

73. Lieut. H. W. Halleck to Mariano Guadalupe Vallejo, Monterey, September 15, 1847, in ibid., 395.

74. Hubert Howe Bancroft, *History of California,* vol. 5, *1846–1848,* 610.

75. Halleck to Sutter, August 16, 1847.

76. John A. Sutter to Lieut. H. W. Halleck, New Helvetia, December 20, 1847, Document 1a, *Contributions of the University of California Archaeological Research Facility*, no. 9 (July 1970): 94–95. See also Albert L. Hurtado, *Indian Survival on the California Frontier*, 65–69.

77. John A. Sutter to William A. Leidesdorff, New Helvetia, September 10, 1847, William A. Leidesdorff Papers, LE 321, Huntington Library, San Marino, Calif.

78. John A. Sutter to William Leidesdorff, New Helvetia, October 13, 1847, LE 340, in ibid.

79. Lieut. William T. Sherman to John Burton, Monterey, September 6, 1847, U.S. Congress, House, 31st Cong., 1st sess., Exec. Doc. 17, 355.

80. Lieut. William T. Sherman to Capt. Henry Naglee, Monterey, September 9, 1847, Pacific Division, Records of the 10th Military Department, Letters Received, 1846–1851, RG 98, Microcopy 210, Roll 1, NA.

81. William Redmond Ryan, *Personal Adventures in Upper and Lower California in 1848–9*, vol. 1, 130–34.

82. Oliver M. Wozencraft, "Indian Affairs, 1849–50," 1877, C-D 204, Bancroft Library, Berkeley, Calif. In December 1850, Chechee, also known as Bautista, led an attack on an American trading post, igniting what became known as the Mariposa Indian War. See Robert Eccleston, *The Mariposa Indian War 1850– 1851, Diaries of Robert Eccleston: The California Gold Rush, Yosemite, and the High Sierra*, ed. C. Gregory Crampton, 15.

83. Ryan, *Personal Adventures*, 134.

84. Ibid., 107–108. During a military operation in Baja California, Naglee also executed two Mexican prisoners. See Col. Richard B. Mason to Gen. R. Jones, Monterey, August 16, 1848, U.S. Congress, House, 31st Cong., 1st sess., Exec. Doc. 17, 512–13.

85. Frank T. Gilbert, *History of San Joaquin County, California, with Illustrations Descriptive of its Scenery*, 20.

86. Sutter et al., *New Helvetia Diary*, 115.

87. James Weeks to Charles Weber, San José, December 28, 1847, Weber Family Papers, C-B 829, Bancroft Library, Berkeley, Calif.

88. Gilbert, *History*, 20. Charles Weber, Deposition, San Francisco, April 3, 1855, Transcript of the proceedings in Case No. 767, Francisco Rico et al., Claimants, vs. the United States, Defendant, for the Place Named Rio Estanislao. U.S. Land Claims 413 ND, 13–14, Bancroft Library, Berkeley, Calif.

89. "California Indian Chiefs," *Sacramento Daily Union*, January 31, 1857.

90. Col. Jonathan D. Stevenson to Andrés Pico, Los Angeles, February 14, 1848, Pacific Division, U.S. Army Continental Commands, 1821–1920, RG 393, Microcopy 210, Roll 3, NA.

91. Capt. Francis J. Lippsitt to Lieut. William T. Sherman, Santa Barbara, February 25, 1848, in ibid.

92. Lieut. John M. Huddart to Capt. Francis J. Lippsitt, Santa Barbara, February 25, 1848, in ibid.

93. Lippsitt to Sherman, February 25, 1848.

94. Col. Richard B. Mason to Juan Price, Monterey, March 21, 1848, U.S. Congress, House, 31st Cong., 1st sess., Exec. Doc. 17, 496–97.

95. Capt. Francis J. Lippsitt to Lieut. William T. Sherman, Santa Bárbara, March 9, 1848, Pacific Division, Records of the 10th Military Department, Letters Received, 1846–1851, RG 98, Microcopy 210, Roll 3, NA. The village may have been Pohalin Tinleu of the Hometwoli (Yokuts), which was located on Kern Lake.

96. Ibid.

97. Lieut. J. L. Bonnycastle to Capt. Francis J. Lippsitt, Los Angeles, April 2, 1848, Pacific Division, U.S. Army Continental Commands 1821–1920, RG 393, Microcopy 210, Roll 3, NA.

98. Capt. Francis J. Lippsitt, Statement, Santa Bárbara, April 18, 1848, Roll 6, in ibid.

99. Charles White to Col. Richard B. Mason, San José, April 29, 1848, Archives of California, Unbound Documents CA-63, Bancroft Library, Berkeley, Calif.

100. Charles White to Col. Richard B. Mason, San José, July 16, 1848, in ibid.

101. Ibid.

102. James Peter Zollinger, *Sutter: The Man and His Empire,* 227.

103. "The Sutter-Marshall Lease with the Yalesumney Indians, 1848," Document 3b, *Contributions of the University of California Archaeological Research Facility,* no. 9 (July 1970): 109–10.

104. Ibid.

105. Henry Bigler, Notes from his diary, January–February, 1848, C-D 45, 66, Bancroft Library, Berkeley, Calif.

106. James W. Marshall to Charles E. Pickett, n.p., January 28, 1856, in John S. Hittell, *Mining in the Pacific States of North America,* 11–12.

107. John A. Sutter to Col. Richard B. Mason, New Helvetia, February 22, 1848, Pioneer Manuscript Collection, 236, California State Library, Sacramento.

108. Col. Richard B. Mason to John A. Sutter, Monterey, March 5, 1848, U.S. Congress, House, 31st Cong., 1st sess., Exec. Doc. 17, 490.

109. John Walton Caughey, *The California Gold Rush,* 20.

110. Col. Richard B. Mason to Gen. R. Jones, Monterey, August 17, 1848, U.S. Congress, House, 31st Cong., 1st sess., Exec. Doc. 17, 533.

111. Col. Richard B. Mason to Gen. R. Jones, San Francisco, November 24, 1848, ibid., 648–49.

112. William Garner to Col. Richard B. Mason, San Luís Obispo, March 15, 1849, Pacific Division, Records of the 10th Military Department, Letters Received, 1846–1851, RG 98, Microcopy 210, Roll 3, NA.

113. Ibid.

114. Gen. Bennett Riley to Lieut. William T. Sherman, Monterey, April 16, 1849, U.S. Congress, House, 31st Cong., 1st sess., Exec. Doc. 17, 900.

115. *San José Pioneer,* April 27, 1878.

116. Ibid.

117. Quoted in James H. Carson, *Recollections of the California Mines,* ed. Joseph A. Sullivan, 13.

118. *San José Pioneer,* April 27, 1878. The individual who escaped took Garner's journal to the coast; see Carson, *Recollections,* 12–13.
119. Asst. Adj. Gen. Edward R. S. Canby to Maj. Anthony S. Miller, Monterey, May 4, 1849, U.S. Congress, House, 31st Cong., 1st sess., Exec. Doc. 17, 904–905.
120. Asst. Adj. Gen. Edward R. S. Canby to Maj. Anthony S. Miller, Monterey, May 7, 1849, in ibid., 906–907.
121. Asst. Adj. Gen. Edward R. S. Canby to Lieut. Clarendon J. L. Wilson, Monterey, June 2, 1849, in ibid., 913–14.
122. Lieut. Clarendon J. L. Wilson to Asst. Adj. Gen. Edward R. S. Canby, Camp Stanislaus, August 20, 1849, Pacific Division, Records of the 10th Military Department, Letters Received, 1846–1851, RG 98, Microcopy 210, Roll 4, NA.
123. Ibid.
124. Gen. Bennett Riley to Gen. R. Jones, Monterey, June 11, 1849, U.S. Congress, House, 31st Cong., 1st sess., Exec. Doc. 17, 917.
125. *San Francisco Weekly Alta California,* May 3, 1849.
126. Gen. Bennett Riley to Col. W. G. Freeman, Monterey, September 20, 1849, U.S. Congress, House, 31st Cong., 1st sess., Exec. Doc. 17, 941–43.
127. Gen. Bennett Riley to Col. J. Hooker, Sacramento City, July 22, 1849, in ibid., 925–26.
128. Gen. Bennett Riley to Gen. R. Jones, Monterey, October 15, 1849, Pacific Division, Records of the 10th Military Department, Letters Received, 1846–1851, RG 98, Microcopy 210, Roll 1, NA.
129. Ibid.
130. Ibid.

CHAPTER 11

1. For the exceptions to traditional historiography, see Sherburne F. Cook, *The Conflict between the California Indian and White Civilization;* James J. Rawls, *Indians of California: The Changing Image;* and Albert L. Hurtado, *Indian Survival on the California Frontier.*
2. Sherburne F. Cook claimed that Indian raids peaked in 1845, but in fact they intensified after that time. See Sherburne F. Cook, "The Physical and Demographic Reaction of the Nonmission Indians in Colonial and Provincial California," in Cook, *Conflict,* 232.
3. For a counter-argument, see George Harwood Phillips, "Indians and the Breakdown of the Spanish Mission System in California," *Ethnohistory* 21 (Fall 1974): 291–302.
4. For an account of Indian life in the pueblo, see George Harwood Phillips, "Indians in Los Angeles, 1781–1875: Economic Integration, Social Disintegration," *Pacific Historical Review* 49 (August 1980): 427–51.
5. Anna Gayton, "Chukchansi—Field Notes," June–July 1938, 79/6c, Bancroft Library, Berkeley, Calif.
6. Robert H. Lowie, *An Introduction to Cultural Anthropology,* 221–22.
7. See, for example, Joseph Jablow, *The Cheyenne in Plains Indian Trade Relations, 1795–1840;* Charles L. Kenner, *A History of New Mexico-Plains Indian*

Relations; and W. W. Newcomb, Jr., "A Re-examination of the Causes of Plains Warfare," *American Anthropologist* 52 (July–September 1950): 317–30.

8. Sherburne F. Cook, "The Mechanism and Extent of Dietary Adaptation Among Certain Groups of California and Nevada Indians," in Cook, *Conflict,* 477–507.

9. See, for example, Arthur J. Ray, *Indians in the Fur Trade: Their Role as Hunters, Trappers, and Middlemen in the Lands Southwest of Hudson Bay, 1660–1870.*

10. David J. Weber, "American Westward Expansion and the Breakdown of Relations between Pobladores and 'Indios Bárbaros' on Mexico's Far Northern Frontier, 1821–1846," *New Mexico Historical Review* 56 (July 1981): 221–38.

11. The classic study of the Santa Fe Trail is Josiah Gregg, *The Commerce of the Prairies,* ed. Milo Milton Quaife.

12. In early 1848, the last major caravan to use the Old Spanish Trail left California with 4,582 animals. See John Adam Hussey, "The New Mexico–California Caravan of 1847–1848," *New Mexico Historical Review* 18 (January 1943): 1–16.

13. LeRoy R. Hafen and Ann W. Hafen, *Old Spanish Trail: Santa Fé to Los Angeles,* 232.

14. *San Francisco Daily Alta California,* July 7, 1851.

15. James Peter Zollinger, *Sutter: The Man and His Empire,* 76.

16. Richard Dillon, *Fool's Gold: The Decline and Fall of Captain John Sutter of California,* 200.

17. See, for example, Hubert Howe Bancroft, *California Pastoral, 1769–1848;* and Nellie Van de Grift Sanchez, *Spanish Arcadia.* The disjointed nature of California historiography is examined by Earl Pomeroy, "Old Lamps for New: The Cultural Lag in Pacific Coast Historiography," *Arizona and the West* 2 (Summer 1960): 105–26; and by David J. Weber, "Mexico's Far Northern Frontier, 1821–1854: Historiography Askew," *Western Historical Quarterly* 7 (July 1976): 279–93.

18. Juan Bautista Alvarado, "History of California," vol. 4, 1838–1842, trans. Earl R. Hewitt, C-D4, Bancroft Library, Berkeley, Calif.

19. Edward Kemble, "Yerba Buena, 1846," *Sacramento Daily Union,* January 6, 1872.

20. Sylvia M. Broadbent, "Conflict at Monterey: Indian Horse Raiding, 1820–1850," *Journal of California Anthropology* 1 (Spring ·1974): 86–101; Charles Hughes, "The Decline of the Californios: The Case of San Diego, 1846–1856," *Journal of San Diego History* 21 (Summer 1975): 1–31.

21. Leonard Pitt, *The Decline of the Californios: A Social History of the Spanish-Speaking Californians, 1846–1890,* 12–13.

22. The law is discussed by David Hornbeck, "The Patenting of California's Private Land Claims, 1851–1885," *Geographical Review* 69 (October 1979): 434–48; and by Paul Gates, "The California Land Act of 1851," *California Historical Society Quarterly* 50 (December 1971): 395–430.

23. See, for example, Neal Harlow, *California Conquered: The Annexation of a Mexican Province, 1846–1850,* 50–51.

Bibliography

GOVERNMENT DOCUMENTS

Annual Report of the Commissioner of Indian Affairs, 1854.
Letters Received by the Office of the Adjutant General (Main Series) 1822–60. Microcopy 567, Roll 483. Record Group 94. National Archives, Washington, D.C.
Records of the 10th Military Department, Pacific Division. Letters Received, 1846–51. Microcopy 210, Rolls 1, 2, 3, 4, 6, 7. Record Group 98. National Archives.
U.S. Army Continental Commands, 1821–1920. Pacific Division. Microcopy 210, Rolls 2, 3, 5, 6. Record Group 393. National Archives.
U.S. Congress. House. 31st Cong., 1st sess., Exec. Doc. 17.
U.S. Congress. Senate. 32nd Cong., 1st sess., Exec. Doc. 110.

NEWSPAPERS

Honolulu Friend, 1846.
Honolulu Sandwich Island Gazette and Journal of Commerce, 1837.
Lewiston Morning Tribune, 1918.
Los Angeles Star, 1853, 1857, 1874.
Monterey Californian, 1846, 1847, 1848.
Sacramento Daily Union, 1857, 1862, 1867, 1872.
San Francisco California Farmer, 1857, 1862.
San Francisco California Star, 1847.
San Francisco Daily Alta California, 1851.
San Francisco Morning Post, 1851.
San Francisco Picayune, 1851.
San Francisco Weekly Alta California, 1849.
San Joaquin Republican, 1852.
San Jose Pioneer, 1878.
Santa Barbara Gazette, 1855.
Stockton Daily Independent, 1881.

UNPUBLISHED PRIMARY SOURCES

Alvarado, Juan Bautista. "History of California." Vols. 2, 4, translated by Earl R. Hewitt. C-D 2, 4. Bancroft Library, Berkeley, California.

Archives of California. Unbound documents. CA-63. Bancroft Library, Berkeley, California.

Archives of the Archdiocese of San Francisco. Documents 735, 1135, 1137, 1139, 1143, 1531, 1535, 1797, 2065, 2593, 2609, 2651, 2652, 2656, 2812, 3047, 3048, 3616, 3988. Mission Santa Barbara Archives, Santa Barbara, California. Photostats.

Bigler, Henry. "Diary of a Morman," January–February, 1848. C-D 45. Bancroft Library, Berkeley, California.

Bowers, Stephen. "The Santa Barbara Indians." 1879. Ms. 532. Southwest Museum Library, Los Angeles, California.

Brown, S. C. Interview. Box 802, Folder 6. George W. Stewart Collection, California State Library, Sacramento.

Buzzell, William. Deposition, San Francisco, September 6, 1853. Transcript of the Proceedings in Case No. 523, Hicks and Martin, Claimants, vs. the United States, Defendant, for the Place Named "Cosumnes." U.S. Land Claims, 240 ND. Bancroft Library, Berkeley, California.

Calendar and Catalogue of Spanish and Mexican Archives (1792–1859) of the Pueblo of San José de Guadalupe. San Jose Public Library, San Jose, California.

Cook, Sherburne F. Papers. 79/21c, G-4. Bancroft Library, Berkeley, California.

Cutter, Donald Colgett, trans. and ed. "Writings of Father Mariano Payeras." Manuscript in possession of Donald Colgett Cutter.

Departmental State Papers. Vol. 17, CA-33. Bancroft Library, Berkeley, California.

Documentos para la Historia de California. Archivo Particular de Sr. Don Mariano Guadalupe Vallejo, C-B 7, 14, 31. Bancroft Library, Berkeley, California.

Dossier regarding the killing of two soldiers by gentile Indians (1790 and 1791). Translated by Maureen Campión de la Necochea, Archivo General de la Nacion-Californias, vol. 46, Mexico City. Transcript on file in U.S. Forest Service, Goleta, California.

Dye, Francis Job. "Recollections of California." 1877. C-D 69. Bancroft Library, Berkeley, California.

Flech, Alpheces. Deposition, San Francisco, September 1, 1853. Transcript of the Proceedings in Case No. 255, Charles M. Weber, Claimant, vs. the United States, Defendant, for the Place Named "Campo de los Franceses." U.S. Land Claims 298 ND. Bancroft Library, Berkeley, California.

Fort Sutter Papers. Vol. 20, Manuscript no. 81. Huntington Library, San Marino, California.

Gayton, Anna H. Chukchansi—Field Notes, June–July, 1938. 79/6c. Bancroft Library, Berkeley, California.

Harrington, John P. Papers, 1916–17. National Anthropological Archives, Smithsonian Institution, Washington, D.C.

Hayes, Benjamin. Missions of Alta California. C-C21, pt. 1. Bancroft Library, Berkeley, California.

————. Scrapbooks. Indians of Santa Barbara, vol. 39. Bancroft Library, Berkeley, California.

Hicks and Martin, Claimants, vs. the United States, Defendant, for the Place Named "Cosumnes." Transcript of the Proceedings in Case No. 523. U.S. Land Claims 240 ND. Bancroft Library, Berkeley, California.

Lausen, Peter. Deposition, San Francisco, September 1, 1853. Transcript of the Proceedings in Case No. 255, Charles M. Weber, Claimant, vs. the United States, Defendant, for the Place Named "Campo de los Franceses." U.S. Land Claims 298 ND. Bancroft Library, Berkeley, California.

Leidesdorff, William A. Papers. LE 22, 32, 74, 122, 129, 137, 138, 164, 321, 340. Huntington Library, San Marino, California.

Marsh, John, Claimant, vs. the United States, Defendant, for the Place Named "Los Meganos." Transcript of the Proceedings in Case No. 213. U.S. Land Claims 107 ND. Bancroft Library, Berkeley, California.

Marsh, John. Collection. Box 240. California State Library, Sacramento.

————. Family Papers. C-B 879. Bancroft Library, Berkeley, California.

Mission San José Register of Baptisms, September 2, 1797–May 8, 1859. Chancery Office, Archdioceses of San Francisco, San Francisco.

Mission Santa Clara Register of Burials, June 22, 1777–December 22, 1866. Orradre Library, University of Santa Clara, Santa Clara, California.

Naglee, Henry. Journal, May 24–June 20, 1847. Naglee Family Collection. MR-116. Bancroft Library, Berkeley, California.

Pioneer Manuscript Collection. Box 236. California State Library, Sacramento.

Reading, Pierson B. Collection. Box 285, 286. California State Library, Sacramento.

Stewart, George W. "Notes of Conservation concerning Yokut Indians." George W. Stewart Collection. Box 802. California State Library, Sacramento.

Sutter, John A. Collection. Miscellaneous Boxes 311, 312. California State Library, Sacramento.

_____. Deposition, San Francisco, September 14, 1853. Transcript of the Proceedings in Case No. 523, Hicks and Martin, Claimants, vs. the United States, Defendant, for the Place Named "Cosumnes." U.S. Land Claims, 240 ND. Bancroft Library, Berkeley, California.

_____. Papers. C-B 631. Bancroft Library, Berkeley, California.

_____. "Personal Reminiscences of General John Augustus Sutter." 1876. C-D 14. Bancroft Library, Berkeley, California.

_____. Statement. 1847. T. Perceval Gerson Collection. 100/51. Department of Special Collections, University of California, Los Angeles.

Upton, Eugene. Scrapbook no. 7. California Historical Society Library, San Francisco.

Vallejo, Mariano Guadalupe. "Historical and Personal Memoirs Relating to Alta California." Translated by Earl R. Hewitt. Vols. 1, 4. C-D 18, 21. Bancroft Library, Berkeley, California.

Vallejo, Salvador. "Notas historicas sobre California." 1874. C-D 22. Bancroft Library, Berkeley, California.

Warner, Juan Jose. "Reminiscences of Early Life in California." Unidentified newspaper article in Missions of Alta California, Benjamin Hayes Collection. C-C 21, pt. 1. Bancroft Library, Berkeley, California.

Weber, Charles M., Claimant, vs. the United States, Defendant, for the Place Named "Campo de los Franceses." Transcript of the Proceedings in Case No. 255. U.S. Land Claims 298 ND. Bancroft Library, Berkeley, California.

_____. Deposition, San Francisco, April 3, 1855. Transcript of the Proceedings in Case No. 767, Francisco Rico, et al, Claimants, vs. the United States, Defendant, for the Place Named "Rio Estanislao." U.S. Land Claims 413 ND. Bancroft Library, Berkeley, California.

Weber Family Papers. C-B 829. Bancroft Library, Berkeley, California.

Wozencraft, O. M. "Indian Affairs, 1849–1850," 1877. C-D 204. Bancroft Library, Berkeley, California.

Wyman, George F. Deposition, San Francisco, September 6, 1853. Transcript of the Proceedings in Case No. 523, Hicks and Martin, Claimants, vs. the United States, Defendant, for the Place Named "Cosumnes." U.S. Land Claims 240 ND. Bancroft Library, Berkeley, California.

_____. Deposition, San Francisco, April 3, 1855. Transcript of the Proceedings in Case No. 767, Francisco Rico, et al, Claimants, vs. the

United States, Defendant, for the Place Named "Rio Estanislao." U.S. Land Claims 413 ND. Bancroft Library, Berkeley, California.

THESES AND DISSERTATIONS

Cutter, Donald Colgett. "Spanish Exploration of California's Central Valley." Ph.D. diss., University of California, Berkeley, 1950.

Johnson, John. "Chumash Social Organization: An Ethnohistorical Perspective." Ph.D. diss., University of California, Santa Barbara, 1988.

Lawrence, Eleanor. "The Old Spanish Trail from Santa Fe to California." M.A. thesis, University of California, Berkeley, 1930.

Wheeler, Mayo Elizabeth. "John A. Sutter, a California Pioneer: An Historical Sketch and Collection of Correspondence." M.A. thesis, University of California, Berkeley, 1924.

PUBLISHED PRIMARY SOURCES

Baker, John. *San Joaquin Vignettes: The Reminiscences of Captain John Baker.* Edited by William Harland Boyd and Glendon J. Rodgers. Bakersfield: Kern County Historical Society, 1955.

Beechey, F. W. *Narrative of a Voyage to the Pacific and Beering's Strait.* Vol. 2. London: Henry Colburn and Richard Bentley, 1831.

Belcher, Edward. *Narrative of a Voyage Round the World, performed in Her Majesty's Ship Sulphur During the Years 1836–1842.* Vol. 1. London: Henry Colburn Publisher, 1843.

Belden, Joseph. "Pastoral California through Gringo Eyes." *Touring Topics* 22, no. 8 (August 1930): 40–47, 53–54.

Bidwell, John. *In California before the Gold Rush.* Los Angeles: Ward Ritchie Press, 1948.

Bryant, Edwin. *What I Saw in California.* Philadelphia: D. Appleton & Company, 1848.

Carson, James H. *Recollections of the California Mines.* Stockton: privately printed, 1852. Edited by Joseph A. Sullivan. Reprint, Oakland: Biobooks, 1950.

Carson, Kit. *Kit Carson's Autobiography.* Edited by Milo Milton Quaife. Lincoln: University of Nebraska Press, 1935.

Clyman, James. *James Clyman: American Frontiersman, 1792–1881.* Edited by Charles L. Camp. San Francisco: California Historical Society, 1928.

Cook, Sherburne F., ed. "Colonial Expeditions to the Interior of California: Central Valley, 1800–1820." *Anthropological Records* 16, no. 6 (May 1960): 239–92.

————, ed. "Expeditions to the Interior of California: Central Valley, 1820–1840." *Anthropological Records* 20, no. 5 (February 1962): 151–213.

Cordua, Theodor. "The Memoirs of Theodor Cordua, the Pioneer of New Mecklenburg in the Sacramento Valley." Edited and translated by Erwin Gustav Gudde. *Quarterly of the California Historical Society* 12, no. 4 (December 1933): 279–311.

Cox, Ross. *The Columbia River*. Vol. 2. London: Henry Colburn and Richard Bentley, 1832.

Crespí, Juan. "Diary Kept During the Exploration that was Made of the Harbor of our Father San Francisco." In Herbert Eugene Bolton, *Fray Juan Crespi: Missionary Explorer on the Pacific Coast, 1769–1774*. Berkeley: University of California Press, 1927.

Davis, William Heath. *Seventy-Five Years in California*. Edited by Douglas S. Watson. San Francisco: John Howell, 1929.

De Anza, Juan Bautista. "Anza's Diary of the Second Anza Expedition, 1775–1776." In *Anza's California Expeditions*, vol. 3, *The San Francisco Colony, Diaries of Anza, Font and Eixarch, and Narratives of Palóu and Moraga*. Translated and edited by Herbert Eugene Bolton. Berkeley: University of California Press, 1930.

De la Guerra Ord, Agustias. *Occurrences in Hispanic California*. Translated and edited by Francis Price and William H. Ellison. Washington: Academy of American Franciscan History, 1956.

Downey, Joseph T. *Filings from an Old Saw: Reminiscences of San Francisco and California's Conquest*. Edited by Fred Blackburn Rogers. San Francisco: John Howell, 1956.

Duflot de Mofras, M. *Duflot de Mofras' Travels on the Pacific Coast*. Vol. 1. Translated and edited by Marguerite Eyer Wilbur. Santa Ana: The Fine Arts Press, 1937.

Duhaut-Cilly, A. "Duhaut-Cilly's Account of California in the Years 1827–28." Translated by Charles Franklin Carter. *Quarterly of the California Historical Society* 8, no. 4 (December 1929): 306–36.

Duran, Narciso. "Expedition on the Sacramento and San Joaquin Rivers in 1817: Diary of Fray Narciso Duran." Edited by Charles Edward Chapman. *Publications of the Academy of Pacific Coast History* 2, no. 5 (December 1911): 329–49.

Duvall, Marius. *A Navy Surgeon in California 1846–1847: The Journal of Marius Duvall*. Edited by Fred Blackburn Rogers. San Francisco: John Howell, 1957.

Eccleston, Robert. *The Mariposa Indian War, Diaries of Robert Eccleston: The California Gold Rush, Yosemite, and the High Sierra*. Edited by C. Gregory Crampton. Salt Lake City: University of Utah Press, 1957.

Estudillo, José María. "Estudillo among the Yokuts: 1819." Translated and edited by Anna H. Gayton. In Robert Lowie, ed., *Essays in Anthropology*, 67–85. Berkeley: University of California Press, 1936.

Fages, Pedro. "Fages's Note to his Diary of 1772." In Herbert Eugene Bolton, "In the South San Joaquin Ahead of Garces," *Quarterly of the California Historical Society* 10, no. 3 (September 1931): 211–19.

Font, Pedro. *Font's Complete Diary: A Chronicle of the Founding of San Francisco*. Translated and edited by Herbert Eugene Bolton. Berkeley: University of California Press, 1933.

Frémont, John Charles. *Memoirs of My Life*. 2 vols. Chicago and New York: Belford, Clark & Company, 1887.

Garcés, Francisco. *On the Trail of a Spanish Pioneer: The Diary and Itinerary of Francisco Garcés in his Travels through Sonora, Arizona, and California, 1775–1776*. Vol. 1. Translated and edited by Elliott Coues. New York: Francis P. Harper, 1900.

Garner, William Robert. *Letters from California, 1846–1847*. Edited by Donald Munro Craig. Berkeley, Los Angeles, and London: University of California Press, 1970.

Gregg, Josiah. *The Commerce of the Prairies*. Edited by Milo Milton Quaife. Chicago: R. R. Donnelley & Sons Company, 1926.

Hammond, George P., ed. *The Larkin Papers: Personal, Business and Official Correspondence of Thomas Oliver Larkin, Merchant and United States Consul in California*. 4 vols. Berkeley and Los Angeles: University of California Press, 1951–53.

Harris, Benjamin Butler. *The Gila Trail: The Texas Argonauts and the California Gold Rush*. Edited by Richard H. Dillon. Norman: University of Oklahoma Press, 1960.

Hartnell, Ella S. "An Indian Ruse." *The Land of Sunshine* 6, no. 1 (December 1896): 27.

Heizer, Robert F., ed. *The Eighteen Unratified Treaties of 1851–1852 Between the California Indians and the United States Government*. Berkeley: Archeological Research Facility, Department of Anthropology, University of California, 1972.

Hittell, John S. *Mining in the Pacific States of North America*. San Francisco: H. H. Bancroft and Company, 1861.

Janssens, Agustín. *The Life and Adventures in California of Don Agustín Janssens, 1834–1856*. Edited by William H. Ellison and Francis Price. San Marino: Huntington Library, 1953.

Johnson, Overton, and William H. Winter. *Route Across the Rocky Mountains*. Lafayette, Ind.: John B. Semans, Printers, 1846. Edited by Carl L. Cannon. Reprint, Princeton: Princeton University Press, 1932.

Johnson, Theodore T. *Sights in the Gold Region and Scenes by the Way*. New York: Baker and Scribner, 1849.

Kelley, Hall J. *Hall J. Kelley on Oregon.* Edited by Fred Wilbur Powell. Princeton: Princeton University Press, 1932.

Kip, William Ingraham. *The Early Days of My Episcopate.* New York: Thomas Whittaker, 1892.

Leonard, Zenas. *Narrative of the Adventures of Zenas Leonard.* Edited by Milo Milton Quaife. Chicago: R. R. Donnelley and Sons Company, 1934.

Librado, Fernando. *Breath of the Sun: Life in Early California as Told by a Chumash Indian, Fernando Librado, to John P. Harrington.* Edited by Travis Hudson. Banning: Malki Museum Press, 1980.

————. *The Eye of the Flute: Chumash Traditional History and Ritual As Told by Fernando Librado Kitsepawit to John P. Harrington.* Edited by Travis Hudson, Thomas Blackburn, Rosario Curletti, and Janice Timbrook. Second edition. Banning: The Malki Museum Press, 1981.

Lienhard, Heinrich. *A Pioneer at Sutter's Fort, 1846–1850: The Adventures of Heinrich Lienhard.* Translated and edited by Marguerite Eyer Wilbur. Los Angeles: The Calafía Society, 1941.

————. *I Knew Sutter.* Translated by George T. Smisor. Sacramento: The Nugget Press, 1939.

Lynch, James. *With Stevenson to California.* Oakland: Biobooks, 1954.

Martínez, José Longinos. *California in 1792: The Expedition of José Longinos Martínez.* Translated by Lesley Byrd Simpson. San Marino: Huntington Library, 1938.

Merriam, C. Hart. "California Mission Baptismal Records." Chapter in *Studies of California Indians,* edited by the staff of the Department of Anthropology of the University of California, 188–225. Berkeley and Los Angeles: University of California Press, 1962.

Palomares, José Francisco. "The Death of Yóscolo." Edited by Robert L. Hoover. *Pacific Historical Review* 51, no. 3 (August 1982): 312–14.

Peard, George. *To the Pacific and Arctic with Beechey: The Journal of Lieutenant George Peard of H.M.S. Blossom, 1825–1828.* Edited by Barry M. Gough. Cambridge: Cambridge University Press, 1973.

Perkins, William. *Three Years in California: William Perkins' Journal of Life at Sonora, 1849–1852.* Edited by Dale L. Morgan and James R. Scobie. Berkeley and Los Angeles: University of California Press, 1964.

Phelps, William Dane. *Alta California 1840–1842: The Journal and Observations of William Dane Phelps, Master of the Ship "Alert."* Edited by Briton Cooper Busch. Glendale: The Arthur H. Clark Company, 1983.

Powers, Stephen. *Tribes of California.* Washington, D.C.: Government Printing Office, 1877. Reprint, Berkeley, Los Angeles, and London: University of California Press, 1976.

Revere, Joseph Warren. *Tour of Duty in California*. New York: C. S. Francis & Co., 1849.

Rich, E. E., ed. *The Letters of John McLoughlin From Fort Vancouver to the Governor of the Committee*. Third Series, 1844–46. Toronto: The Champlain Society, 1944.

Ripoll, Antonio. "Fray Antonio Ripoll's Description of the Chumash Revolt at Santa Barbara in 1824." Translated and edited by Maynard Geiger. *Southern California Quarterly* 52, no. 4 (December 1970): 345–64.

Ryan, William Redmond. *Personal Adventures in Upper and Lower California in 1848–9*. 2 vols. London: William Shoberl, Publisher, 1850.

Smith, Jedediah. *The Southwest Expedition of Jedediah S. Smith: His Personal Account of the Journey to California, 1826–1827*. Edited by George R. Brooks. Glendale: Arthur H. Clark Company, 1977.

Spence, Mary Lee, and Donald Jackson, eds. *The Expeditions of John Charles Frémont*, vol. 2, *The Bear Flag Revolt and the Court Martial*. Urbana, Chicago, and London: University of Illinois Press, 1973.

Stewart, George W. "The Yokut Indians of the Kaweah Region." *Sierra Club Bulletin* 12, no. 4 (1927): 385–400.

Sutter, John A. Letter to H. W. Halleck, New Helvetia, December 20, 1847. "Document 1a." *Contributions of the University of California Archaeological Research Facility*, no. 9 (July 1970): 94–95.

————. Letter to Mariano Guadalupe Vallejo, New Helvetia, June 1, 1846. "Documentary: The Fremont Episode." *California Historical Society Quarterly* 6, no. 2 (June 1927): 181–91.

————. *The Diary of Johann August Sutter*. San Francisco: The Grabhorn Press, 1932.

————, et al. *New Helvetia Diary: A Record of Events Kept by John A. Sutter and his Clerks at New Helvetia, California, From September 9, 1845, to May 25, 1848*. San Francisco: The Grabhorn Press, 1939.

Swasey, F. W. *The Early Days and Men of California*. Oakland: Pacific Press Publishing Company, 1891.

"The Sutter-Marshall Lease with the Yalesumney Indians, 1848." "Document 3b." *Contributions of the University of California Research Facility*, no. 9 (July 1970): 109–10.

Tibesar, Antonine, trans. and ed. *Writings of Junípero Serra*, vol. 3. Washington, D.C.: Academy of American Franciscan History, 1956.

Townsend, E. D. *The California Diary of General E. D. Townsend*. Edited by Malcolm Edwards. Los Angeles: The Ward Ritchie Press, 1970.

Turner, Henry Smith. *The Original Journals of Henry Smith Turner with Stephen Watts Kearny to New Mexico and California, 1846–1847*. Edited by Dwight L. Clark. Norman: University of Oklahoma Press, 1966.

Vischer, Edward. "Edward Vischer's First Visit to California." Translated and Edited by Erwin Gustav Gudde. *California Historical Society Quarterly* 19, no. 2 (September, 1940): 193–216.

Warner, Juan José. "Reminiscences of Early California from 1831 to 1846." *Annual Publications of the Historical Society of Southern California* 7 (1907–1908): 176–93.

———, Benjamin Hayes, and J. P. Widney. *An Historical Sketch of Los Angeles County, California.* Los Angeles: Louis Lewin and Co., 1876. Reprint, Los Angeles: O. W. Smith, Publisher, 1936.

Waseurtz af Sandels, G. M. *A Sojourn in California by the King's Orphan: The Travels and Sketches of G. M. Waseurtz af Sandels, a Swedish gentleman who visited California in 1842–1843.* Edited by Helen Putnam Van Sicklen. San Francisco: The Book Club of California, 1945.

Wierzbicki, Felix Paul. *California As It Is and As It May Be.* San Francisco: Washington Bartlett, 1849. Reprint, New York: Burt Franklin, 1970.

Wilkes, Charles. *Narrative of the United States Exploring Expedition during the Years 1838, 1839, 1840, 1841, 1842.* Vol. 5. Philadelphia: Lea and Blanchard, 1845.

Work, John. *Fur Brigade to Bonaventura: John Work's California Expedition of 1832–1833 for the Hudson's Bay Company.* Edited by Alice Bay Maloney. San Francisco: California Historical Society, 1945.

SECONDARY SOURCES

Anderson, Robert T. "Anthropology and History." *Bucknell Review* 15, no. 1 (March 1967): 1–8.

Anonymous. *History of Sacramento County California.* Oakland: Thompson and West, 1880.

Applegate, Richard B. "The Datura Cult among the Chumash." *Journal of California Anthropology* 2, no. 1 (Summer 1975): 7–17.

Axtell, James. "Ethnohistory: An Historian's Viewpoint." Chapter in *The European and the Indian: Essays in the Ethnohistory of Colonial North America,* 3–15. New York, Toronto, and Melbourne: Oxford University Press, 1981.

Bancroft, Hubert Howe. *California Pastoral, 1769–1848.* San Francisco: The History Company, Publishers, 1888.

———. *History of California.* 7 vols. San Francisco: The History Company, Publishers, 1886–1890.

Baumhoff, Martin A. "Ecological Determinants of Aboriginal California Populations." *University of California Publications in American Archaeology and Ethnology* 49, no. 2 (May 1963): 155–236.

Beals, Ralph L., and Joseph A. Hester, Jr. "A New Ecological Typology of the California Indians." In *Men and Cultures,* edited by Anthony F. C. Wallace, 411–19. Philadelphia: University of Pennsylvania Press, 1960.

Beattie, George William. "California's Unbuilt Missions: Spanish Plans for an Inland Chain." *Historical Society of Southern California Annual Publications* 14, pt. 2 (1929): 243–64.

Beeler, Madison S. "Noptinte Yokuts." In *Studies in American Indian Languages.* University of California Publications in Linguistics, Vol. 65, 11–76. Edited by Jesse Sawyer. Berkeley and Los Angeles: University of California Press, 1971.

Bennyhoff, James A. *Ethnogeography of the Plains Miwok.* Center for Archaeological Research at Davis, Publication No. 5. Davis: University of California, 1977.

Berkhofer, Robert F., Jr. "The Political Context of a New Indian History." *Pacific Historical Review* 15, no. 3 (August 1971): 357–82.

Biggs, Donald C. *Conquer and Colonize: Stevenson's Regiment and California.* San Rafael: Presidio Press, 1977.

Bolton, Herbert Eugene. "In the South San Joaquin Ahead of Garcés." *Quarterly of the California Historical Society* 10, no. 3 (September 1931): 211–19.

Bowman, J. N. "The Resident Neophytes *(Existentes)* of the California Missions, 1769–1834." *Southern California Quarterly* 40, no. 2 (June 1958): 138–48.

Broadbent, Sylvia M. "Conflict at Monterey: Indian Horse Raiding, 1820–1850." *Journal of California Anthropology* 1, no. 1 (Spring 1974): 86–101.

———. *The Southern Sierra Miwok Language.* University of California Publications in Linguistics, Vol. 38. Berkeley and Los Angeles: University of California Press, 1964.

Caughey, John Walton. *The California Gold Rush.* Berkeley, Los Angeles, and London: University of California Press, 1948.

Chartkoff, Joseph L., and Kerry Kona Chartkoff. *The Archaeology of California.* Stanford: Stanford University Press, 1984.

Cook, Sherburne F. "Smallpox in Spanish and Mexican California, 1770–1845." *Bulletin of the History of Medicine* 7, no. 2 (February 1939): 153–91.

———. "The Aboriginal Population of Alameda and Contra Costa Counties, California." *Anthropological Records* 16, no. 4 (June 1957): 131–55.

———. "The Aboriginal Population of the San Joaquin Valley, California." *Anthropological Records* 16, no. 2 (July 1955): 31–78.

———. "The American Invasion, 1848–1870." *Ibero-Americana* 23

(1943). Chapter in Sherburne F. Cook, *The Conflict between the California Indian and White Civilization,* 252–361. Berkeley and Los Angeles: University of California Press, 1976.

————. "The Epidemic of 1830–1833 in California and Oregon." *University of California Publications in American Archaeology and Ethnology* 43, no. 3 (1955): 303–25.

————. "The Indian versus the Spanish Mission." *Ibero-Americana* 21 (1943). Chapter in *The Conflict between the California Indian and White Civilization,* 1–194. Berkeley and Los Angeles: University of California Press, 1976.

————. "The Mechanism and Extent of Dietary Adaptation Among Certain Groups of California and Nevada Indians." *Ibero-Americana* 18 (1941). Chapter in *The Conflict between the California Indian and White Civilization,* 447–507. Berkeley and Los Angeles: University of California Press, 1976.

————. "The Physical and Demographic Reaction of the Nonmission Indians in Colonial and Provincial California." *Ibero-Americana* 22 (1943). Chapter in *The Conflict between the California Indian and White Civilization,* 195–251. Berkeley and Los Angeles: University of California Press, 1976.

————. *The Population of the California Indians, 1769–1970.* Berkeley, Los Angeles, and London: University of California Press, 1976.

Cook, Sherburne F., and Woodrow Borah. *Essays in Population History: Mexico and California.* Berkeley, Los Angeles, and London: University of California Press, 1979.

Coombs, Gary B. "With What God Will Provide: A Reexamination of the Chumash Revolt of 1824." *Noticias* 26, no. 2 (Summer 1980): 21–29.

Davis, James T. *Trade Routes and Economic Exchange among the Indians of California.* University of California Archaeological Survey Report No. 54 (1961). Reprint, Ballena Press Publications in Archaeology, Ethnology and History, No. 3. Ramona, Calif.: Ballena Press, 1974.

Dening, Gregory. "Ethnohistory in Polynesia: The Value of Ethnohistorical Evidence." *Journal of Pacific History* 1 (1966): 23–42.

————. *Islands and Beaches: Discourse on a Silent Land, Marquesas, 1774–1880.* Honolulu: University Press of Hawaii, 1980.

Dillon, Richard. *Fool's Gold: The Decline and Fall of Captain John Sutter of California.* New York: Coward-McCann, 1967.

Engelhardt, Zephyrin. *The Missions and Missionaries of California.* 4 vols. San Francisco: James H. Barry Company, 1908–1915.

————. *Mission San Luis Obispo in the Valley of the Bears.* Santa Barbara: Mission Santa Barbara, 1933.

————. *San Miguel, Arcangel, The Mission on the Highway.* Santa Barbara: Mission Santa Barbara, 1929.

Evans-Pritchard, E. E. "Anthropology and History." Chapter in *Social Anthropology and Other Essays,* 172–91. New York: The Free Press of Glèncoe, 1962.

Fenton, William N. "Ethnohistory and Its Problems." *Ethnohistory* 9, no. 1 (Winter 1962): 1–23.

Fisher, Nora, ed. *Spanish Textile Tradition of New Mexico and Colorado.* Santa Fe: Museum of New Mexico Press, 1979.

Forbes, Jack D. "Frontiers in American History and the Role of the Frontier Historian." *Ethnohistory* 15, no. 2 (Spring 1968): 203–35.

————. "Indian Horticulture West and Northwest of the Colorado River." *Journal of the West* 2, no. 1 (January 1963): 1–14.

Garr, Daniel. "Planning, Politics and Plunder: The Missions and Indian Pueblos of Hispanic California." *Southern California Quarterly* 54, no. 4 (Winter 1972): 291–312.

Gates, Paul. "The California Land Act of 1851." *California Historical Society Quarterly* 50, no. 4 (December 1971): 395–430.

Gayton, Anna H. "Yokuts and Western Mono Social Organization." *American Anthropologist* 47, no. 3 (July–September 1945): 409–26.

————. "Yokuts-Mono Chiefs and Shamans." *University of California Publications in American Archaeology and Ethnology* 24, no. 8 (October 1930): 361–420.

————, and Stanley S. Newman. "Yokuts and Western-Mono Myths." *Anthropological Records* 5, no. 1 (October 1940): 1–110.

Gifford, Edward Winslow. "Miwok Lineages and the Political Unit in Aboriginal California." *American Anthropologist* 28, no. 2 (April 1926): 389–401.

Gilbert, Frank T. *History of San Joaquin County, California, with Illustrations Descriptive of its Scenery.* Oakland: Thompson and West, 1879.

Goldschmidt, Walter. "Social Organization in Native California and the Origin of Clans." *American Anthropologist* 50, no. 3 (July–September 1948): 444–56.

Grant, Campbell. "Interior Chumash." In *California,* edited by Robert Heizer, vol. 8, 530–34. *Handbook of North American Indians,* edited by William C. Sturtevant. Washington: Smithsonian Institution, 1978.

Grivas, Theodore. *Military Governments in California 1846–1850.* Glendale: The Arthur H. Clark Company, 1963.

Guest, Francis F. *Fermin Francisco de Lasuen (1736–1803): A Biography.* Washington: Academy of American Franciscan History, 1973.

————. "Junípero Serra and His Approach to the Indians." *Southern California Quarterly* 67, no. 3 (Fall 1985): 223–61.

Gutiérrez, Ramón A. *When Jesus Came, the Corn Mothers Went Away: Marriage, Sexuality, and Power in New Mexico, 1500–1846.* Stanford: Stanford University Press, 1991.

Hafen, LeRoy R. "The Old Spanish Trail, Santa Fe to Los Angeles." *Huntington Library Quarterly* 11, no. 2 (February 1948): 149–60.

———, and Ann W. Hafen. *Old Spanish Trail: Santa Fé to Los Angeles.* Glendale: The Arthur H. Clark Company, 1954.

Hall, Frederic. *The History of San José and Surroundings with Biographical Sketches of the Early Settlers.* San Francisco: A. L. Bancroft and Company, 1871.

Hammond, George P., and Dale L. Morgan. *Captain Charles M. Weber: Pioneer of the San Joaquin and Founder of Stockton, California.* Berkeley: Friends of the Bancroft Library, 1966.

Harlow, Neal. *California Conquered: The Annexation of a Mexican Province, 1846–1850.* Berkeley, Los Angeles and London: University of California Press, 1982.

Heizer, Robert F. "The Direct-Historical Approach in California Archaeology." *American Antiquity* 7, no. 2 (October 1941): 98–122.

———. "Walla Walla Indian Expeditions to the Sacramento Valley." *California Historical Society Quarterly* 21, no. 1 (March 1942): 1–7.

———, and Albert B. Elsasser. *The Natural World of the California Indians.* Berkeley, Los Angeles, and London: University of California Press, 1980.

Hill, Joseph J. "Ewing Young in the Fur Trade of the Far Southwest, 1822–1834." *Quarterly of the Oregon Historical Society* 24, no. 1 (March 1923): 1–35.

———. "The Old Spanish Trail: A Study of Spanish and Mexican Trade and Exploration Northwest from New Mexico to the Great Basin and California." *Hispanic American Historical Review* 4, no. 3 (August 1921): 444–73.

Hittell, Theodore H. *History of California.* 4 vols. San Francisco: Pacific Press Publishing House and Occidental Publishing Company, 1885.

Holmes, Kenneth L. *Ewing Young: Master Trapper.* Portland, Binfords & Mort, 1967.

Holterman, Jack. "The Revolt of Estanislao." *The Indian Historian* 3, no. 1 (Winter 1970): 43–54.

Hornbeck, David. "Land Tenure and Rancho Expansion in Alta California, 1784–1846." *Journal of Historical Geography* 4, no. 4 (1978): 371–90.

———. "The Patenting of California's Private Land Claims, 1851–1885." *Geographical Review* 69, no. 4 (October 1979): 434–48.

Hudson, Travis, and Thomas Blackburn. "The Integration of Myth and Ritual in South-Central California: The 'Northern Complex.'" *Journal of California Anthropology* 5, no. 2 (Winter 1978): 225–50.

Hughes, Charles. "The Decline of the Californios: The Case of San

Diego, 1846–1856." *Journal of San Diego History* 21, no. 3 (Summer 1975): 1–31.

Hurtado, Albert L. *Indian Survival on the California Frontier.* New Haven and London: Yale University Press, 1988.

Hussey, John Adam. "The New Mexico–California Caravan of 1847–1848." *New Mexico Historical Review* 18, no. 1 (January 1943): 1–16.

_____, and George Walcott Ames, Jr. "California Preparations to Meet the Walla Walla Invasion, 1846." *California Historical Society Quarterly* 21, no. 1 (March 1942): 9–21.

Hutchinson, C. Alan. "The Mexican Government and the Mission Indians of Upper California, 1821–1835." *The Americas* 21, no. 4 (April 1965): 335–62.

Jablow, Joseph. *The Cheyenne in Plains Indian Trade Relations, 1795–1840.* Monographs of the American Ethnological Society, 19. New York: J. J. Augustin Publisher, 1950.

Jackson, Robert H. "Gentile Recruitment and Population Movements in the San Francisco Bay Area Missions." *Journal of California and Great Basin Anthropology* 6, no. 2 (1984), 225–39.

James, Steven R., and Suzanne Graziani. "California Indian Warfare." *Contributions of the University of California Archaeological Research Facility,* no. 23 (March 1975): 47–109.

Jennings, Francis. "A Growing Partnership: Historians, Anthropologists and American Indian History." *Ethnohistory* 29, no. 1 (1982): 21–34.

Johnson, John R. "Indian History in the Santa Barbara Back Country." *Los Padres Notes* 3 (Spring 1984): 1–23.

_____. "Mission Registers as Anthropological Questionnaires: Understanding the Limitations of the Data." *American Indian Culture and Research Journal* 12, no. 2 (1988): 9–30.

Jones, Oakah L., Jr. *Pueblo Warriors and Spanish Conquest.* Norman: University of Oklahoma Press, 1966.

Kenner, Charles L. *A History of New Mexico–Plains Indian Relations.* Norman: University of Oklahoma Press, 1969.

Kroeber, Alfred L. *An Anthropologist Looks at History.* Edited by Theodora Kroeber. Berkeley and Los Angeles: University of California Press, 1966.

Kunkel, P. H. "The Pomo Kin Group and the Political Unit in Aboriginal California," *Journal of California Anthropology* 1, no. 1 (Spring 1974), 7–18.

Latta, Frank F. *Handbook of Yokuts Indians.* 2d ed. Santa Cruz: Bear State Books, 1977.

Lawrence, Eleanor. "Mexican Trade between Santa Fe and Los Angeles, 1830–1848." *California Historical Society Quarterly* 10, no. 1 (1931): 27–39.

Layton, Thomas N. "Traders and Raiders: Aspects of Trans-Basin and California-Plateau Commerce, 1800–1830." *Journal of California and Great Basin Anthropology* 3, no. 1 (Summer 1981), 127–37.

Lévi-Strauss, Claude. "Introduction: History and Anthropology." Chapter in *Structural Anthropology,* 1–28. Translated by Claire Jacobson and Brooke Grundfest Schoepf. Garden City, N.Y.: Anchor Books, Doubleday and Company, 1967.

Lewis, Henry T. *Patterns of Indian Burning in California: Ecology and Ethnohistory.* Ballena Press Anthropological Papers, No. 1. Ramona, Calif.: Ballena Press, 1973.

Lewis, I. M. "Introduction." In *History and Social Anthropology,* ix–xxvii. Edited by I. M. Lewis. London, New York, Sidney, Toronto, and Wellington: Tavistock Publications, 1968.

Limerick, Patricia Nelson. *The Legacy of Conquest: The Unbroken Past of the American West.* New York & London: W. W. Norton, 1987.

Lothrop, Marion Lydia. "The Indian Campaigns of General M. G. Vallejo, Defender of the Northern Frontier of California." *Quarterly of the Society of California Pioneers* 9, no. 3 (September 1932): 161–205.

Lowie, Robert H. *An Introduction to Cultural Anthropology.* New York: Farrar and Rinehart, 1934.

Lyman, George D. *John Marsh, Pioneer: The Life Story of a Trail-Blazer on Six Frontiers.* San Francisco: The Chatauqua Press, 1931.

Martin, Calvin, ed. *The American Indian and the Problem of History.* New York and Oxford: Oxford University Press, 1987.

McCarthy, Francis Florence. *The History of Mission San Jose, California, 1797–1835.* Fresno: Academy Library Guild, 1958.

Morgan, Dale L. *Jedediah Smith and the Opening of the West.* Lincoln: University of Nebraska Press, 1953.

Newcomb, W. W., Jr. "A Re-examination of the Causes of Plains Warfare." *American Anthropologist* 52, no. 3 (July–September 1950): 317–30.

Ortiz, Alfonso. "Indian/White Relations: A View from the Other Side of the 'Frontier.'" In *Indians in American History: An Introduction,* 1–16. Edited by Frederick E. Hoxie. Arlington Heights, Ill.: Harlan Davidson, 1988.

Phillips, George Harwood. *Chiefs and Challengers: Indian Resistance and Cooperation in Southern California.* Berkeley and Los Angeles: University of California Press, 1975.

————. "Indians and the Breakdown of the Spanish Mission System in California." *Ethnohistory* 21, no. 4 (Fall 1974): 291–302.

————. "Indians in Los Angeles, 1781-1875: Economic Integration, Social Disintegration." *Pacific Historical Review* 49, no. 5 (August 1980): 427–51.

_____. "The Alcaldes: Indian Leadership in the Spanish Missions of California." In *The Struggle for Political Autonomy: Papers and Comments from the Second Newberry Library Conference on Themes in American History.* Occasional Papers in Curriculum Series, no. 11, 83–87. Chicago: The Newberry Library, 1989.

Pitt, Leonard. *The Decline of the Californios: A Social History of the Spanish-Speaking Californians, 1846–1890.* Berkeley and Los Angeles: University of California Press, 1968.

Pomeroy, Earl. "Old Lamps for New: The Cultural Lag in Pacific Coast Historiography." *Arizona and the West* 2, no. 2 (Summer 1960): 105–26.

Preston, William L. *Vanishing Landscapes: Land and Life in the Tulare Lake Basin.* Berkeley, Los Angeles, and London: University of California Press, 1981.

Rawls, James J. *Indians of California: The Changing Image.* Norman: University of Oklahoma Press, 1984.

Ray, Arthur J. *Indians in the Fur Trade: Their Role as Hunters, Trappers, and Middlemen in the Lands Southwest of Hudson Bay, 1660–1870.* Toronto and Buffalo: University of Toronto Press, 1974.

Richman, Irving Berdine. *California Under Spain and Mexico, 1535–1847.* Boston and New York: Houghton Mifflin Company, 1911.

Robinson, W. W. *Land in California.* Berkeley and Los Angeles: University of California Press, 1948.

Sahlins, Marshall. "Other Times, Other Customs: The Anthropology of History." *American Anthropologist* 85, no. 3 (September 1983): 517–44.

Sample, L. L. "Trade and Trails in Aboriginal California." *Reports of the University of California Archaeological Survey,* no. 8 (September 1950): 1–30.

Sanchez, Nellie Van de Grift. *Spanish Arcadia.* San Francisco, Los Angeles, and Chicago: Powell Publishing Company, 1929.

Sandos, James A. "Levantamiento!: The 1824 Chumash Uprising Reconsidered." *Southern California Quarterly* 67, no. 2 (Summer 1985): 109–33.

Schapera, I. "Should Anthropologists be Historians?" *Journal of the Royal Anthropological Institute of Great Britain and Ireland* 92, pt. 2 (July–December 1962): 143–56.

Schenk, W. Egbert. "Historic Aboriginal Groups of the California Delta Region." *University of California Publications in American Archaeology and Ethnology* 23, no. 2 (1926), 123–46.

Shipley, William F. "Native Languages of California." In *California,* edited by Robert Heizer, vol. 8 in *Handbook of North American Indians,* 80–90. Edited by William C. Sturtevant. Washington: Smithsonian Institution, 1978.

————. "Spanish Elements in the Indigenous Languages of Central California." *Romance Philology* 16, no. 1 (August 1962): 1–21.

Steward, Julian H. "Ethnography of the Owens Valley Paiute." *University of California Publications in American Archaeology and Ethnology* 33, no. 3 (September 1933): 233–350.

Sturtevant, William C. "Anthropology, History, and Ethnohistory." *Ethnohistory* 13, nos. 1 and 2 (Winter–Spring, 1966): 1–51.

Sullivan, Maurice S. *The Travels of Jedediah Smith: A Documentary Outline, Including the Journal of the Great American Pathfinder.* Santa Ana: The Fine Arts Press, 1934.

Sutton, Mark Q. "Some Aspects of Kitanemuk Prehistory." *Journal of California and Great Basin Anthropology* 2, no. 2 (Winter 1980): 214–25.

Taylor, George Rogers, ed. *The Turner Thesis Concerning the Role of the Frontier in American History.* Lexington, Mass., Toronto, and London: D. C. Heath and Company, 1972.

Teilman, I., and W. H. Shafer. *The Historical Story of Irrigation in Fresno and Kings Counties in Central California.* Fresno: Williams and Son, 1943.

Thomas, Keith. "History and Anthropology." *Past and Present: A Journal of Historical Studies* no. 24 (April 1963): 3–24.

Thompson, Joseph A. *El Gran Capitan, Jose de la Guerra: A Historical Biographical Study.* Los Angeles: Cabrera and Sons, 1961.

Thompson, Leonard, and Howard Lamar. "Comparative Frontier History." In *The Frontier in History: North America and South Africa Compared,* 3–13. Edited by Howard Lamar and Leonard Thompson. New Haven and London: Yale University Press, 1981.

Timbrook, Jan. "Virtuous Herbs: Plants in Chumash Medicine." *Journal of Ethnobiology* 7, no. 2 (Winter 1987): 171–80.

————, John R. Johnson, and David D. Earle. "Vegetation Burning by the Chumash." *Journal of California and Great Basin Anthropology* 4, no. 2 (Winter 1982): 163–86.

Tinkham, George H. *A History of Stockton.* San Francisco: W. M. Hinton & Co., Printers, 1880.

————. *History of San Joaquin County.* Los Angeles: Historic Record Company, 1923.

Trigger, Bruce G. "Ethnohistory: Problems and Prospects." *Ethnohistory* 29, no. 1 (Winter 1982): 1–19.

————. *The Children of Aataentsic I: A History of the Huron People to 1660.* Montreal and London: McGill-Queen's University Press, 1976.

Uldall, Hans Jørgen, and William Shipley. *Nisenan Texts and Dictionary.* University of California Publications in Linguistics, Vol. 46. Berkeley and Los Angeles: University of California Press, 1966.

Wallace, William J. "Southern Valley Yokuts." In *California,* edited by Robert Heizer, vol. 8, in *Handbook of North American Indians,* 448–61. Edited by William C. Sturtevant. Washington: Smithsonian Institution, 1978.

Weber, David J. "American Westward Expansion and the Breakdown of Relations between Pobladores and 'Indios Bárbaros' on Mexico's Far Northern Frontier, 1821–1846." *New Mexico Historical Review* 56, no. 3 (1981): 221–38.

————. "Mexico's Far Northern Frontier, 1821–1854: Historiography Askew." *Western Historical Quarterly* 7, no. 3 (July 1976): 279–93.

————. *The Californios versus Jedediah Smith, 1826–1827: A New Cache of Documents.* Spokane: The Arthur H. Clark Company, 1990.

Wells, Robin F. "Frontier Systems as a Sociocultural Type." *Papers in Anthropology* 14, no. 1 (Spring 1973): 6–15.

Winther, Oscar Osburn. "The Story of San Jose, 1777–1869: California's First Pueblo," pt. 1. *California Historical Society Quarterly* 14, no. 1 (1935): 3–27.

Wyman, Walker D., and Clifton B. Kroeber, "Introduction." In *The Frontier in Perspective,* xiii–xx. Edited by Walker D. Wyman and Clifton B. Kroeber. Madison: University of Wisconsin Press, 1957.

Zollinger, James Peter. *Sutter: The Man and His Empire.* New York, London, and Toronto: Oxford University Press, 1939.

Index

Acorns: as food source, 17, 21–22; leaching of, 22
Africa, historian focus on, 3
Agriculture, California Indians and, 99–100, 122, 143
Alta California. *See* California
Alvarado, Juan Bautista, 110, 113, 118, 125, 126, 162
Anashe (Miwok chief), 117, 121, 122
Animals, Indian dependence on, 16, 18, 20–21, 24, 26, 104–105. *See also* Cattle; Horses; Mules
Anthropology, history and, 3–7. *See also* Ethnohistory
Anza, Juan Bautista de, 34–37
Apiachi. *See* Yokuts
Argüello, Luís Antonio, 54–55, 75
Artifacts, early Indian, 18
Atrocities: Californio, 72, 81, 90, 114; of Indians, 79; of trappers, 90–91; by U.S. Army, 147; by U.S. settlers, 145–46

Baptism, of Indians, 38, 46–51, 54–57, 61, 98, 118. *See also* Neophytes, mission
Birds, of early California, 20
Burial rituals, early Indian, 18

Cabot, Juan, 66, 77, 85
California, state of: geological history of, 14–16; Indian occupation of, 16–31 (*see also* California Indians); Mexican residents of (*see* Californios); Spanish in (*see* Spaniards, California colonized by); United States and, 135–56, 164–65 (*see also* California Battalion; Frémont, John; Larkin, Thomas; Mason, Richard B.; New York Volunteers). *See also* California Indians; Central Valley; Coastal zone; Gold

California Battalion, 135, 136, 138–39; Walla Walla in, 138. *See also* Frémont, John; José Jesús; Walla Walla
California Indians: background of, 19–31; Californios vs., 65–68, 70–73, 76–84, 89–90, 103, 112–16, 118, 145, 160–61, 178n.67; earliest, 16–19; external forces on, 157; intertribal friction among, 41–43; "Mission" (*see* Neophytes, mission); Nuevomexicanos and, 82, 84–87, 92, 96, 102, 104, 160, 180; political patterns of, 97; social patterns of, 26; Spanish vs., 42, 46–47, 50–55, 57–59, 61; as Spanish allies, 41–42; Spanish-speaking, 100–101; vs. trappers, 87–88; U.S. government vs., 139–50, 154–57, 181n.7; U.S. settlers vs., 136–39, 145–50, 152–53, 193n.46 (*see also* Garner, William). *See also* Chumash; Esselen; Karkin; Kitanemuk; Miwok; Mohaves; Monache; Neophytes, mission; Nisenan; Ohlone; Paiutes; Salinan; Yokuts
Californios, 64, 65, 157–63; Indians and (*see* California Indians, Californios vs.); Marsh and, 112; and Mexican War, 136; and Sutter, 126; vs. trappers, 75; U.S. and, 140, 148–50, 152–53, 164–65; vs. U.S. settlers, 137–39. *See also* Alvarado, Juan Bautista; Castro, José; Figueroa, José; Vallejo, M. G.
Canby, Edward R. S., 153–54
Carrillo, Pedro, 149–50
Carson, Kit, 84
Castec. *See* Chumash
Castro, José, 113, 128, 129, 132–33; vs. Sutter, 133, 134
Catholicism, California Indians and, 32, 37, 122. *See also* Baptism; Franciscans

219